THE FUTURE OF NATO

THE FUTURE
OF
NATO

Edited by

TED GALEN CARPENTER

FRANK CASS • LONDON

First published in 1995 in Great Britain by
FRANK CASS & CO. LTD.
2 Park Square, Milton Park,
Abingdon, Oxon, OX14 4RN

and in the United States of America by
FRANK CASS
270 Madison Ave,
New York NY 10016

Transferred to Digital Printing 2005

British Library Cataloguing in Publication Data

Future of N.A.T.O. – (Strategic Studies,
ISSN 0140-2390)
I. Carpenter, Ted Galen II. Series
355.031091821

ISBN 0-7146-4647-4 (cloth)
ISBN 0-7146-4171-5 (paper)

Library of Congress Cataloging-in-Publication Data
A catalog record for this book is available
from the Library of Congress

This group of studies first appeared in a Special Issue on 'The Future of
NATO' of The Journal of Strategic Studies, Vol. 17, No. 4 (Dec. 1994)
published by Frank Cass & Co. Ltd.

Typeset by Regent Typesetting, London

Contents

Introduction
The Post-Cold War NATO Debate

TED GALEN CARPENTER

The end of the Cold War, culminating in the collapse of the Warsaw Pact and the disintegration of the USSR itself, raises profound questions about the future of NATO. A series of stunning events have utterly transformed the political landscape of Europe and erased the original rationale for the Alliance – the defense of Western Europe from a powerful and aggressively expansionist Soviet Union.

NATO's defenders insist that the Alliance is even more important in the post-Cold War era than it was during the Cold War. Not only do they contend that NATO is essential to prevent the resurgence of the instability and national rivalries that spawned two world wars in Europe, they argue that a continuation of Washington's Alliance leadership role, symbolized by the continued deployment of American troops on the Continent, is imperative as well. NATO is the only institutional vehicle for US influence in European affairs, Atlanticists argue; any US retrenchment on security issues would, therefore, jeopardize important American political and economic interests.

Instead of considering the fundamental question of whether an alliance created to wage the Cold War is truly relevant in the vastly altered setting of post-Cold War Europe, the focus of most discussions about NATO is on whether the Alliance should enlarge its membership by incorporating some or all of the Central and East European states. Yet even that relatively narrow debate raises an assortment of troubling questions. Which nations should be brought into the fold, and how quickly should expansion occur? What conditions ought to be met before a new member is granted admission? Can or should enlargement take place without new members being offered the explicit security guarantees contained in Article 5 of the North Atlantic Treaty? Should an enlarged NATO include Russia, or should the Alliance have an implicit anti-Russian purpose in the post-Cold War period as it did throughout the Cold War? Would the inclusion of Russia so transform the security focus and geographic coverage of the Alliance that it would lack cohesion and be unable to fulfill any meaningful security role? And can expansion occur without entangling the existing members of NATO in the numerous parochial quarrels and conflicts that bedevil much of Eastern Europe?

It is unclear whether the Partnership for Peace (PFP) program, adopted by

NATO leaders at the Alliance summit in January 1994, is an honest effort to address and resolve such matters in an orderly manner. Although it may have that potential, some skeptics contend that the PFP is merely an attempt on the part of NATO policymakers to avoid invidious choices. Other critics fear that the PFP is the first stage of a gradual, covert attempt to expand the Alliance's security obligations and membership without giving the publics in Western Europe and the United States an opportunity to debate the merits of enlargement.

Beyond the issue of NATO's expansion lie other, in some ways more important, issues. For example, the original premise for the Alliance was a fundamental compatibility of interests between the United States and its European allies. Although that premise seemed convincing during the Cold War when the Western democracies faced a powerful common adversary, the validity of beliefs about transatlantic solidarity is far more questionable in the post-Cold War era when no such adversary exists. Likewise, throughout the Cold War it did not appear that any other security organization could be an adequate substitute for NATO. With the growing prominence and capabilities of such institutions as the Conference on Security and Cooperation in Europe (CSCE) and the Western European Union (WEU), that assumption is no longer indisputable. Indeed, some policy experts argue that without a global hegemonic threat, such organizations are better suited than NATO for managing and resolving the local and regional conflicts of post-Cold War Europe.

The belief that US leadership is irreplaceable is also now open to question. In large part that belief was based on the recognition that only a superpower could effectively neutralize the threat posed by another superpower. But the security problems facing Europe in the post-Cold War era are those posed by small revisionist states and the internal conflicts generated by feuding factions within unstable multinational states, not the threat of continental domination by an expansionist great power. Given that greatly altered geopolitical environment, it is at least pertinent to ask whether Europe cannot manage its affairs without US supervision.

The related argument that the absence of US leadership would automatically lead to a renationalization of Western Europe's defenses and the renewal of the national rivalries that produced two world wars should not pass unexamined. Although renationalization is a worrisome possibility, patterns of political and economic cooperation among the nations of Western Europe have had nearly a half century to develop. Is it certain, or even probable, that such institutional linkages and important shared interests would prove insufficient for continued regional cohesion? Conversely, if renationalization is such a strong, lurking menace, is it credible that continued US leadership of NATO will be enough to prevent its emergence?

The contributors to this volume discuss the vast array of issues relevant to the future of NATO. They offer a variety of perspectives and policy prescriptions, and although they frequently disagree about important matters, they share a willingness to challenge the conventional wisdom.

Joseph Lepgold outlines the crucial choices about the future of NATO now confronting Western leaders and concludes that there are three general options. One alternative would be to continue the Partnership for Peace course, offering the Central and East European nations a limited political and military relationship devoid of the firm security guarantees in Article 5. The most important argument for that strategy, according to Lepgold, is its flexibility. Although the PFP commits NATO to expansion in principle, the timing and scope of expansion could be adjusted to reflect political developments throughout the region. A second option would be to accelerate the expansion of the Alliance and immediately confront the thorny issues of which nations to admit and whether an enlarged NATO should take on the task of containing a neo-imperial Russia. The third alternative would be to deemphasize NATO and seek a new Euro-Atlantic security arrangement more appropriate for the challenges of the post-Cold War era. Lepgold concludes that, on balance, the third course is preferable – although the first option may prove to be adequate and may, in fact, ultimately lead to the third. The second course, he believes, is the best policy only if the West finds it necessary to thwart a revanchist Russia. Lepgold cautions, however, that choosing rapid enlargement on that premise could be a self-fulfilling prophecy.

Coral Bell is even more adamant that Western policymakers should not regard Russia as an inevitable enemy. Instead, Russia must be seen as an essential component of a new post-Cold War concert of great powers and a partner in efforts to stabilize Europe. She warns that enlarging NATO while excluding Russia from membership would be highly provocative to Moscow and risk once again dividing Europe into antagonistic military blocs. Such a flagrant disregard of Russian interests and sensibilities could also have undesirable political consequences inside that country, undermining the 'Westernizers' who are now in power and playing into the hands of the aggressively nationalistic 'Slavophiles'. Bell contends that only transforming NATO into a pan-European security arrangement that specifically includes Russia as a partner can such perils be avoided.

Jonathan G. Clarke believes that a possible confrontation with Moscow is only one of several reasons why proposals to enlarge NATO are ill-advised. He notes that democratic institutions are still extremely fragile throughout Central and Eastern Europe and that the proposed new members could be unstable and unreliable allies. Even worse, Clarke points out, there is a plethora of unresolved territorial, ethnic, and religious grievances that could easily explode into armed conflict. As the security guarantor for the region, NATO would become responsible for resolving such conflicts. Not only might that mission prove costly in terms of lives and treasure, most of the disputes have deep and tangled historical roots. NATO leaders would frequently find it nearly impossible to determine the merits of individual cases. Incorporating the nations of Central and Eastern Europe into NATO, Clarke warns, would soon end in frustration and mutual recrimination.

Hugh De Santis fears that the Partnership for Peace and the lure of ultimate membership in NATO may be creating expectations among the Central and East European nations that cannot be fulfilled. He doubts whether the United States or the existing European members of NATO are prepared to extend meaningful security commitments to their eastern neighbors, given the various risks entailed. Yet the hope of NATO membership has led the nations of Central and Eastern Europe to abandon their own promising efforts at mutual political, economic, and security cooperation. Instead, the PFP has encouraged them in an unseemly and potentially dangerous rivalry for NATO's affections. De Santis concludes that the entire enlargement debate has an aura of unreality. NATO partisans seek improbable new missions for the Alliance because they will not admit that NATO has lost most of its relevance with the end of the Cold War. He urges US leaders to foster greater realism by encouraging the Europeans to form new, post-Cold War security organizations on the Continent and by devolving security responsibilities to Washington's European allies.

Benjamin C. Schwarz contends that powerful economic factors inhibit American policymakers from making such a drastic change in their policy toward Europe. Schwarz argues that preventing Soviet expansionism was only a secondary reason for Washington's intense commitment to NATO during the Cold War. A more important motive was to incorporate the nations of Western Europe (especially Germany) into a US-dominated security network. Without American hegemony to stabilize the international system, a succession of US leaders concluded, an open global economy could not flourish. Schwarz argues that despite the demise of the Soviet Union and the lack of any other serious threat to the security of the United States, that rationale has not changed. Washington still must 'smother' its democratic allies, lest they renationalize their defenses and again pursue normal great power politics – a step that would undermine the necessary conditions for an open international economic system. US leaders are caught in a dilemma, according to Schwarz. Relinquishing the smothering role would threaten America's own economic preeminence, but the costs and risks of maintaining that policy may prove to be both politically and economically unsustainable.

Whatever their motives, American leaders are wedded to an excessively 'NATO-centric' policy, according to Daniel N. Nelson. Although Nelson believes that NATO is an important part of Europe's post-Cold War security structure, he argues that the Alliance is ill-suited to perform increasingly essential conflict prevention and conflict resolution. Those tasks require a pan-European collective security organization. Nelson maintains that such an organization, the CSCE (now OSCE), already exists and merely needs adequate powers. Thus far, however, most Western – especially US – leaders have failed to appreciate the CSCE's potential and have treated it as an insti-tution of only slight relevance to future European security and stability. That attitude needs to change quickly, Nelson argues, or Eastern Europe will become the arena for numerous Bosnia-style conflicts.

David Garnham contends that NATO has enabled the nations of Western Europe to perpetuate a security dependence on the United States that is unhealthy for all concerned. He points out that the US defense budget is far higher than the budgets of the principal West European states and that American taxpayers continue to subsidize the defense of Washington's allies at considerable cost, despite the disappearance of the Soviet threat. In his view, an array of perverse political and economic incentives in both the United States and Western Europe ossifies sterile status quo policies. Given Western Europe's considerable actual and potential military capabilities, and the need for the United States to address pressing domestic problems, Garnham believes that the time has come for Washington to adopt a lower profile on the Continent and encourage its allies to become more self-reliant through such organizations as the WEU.

In the final essay, I review the ongoing debate in the American and European foreign policy communities about the future of NATO and assess the policy agendas of the various parties. A striking feature of the discussion is that although it is widely agreed that the Alliance has an important role in the security affairs of post-Cold War Europe, there is a great variance in goals and expectations. For example, the East Europeans want full member-ship in NATO as protection from Russia, while Moscow seeks to be included in the Alliance to convert it into a toothless pan-European security forum. Most of the West European powers are ambivalent about enlarging NATO, but they want to retain the Alliance as an insurance policy against hegemonic aspirations by either Russia or Germany. American policymakers see NATO as the only credible institutional vehicle for preserving a dominant US posi-tion in Europe and preventing the West Europeans from becoming more assertive and thereby undermining important US political and economic interests. I question whether any single institution can satisfy such conflict-ing, if not fundamentally incompatible, policy goals, and I explore how America might be able to protect its legitimate European interests without NATO.

The essays in this volume are presented in the hope that they will act as a catalyst to expand and intensify the debate on both sides of the Atlantic about the future of NATO. Policymakers in the United States and Europe have already adopted measures such as the Partnership for Peace, and are contemplating further steps, that may have far-reaching ramifications. Before they take action to consolidate and perpetuate NATO – much less before they expand and transform the Alliance – there are many crucial issues that need to be addressed. The authors in *The Future of NATO* have helped focus attention on those issues and the implications of the various policy options now being considered.

The Next Step Toward a More Secure Europe

JOSEPH LEPGOLD

The discussion over Europe's post-Cold War security system has reached a turning point, although few people have framed it as such. NATO's January 1994 summit, unusually harmonious by recent standards, produced the Partnership for Peace (PFP), under which former members of the Warsaw Pact and European neutrals can become candidate members. On their way into the alliance these countries can participate in various joint projects with NATO members and one another, but initially at least they will do so without NATO's mutual security guarantee. The United States has promised to support eventual full membership for all countries that meet certain criteria, although no NATO member will publicly commit itself to a timetable. Twenty-one of the eligible governments have nevertheless signed up, including Russia. Yet this apparent success should not induce NATO members to continue sidestepping the basic issues raised by the membership controversy, few of which have been settled. The PFP train may have left the station, but its passengers now need a sense of where it is ultimately headed. There are still major choices to be made about how Europe's security should be organized, and the United States should not be indifferent to their very distinct opportunities and risks.

A turning point is evident if one considers that the Cold War ended, as it began, in discrete stages. Soviet President Mikhail Gorbachev's movement toward truly mutual East-West security foreshadowed the first step, the fall of the Berlin Wall. German unification and the demise of the Warsaw Pact constituted a second major stage, and the dissolution of the USSR itself was a third. Russia's entry into the PFP can be seen as part of a fourth major stage, in which its leaders seek a role for their country as a 'normal' part of Europe. The strategic bargaining among Europeans, Russians, and Americans to define that role will help shape the international system in the next century. Meanwhile, however, several distinct political options for the United States and its NATO allies are implicitly on the table. As its spokesman admits, NATO is now an alliance that opposes no one.[1] Apart perhaps from the post-1815 Vienna system, that situation is historically if not logically anomalous. NATO could, perhaps, build on its Cold War success and try to find a new role. Without a crisis compelling quicker adaptation, cautious change might ensure that existing security structures do not atrophy before new ones emerge. Yet NATO, as a Cold War edifice that must be retrofitted to survive, may not ultimately be the best institution to tackle Europe's security problems. Perhaps now, when there is no looming threat to NATO's members, is the time to think closely about the alliance's future.

This study aims to stimulate such a dialogue. It asks four questions: How fast should NATO expand, if at all? If it does expand, how far east should it go? If it expands, what is the ultimate purpose of the expansion? Finally, is NATO itself the best instrument to secure and stabilize post-Cold War Europe? Three major options for dealing with these issues are considered. One involves incrementally deepening the NATO Partnerships. This approach would continue what has been Clinton administration policy, but aim for longer-term results. A second option, immediate expansion, could take two forms. One would accelerate NATO membership for at least the Visegrad countries (Poland, Hungary, the Czech Republic, and Slovakia) and perhaps Ukraine and the Baltic states, but leave Russia out. This would recast post-Cold War NATO as an instrument to contain Russian expansion. Another way to expand quickly would be less anti-Russian, and would instead admit those countries that have most met the membership 'requirements' PFP lays out. A third option would be to scrap NATO and replace it with a genuinely post-Cold War Euro-American security system. I conclude that the first poses the fewest short-term risks and some major long-term benefits for NATO as a whole, but that it is best pursued as a stage on the way to the ultimately more satisfactory third option. The more that the existing Partnerships are deepened step by step, the less one needs to restructure European security radically along the lines of the third option.

Option One: Incrementally Deepen the NATO Partnerships

Partnership For Peace emerged as the most politically expedient way for NATO to deal with Central and East European security concerns because it hedges bets in several ways. It leaves open the possibility of NATO membership for the Visegrad group, the Baltic republics, and perhaps Ukraine or other parts of the former East bloc, while deferring hard choices about whom to admit and under what arrangements. It assumes either that the Europeans can work toward mutual security with Russia or, if Russia resumes expansion, that those nations that are threatened will have time to mobilize effectively. Meanwhile, it avoids isolating Russia and taking steps that could be seen by Moscow as encirclement. Russia and its former imperial possessions are instead invited gradually to join the West.

Governments joining the PFP commit themselves to five goals: transparent defense budgets and budget processes; democratic control of armed forces;

capacity and willingness to contribute to NATO operations authorized by the United Nations or the Conference on Security and Cooperation in Europe (CSCE); joint planning and training with NATO members to accomplish these tasks; and, over the long term, the development of military forces that can operate side-by-side with those of NATO members.[2] All Partners sign a general Framework Agreement affirming these goals (bilaterally with NATO rather than with specific members) and individual Presentation Agreements that specify how the goals will be achieved.[3] Because this defense coordination can be tightened in stages, the program ideally is consistent either with having a benign Russia inside a loosely structured European security system or facing a more menacing Russia that NATO members believe they must again actively deter.

Nevertheless, PFP showed signs of being a bad internal compromise. In late 1993 Czech and Polish leaders, their fears about a security vacuum in Central Europe heightened by the nationalists' strength in the Russian elections, lobbied for quick entry into NATO. Germany's defense minister Volker Rühe and three American RAND Corporation analysts, Ronald Asmus, Richard Kugler and F. Stephen Larrabee, made similar arguments.[4] One faction in the US State Department likewise wanted to open NATO fairly quickly. Opposed to that action were Washington officials who worried that rapid expansion would strengthen Russian hardliners, exacerbate Moscow's fear of encirclement, and heighten tensions in Europe. Some policy-makers apparently believed that these problems might even dissuade Ukraine from giving up its nuclear weapons. There was also concern about extending NATO's security guarantee at a time of declining defense budgets and public support for military intervention.[5] PFP seemingly reconciled these deep differences in several ways. No automatic NATO membership is promised to those wanting to join the alliance now; it is suggested only that their applications will be strengthened by having appropriate PFP experience and evidence of compatible institutional reform on their resumés. Moreover, there is no concrete timetable for action on membership. As one US official put it,

> The 'partnership for peace' proposal was a very skillful compromise between people who said we should do nothing to offend the Russians and people who said we should let the Eastern Europeans in now. But the Eastern Europeans are not ready for that yet. The beauty of the proposal is that it's a frame on whose canvas we can paint whatever we want.[6]

Seen this way, PFP seemingly allowed NATO members to avoid difficult choices and tradeoffs. Nevertheless, since the aspiring Central and East European members are looking for tangible hoops that they can jump through to join the Alliance, and most present members do not want to make that firm a promise, there could be some disappointments down the road as those rather different expectations clash.[7]

Nevertheless, the significance of PFP should not be dismissed too quickly. PFP can be also be seen as a coherent way to hedge temporarily the opportunities, risks, and domestic political constraints entailed in creating a post-Cold War European security system. It does so, first, by avoiding actions that could deepen Moscow's sense of encirclement and isolation. Such restraint is rare in international relations. It acknowledges the undesirable effects of the security dilemma, in which states can inadvertently threaten their rivals even when they mean only to preserve the status quo. In this view, the status quo that the major Western countries want to preserve in Central and Eastern Europe – continued development of a pluralistic, stable, and prosperous zone from Germany eastward to Russia, or at least to the Baltics and Ukraine – need not challenge essential Russian interests. Russia is encouraged to join that project enthusiastically, and an open Russia, unlike Stalin's, should be strongly inclined to do so.

PFP thus seeks to avoid a new division of Europe, unless Russian expansion is seen to require that step. To the extent that there is a struggle among nationalists and more Western-leaning elements for power in Russia, a conciliatory Western hand helps to avoid provoking the former.[8] A widely inclusive NATO is also consistent with Secretary of State James A. Baker's promise to Soviet leaders when Germany was reunified that NATO would not try move further east in a competitive fashion.[9] Although that pledge was made to a state which no longer exists, its rationale remains: provoke as little insecurity in others as necessary.

Second, PFP can help catalyze further internal reforms in the East European countries and make their behavior generally more transparent. For example, in countries where political commissars effectively ran defense policy for 40 years, effective civilian control of the military is slow in coming. Indeed, in some former Warsaw Pact governments, civilian officials and parliamentarians seeking defense information to which they are legally entitled are still being patronized by military organizations not yet used to civilian oversight.[10] Deeper and more extensive working links between new PFP members and NATO governments can help strengthen civilian control of military institutions in compatible ways, although achieving that goal will take time. More direct security arguments are also made for a gradual approach to security integration. Emphasizing the added transparency PFP can offer, one US official said that it 'gives us a way to be associated with Russia on the one hand, and keep an eye open on the other, thereby hedging our bets'.[11]

Third, PFP prepares candidate NATO members to function effectively in NATO's integrated military command system. Interoperable military procedures and equipment, developed over decades by the 14 alliance members that serve under the Supreme Allied Commander for Europe (SACEUR), are seen by these governments as the key to working together effectively. The kinds of activities the Partners will participate in during the transition period to membership – peacekeeping with NATO members, joint exercises and strategic planning, and exchanges of staff officers – will build working-level relationships and demonstrate that these countries can contribute something to NATO as well as consume the protection it offers. In short, these interim activities prepare former Warsaw Pact countries to be effective allies.[12]

A fourth factor, not always stated explicitly, is that few if any NATO members are yet prepared to extend the alliance's security guarantee.[13] Peace Partners are formally entitled to consult NATO on security issues, a right they lacked before, but there is little evident political support for a further explicit defense commitment.

That no current NATO member had to meet such stringent conditions to join[14] is beside the point. NATO is attractive largely because it offers real military protection. That capability derives partly from a coordinated, multi-national command structure built gradually during the 1950s. Rather than dilute the existing military readiness and interoperability, it may make sense to bring new members up to existing standards. Some applicants in fact recognize that need.[15] The process can be pursued gradually because the European states face no military threat comparable in terms of offensive enemy strength or short warning time to that posed by Moscow before the early 1990s. The Bosnian war – the only possible counterexample to date – has been a humanitarian tragedy but not yet a threat to the balance of power outside the Balkans. If such a threat were to emerge, the geopolitical rationale for quicker membership would strengthen, while the institutional and political barriers would diminish.

There is also a longer-term rationale for carefully building new security ties through the PFP – using the PFP to help create in East-Central Europe, and perhaps even in Russia, an environment in which the use or threat of force is considered illegitimate. Although political elites sometimes allude to that rationale, its possibilities have not been explored in depth. The former Warsaw Pact countries sorely need to make that transformation; indeed, doing so would help solve many of their real security problems.

Many of those countries face ethnic disputes arising from scattered minority groups living outside their national homes. Mistreatment of these groups by ethnic majorities, irredentism, or an unhealthy combination of the two factors has produced ongoing sources of tension. Most of the problems originated in the dissolution of the Russian, Ottoman, and Austro-Hungarian Empires after World War I and the often arbitrary delineation of boundaries that followed. Several pairs of states experience those problems: Poland and

Belarus; Poland and Ukraine; Poland and Lithuania; Hungary and Romania; Hungary and Serbia; Hungary and Slovakia; Serbia and Albania; Serbia and Bulgaria; Greece and Macedonia; Moldova and Romania; Bulgaria and Turkey; Bulgaria and Romania.[16] Not all of the disputes are equally serious, and some progress on the underlying problems has resulted from the CSCE's efforts to formulate guidelines for the rights of cultural and linguistic minorities. Still, nationalist regimes representing majority constituencies have resisted applying such norms, and the disputes have intensified without an effective multilateral security structure or a regional hegemon.[17]

Consequently, much of the former Soviet bloc lacks the stability and safety in which economies thrive. Several East European leaders, for instance, have said that foreign investment will continue to lag until the security situation is seen as having stabilized.[18] An analogy to the late 1940s is inescapable: then too, Europeans sought security guarantees from the United States, largely so that economic reconstruction could take off.

Deepening NATO's Partnerships incrementally might provide some of the missing confidence even without formal security guarantees. The goal would be to create as deep a pluralistic security community among as many countries as possible. As Karl Deutsch defined it, a security community consists of two or more states that reject the use or threat of force between them; empirically, one exists if no member devotes any significant planning or resources to a possible war with any other member.[19] In practice, that condition can be ambiguous. It might take decades for states' pacific intentions toward one another to be clarified. Moreover, to the extent that military forces are threatening by virtue of their own size and capabilities, states could be able to threaten one another even without that specific intent.[20] Yet, practically speaking, it is usually fairly clear when political leaders have ruled out war against some other state(s).[21] The first option would use PFP to make pacific intentions manifest among most or all prospective NATO members.

Of course, this assumes that the PFP states want to reassure rather than deter or dominate their neighbors. Those who think that Russia retains imperial ambitions will reject a go-slow approach to NATO expansion. In any case, the Visegrad countries seem overtly wedded to peaceful means of conflict resolution as well as internal reform. Hungary and the Czech Republic have tried to strengthen CSCE codes of conduct designed to defuse conflicts and manage crises peacefully. The CSCE lacks any collective means of enforcement, so these confidence-building measures cannot stand alone, but the detailed work thus far on such measures shows a willingness to accept the status quo.[22] A gradual approach to security integration requires a general acceptance of the status quo, since states will otherwise lack the confidence within which new defense ties can develop.

Even so, most security regimes confront the chicken-and-egg problem:

where norms of restraint are most needed they are hardest to achieve, and vice versa. As the above discussion indicates, security problems abound in Central and Eastern Europe. How might PFP help ameliorate them?

One way is by reshaping the strategies, procurement patterns, and dependencies of military organizations in the former Warsaw Pact countries.[23] As arguments for integration suggest, pooling resources to perform joint tasks creates cross-cutting communities that then make it harder for governments to act independently, especially in ways that threaten others. For example, not every NATO nation needs a fully-developed logistics, communications, or medical supply system in wartime; specialization enhances efficiency as well as the kind of dependencies that promote mutual security. The lesson may be that NATO's integrated command structure has important effects beyond military efficiency and a better ability to coordinate operations. As a result, the military structures of NATO states have become exceptionally transparent to one another, which makes it hard for them to threaten a treaty ally. Gradually extending similar integration through practical PFP programs would help to reassure other members of a country's benign intentions.[24]

Another way is by educating defense policymakers to use compatible internal norms and practices. For example, the US Defense Department's new George C. Marshall Center (dedicated June 1993) in Garmisch, Germany is teaching military officers from Eastern and Central Europe how to build democratically accountable military organizations, and NATO is trying to work out a similar program. Russian Foreign Minister Andrei Kozyrev has similarly suggested that the 'disproportionate influence' of the military-industrial complex in Russian life might be diluted by close collaboration with the West in peacekeeping, since that would give the military an internationally accepted, and thus limited, role to play.[25]

More generally, making defense policy within a consensual alliance teaches multilateralism. Justifying one's military plans each year to a room of foreign officials allows governments to see how their actions affect others, and the resulting transparency about others' intentions and capabilities offers another potent kind of reassurance.[26]

PFP can also reinforce the East-West economic integration symbolized by Russia's association agreement with the European Union (EU) and the prospect that the Visegrad countries will join the EU before the end of the century. Here a Cold War analogy is instructive. Beginning with the European Coal and Steel Community (1951), German power has been tied into the rest of Western Europe. Anything that embeds Russia and its former satellites into the West economically is likewise beneficial on security grounds, since it creates another set of cross-cutting constituencies who favor a security community.

There are numerous practical ways to implement this option. One is to broaden the function of the North Atlantic Cooperation Council. NACC consists of NATO plus the former Warsaw Pact countries; when the Pact crumbled, it gave the East Europeans a minimal but formal communications channel to NATO. Although NACC has been faulted for a lack of military substance, it was never meant to provide one. Now, NACC's work on the environment, science, and European airspace control could be broadened into PFP programs. Ukrainians, Poles, and Czechs would join NATO working groups and contribute to its governance, 'slowly building the familiarity, shared experience, and unity of purpose that is one of the most valuable benefits of NATO structures'.[27] Some PFP countries might begin participating in NATO's Annual Review, which sets out force goals, easing their way into the detailed work done by the planning staffs.[28] Meanwhile, some PFP governments could join NATO in peacekeeping missions. Overall, this would deliberately blur the status of 'NATO membership' by creating multiple, overlapping forms of participation in various programs, with no *a priori* limit on how far the integration could go.[29]

None of this satisfies those who dismiss PFP as a way to avoid the crucial issue of promptly admitting nations that want to join NATO. According to that view, PFP does not satisfy those members that want protection against Russia; they are no more secure now than they were before the PFP was proposed. Russia's ambiguous status as a PFP country that continues to grouse about the program indicates that blurring the line between membership and nonmembership is, as Senator Lugar put it, 'a band-aid offered in place of corrective surgery'.[30]

Yet dodging a difficult issue is not necessarily bad, especially if an interim period is used wisely. Except for Britain and Italy, which have been ambivalent about the matter, all NATO members support eventual expansion. The enlargement process will likely be accelerated if Russia becomes more unstable, authoritarian, or interventionist on its periphery. But if Russia becomes a nonimperial, democratic state, a wider European security community should begin to develop. In that case, the tension between Russian and Western conceptions of NATO's ultimate purpose will fade. The West sees military contacts with Russia as a way to ease that country's isolation and insecurity. Russia, in contrast, wants eventually to transform NATO into a pan-European security organization completely divorced from its Cold War roots.[31]

These certainly conflict in the short run, but may not over the longer term. A wider European security institution is not necessarily harmful to the West if it ties in the United States and Russia acts consistently in nonthreatening ways. Either way, NATO is prepared.

In sum, there are two justifications for gradually deepening the PFP relationships in lieu of more rapid changes in NATO. First, gradualism minimizes the risks entailed in quickly changing an institution that has helped stabilize Western Europe, while also dealing with fears of abandonment in Central and Eastern Europe. NATO should not admit new members it is not ready to defend, and choosing to extend defense commitments entails long-term resource requirements that should be carefully considered. The first option thus implies eventual NATO expansion, but only when applicants are truly ready internally to participate fully and other circumstances justify it. By bringing candidate members gradually into a developed security community, it can foster compatible military institutions, constructive ways of thinking about mutual security, and helpful military dependencies. All of this will make it harder for those nations to threaten one another and will be valuable whether or not Russia eventually joins the security community. Second, this option avoids prematurely drawing new lines across Europe and, in so doing, further legitimizing nationalist, neo-imperial strains in Russian foreign policy.

Option Two: Quickly Accelerate NATO Membership

This option has two variants, depending on who is admitted and for what purposes. Variant A is the narrower of the two. It would bring the Visegrad countries and perhaps the Baltic republics and Ukraine fairly quickly into NATO to protect them from Russia. It sees Russia as the security problem in Europe, not as part of the solution. In considering such a policy, one might be optimistic and expect Russia to become more cooperative if the West is firm: this assumes that strong fences make good neighbors. But if such firmness produces a more insecure, aggressive Russia, advocates of variant A see the price as unavoidable. Where the first option defers basic decisions about how the West should deal with Russia on security issues, 2(A) seeks clarity by dealing with a Russian problem first. Quick NATO membership for states legitimately worried about Russia is the solution. It would reassure the new members, but it would also bring fairly high risks.

Henry Kissinger and Zbigniew Brzezinski have made arguments for rapid expansion in several articles critical of PFP.[32] While their positions are not identical – Brzezinski would try a bit harder to reassure Russia about Western intentions if NATO expanded – the reasoning is similar. Four main points are made. First, PFP risks diluting NATO to the point of meaninglessness; according to Kissinger: 'Refused a security guarantee and offered the placebo of nebulous joint missions, which have not been defined and which do not respond to their concerns, Poland, the Czech Republic and Hungary must have noted the absence of any distinction between Russia, the cause of their anxiety, and themselves, the historical victims of Russian aggression.'[33] That argument reflects a venerable *realpolitik* assumption: an alliance ultimately must stand against some security threat. If it includes everyone, it cannot deal with real rivalries.

Second, Russian pretensions to intervene freely in the countries on its periphery make it inopportune to put off the pleas of East-Central Europeans for real protection. Proponents of rapid enlargement assume that Russia is effectively trying to recreate large chunks of the Soviet Union by destabilizing and bullying its neighbors. Central and East Europeans have good reason to worry about Moscow's actions; now is not the time for those countries to languish in a security vacuum. Historically, the existence of such a vacuum has tempted aggressors in Europe rather than reassured them. In fact, rewarding Russia with a special status in the Partnership – which key NATO members have agreed that Moscow must have due to its geopolitical weight – smacks more of a so-called 'second Yalta' than the creation of a bloc-free Europe, a key rationale for PFP.

Third, avoiding a decision on expanded membership will not make it any easier to decide later. If NATO fears to draw new security lines when Russia is weak, these analysts argue, why would it be willing to extend security guarantees eastward in the future, when Russia may be stronger? The conclusion is then obvious: NATO should expand before Russia recovers. If political developments in Russia do turn out badly, Europe might be much more threatened than it is now.[34]

Fourth, the West must set clear limits around Russia because that country is relentlessly expansionist. Assumptions that capitalism and democracy will change that tendency are too optimistic. History and culture make it unlikely that Russia will become a stable democracy, and the imperial temptation will be much stronger in an authoritarian system. Evidence is adduced that Russia is increasingly coercing the states on its periphery in ways quite similar to those of the Soviet era.[35] Kissinger put it bluntly: 'Perhaps the most serious misapprehension of the Partnership for Peace proposal is that a reformist Russian government would automatically abandon traditional foreign policy goals.'[36]

Of course, the risks in admitting the Baltic republics and Ukraine could be greater than for incorporating the Visegrad group, since the former were part of Moscow's 'inner' rather than 'outer' empire. Russian leaders will probably be more committed to a sphere of influence inside the Commonwealth of Independent States (CIS) than outside of it. Brzezinski, in noting a strong and increasingly explicit Russian consensus to recreate a sphere of influence within the CIS, implicitly acknowledges that point.[37] Yet he does not seem to reach a plausible policy implication for such a distinction among NATO aspirants: that NATO's eventual security perimeter might prudently stop short of the old Soviet Union rather than come to rest inside it.

A renewed clarity about allies and adversaries is the main attraction of a rapid enlargement policy. It would admit to NATO those countries that want to join unconditionally and draw a line around Russia, the 'difficult' partner that continually wants to negotiate special understandings and arrangements. The fear that NATO could eventually be expanded only on Russian terms, tacit or explicit, would then be gone. There is a logic to that approach: even strong advocates of PFP admit that the West will have a difficult, uncertain relationship with Russia for a long time to come. Setting firm, defensive limits along its borders now would at least remove some major ambiguities. Along with such clarity, NATO could perform the deterrent mission to which it is best suited, and for which it might be irreplaceable.

On the other hand, that policy would risk a self-fulfilling prophecy by heightening Russian insecurity and hostility. The Versailles Treaty surely did not create Hitler, but it helped legitimize him inside Germany. While it is foolish to overestimate the West's impact on Russia's internal evolution – its size and distinctive political culture make it hard for outsiders to mold – underestimating that impact would also be a mistake. Elites that want to cooperate with the West are still in power in Russia, they have survived two attempts by hardliners to derail reform, and their policies are better for Russia's neighbors than those of their nationalist rivals. Advocates of option 2(A) ignore evidence that supports that conclusion. Russia has withdrawn its troops from eastern Germany on schedule, withdrawals from the Poland and Baltics are proceeding on schedule, and Moscow is now willing to share peacekeeping in Georgia with UN troops.[38] With those indicators in mind, should NATO take an action that can only strengthen the nationalists at the reformers' expense? Few doubt that a rapid enlargement of NATO would undermine the reformers. Are the likely marginal benefits of quick expansion worth such risks? Would Poland, the Czech Republic or any other country gain enough additional security, given the modest threats any of them faces from Russia now, to risk the results of provoking a major nationalist backlash there?

The question is moot if Russia is indeed relentlessly authoritarian and imperialist, but that assumption may be too pessimistic. Stephen Sestanovich argues that Russia seeks a traditional sphere of influence in its 'near abroad,' not a restored empire, and that the distinction matters. Comparing recent Russian behavior abroad to that of the Soviet Union lends some support to Sestanovich's view. Seeking leases to military bases in Azerbaijan and Georgia is different from thoroughly dominating these nations, and Russian acquisition of Ukrainian oil refineries is hardly the same as efforts to dismember that country. Admittedly, Russian efforts to crush Chechen independence do not bode well, but this is an internal matter. There is also no evidence that Russia is threatening or intimidating nations in its former outer empire. It is unlikely that situation will change unless Russian extremists take power. In fact, a moderately assertive Russian foreign policy, one that stops well short of domination in the near abroad, may be good insurance against more fundamental expansionism insofar as it helps legitimize non-nationalist democrats inside the Russian Federation.[39]

Quickly adding members to NATO would also require premature, counter-productive decisions about where security lines should be drawn *among* applicants. Kissinger and Brzezinski aside, relatively few people suggest that Ukraine, Belarus, Moldova, and the Baltic states should be brought in at the same time as the Visegrad group. But leaving them demonstrably out could heighten their insecurity, and might, despite Western efforts to the contrary, be taken as a tacit signal to Russia that they were now more firmly in Moscow's sphere. Why then should a new line be drawn at Ukraine's border without a more serious threat to its essential security interests?

If this analysis is correct, even the Visegrad countries would gain little added security from joining an anti-Russian NATO quickly, and quick expansion could hurt the forces within Russia that are likeliest to treat them well. Drawing new lines around Russia could delegitimize moderates at home. By the same token, trying to put Ukraine in NATO would be provocative and of little practical help. Since Russia will likely at times act in ways that make the West uncomfortable, but will probably not try to recreate its outer empire, what is the West's best response? Can NATO really deny Russia a sphere of influence in contiguous areas? If not, should it work to moderate Russian behavior within multilateral institutions from which Russia does not want to be excluded? If the last question is answered affirmatively, caution about any version of an anti-Russian NATO is in order.

A second, broader argument for adding members promptly can also be made. Two premises underpin it: 'NATO must go out of area or it will go out of business'; and nothing short of expanded membership can help stabilize East-Central Europe.[40] What distinguishes 2(B) from 2(A) is that in the latter version, NATO is not intended primarily to contain Russia and would not add members based on that threat alone. Instead, it would seek to prevent the emergence of an 'arc of instability' running through much of the area between Germany and Russia by embedding the East-Central European nations into an established security institution whose members work and plan together. Democracy and capitalism are seen in this argument as very fragile in the region without real security guarantees, which PFP does not provide. Ideally, NATO would expand along with the European Union, since it is not in the US interest for Europeans to have defense commitments through the Western European Union (WEU), EU's defense arm, in which the United States has no input.[41] Nothing in this idea is seen as necessarily anti-Russian, according to Asmus, Kugler and Larrabee:

[I]t is hard to understand how supporting democracy and stability in Eastern Europe can undercut democracy in Russia. It is not in the interests of Russia, above all Russian democrats, to have a zone of instability, renewed nationalism and potential conflict on its western flank.[42]

These problems, they argue, can be best alleviated by a wider NATO.

That thesis still leaves the question of which nations to admit and when, since not everyone would join at once.[43] One criterion would be to admit first those countries that have gone furthest toward democracy, civilian control of the military, market economies, and the other characteristics of Western societies – in other words, those that have become most NATO-like on their own. Expansion on that basis could be seen as a quicker way to create the security community envisaged through Option One. Using the standard of 'readiness,' Poland, the Czech Republic and perhaps one or more of the Baltic states would be eligible to join soon. Implicit in this policy is the idea that Westernization naturally would create a natural distinction between the Visegrad group and Russia or Ukraine, because the most eastern east nations are least likely on grounds of internal reform to be suitable NATO members in the near future.

At first glance the main difference between current policy and 2(B) would seem to be timing; after all, US and many other NATO officials have said repeatedly that NATO membership is highly probable for qualified PFP candidates at some point. Yet there is a critical difference. Option one deliberately would sidestep the membership issue for some time to see what PFP could achieve on its own. There are several reasons to do that. First, NATO works fairly well now with 16 members. Without a specific security emergency, which Asmus and his colleagues do not demonstrate is imminent, an evolutionary expansion of the alliance is likely to be more productive than a swift one. Eastern Europe has a very different recent history than that of the NATO countries; it also has distinct political and military structures and decision-making traditions. These governments need to get used to working with one another and with current NATO members and that is best done gradually.

Second, full NATO membership for East-Central European countries creates a commitment to protect an unstable status quo. That point obviously can be cited as a reason to make the commitment in the first place, but it also ought to induce caution. Does NATO want more problems similar to those posed by the rivalry between Greece and Turkey? And even if is willing to assume them, can it prudently extend its security perimeter when defense budgets throughout the alliance are falling? The more time that passes, all else being equal, the firmer the post-Cold War status quo will become, and the less serious this problem will be.

Third, admitting some members soon increases the risks that those left out will become alienated. This could have serious internal consequences for those states. Asmus and his associates recognize the problem: they claim that Eastern Europe's 'lack of a stable security arrangement has already helped to undermine progress toward democracy and reform.'[44] Arguably if some former Warsaw Pact states enter NATO soon but others do not, Western-leaning elites in the latter may find less value in Westernization than before. That risk is hard to calculate, and could be quite different from one country to another, but it ought to induce caution about quickly adding new members to NATO.

Finally, the argument that a wider NATO is needed to underpin a wider EU does not hold up. Asmus *et al.* claim that opening the EU is the best insurance against backsliding on reform and that NATO, for reasons mentioned above, must include any new EU members. That logic is flawed, since EU expansion will take some time. New members will have to enter the Union gradually so as not to be crushed by the competitive European market. Moreover, existing EU states will want to plan carefully for the massive resource transfers that these relatively poor countries will need. For these reasons, the entire process of extending the Western economic and security system eastward will be slower than the advocates of option 2(B) believe.

Option Three: Build a New European Security Institution

A third option sees NATO itself as the long-term problem in dealing with European security: it is too tied to Europe's past to be of much use in the future. The remedy is usually thought to be some new vehicle for pan-European integration. That option could be pursued directly. Alternatively, to the extent that the first option works, NATO's character could become so different that it would in effect become the vehicle for European security integration.

As with both variants of the second option, a direct approach might begin with Russia. As an initial step, Moscow might be induced to respect the political and military status quo in the former Warsaw Pact countries. If Russia made credible promises to do so, and after a reasonable transition period, it could help build the 'Common European Home' it has long sought, one that would transcend NATO and Russia's defeat in the Cold War. The necessary enforcement stick in this package would be a credible collective security pact involving all interested European states; if key lines were crossed by aggression or intimidation, a collective response to the aggression could be expected. To avoid even the appearance of a Western-Russian condominium over the heads of East-Central Europeans, those countries would be made charter members of the new institution. Such commitments would be phased in gradually, and only when the requisite military forces to guarantee them had been credibly committed. Unlike the CSCE, the new body would then have collective means of enforcement at its immediate disposal.

Such a radical departure would rest on the belief that NATO has outlived its usefulness – that it carries too much Cold War baggage to address today's issues.[45] Aside from peacekeeping and peace-enforcement operations, which often require more collective will than NATO members have recently shown, NATO now has little coherent purpose. Off the record, government officials admit that it is seeking ways to justify its continued existence. That in itself is not sufficient reason to start over with a fresh institution and mandate, but there are other fundamental problems. By keeping Europeans dependent on the US military guarantee, NATO makes them less willing to define and pay for their own 'security pillar', an oft-stated goal. A new organization with less historical baggage would gain more European support, and would allow the United States to define a more realistic transatlantic security role.

Several commentators have made this last point in recent years. NATO persists, they say, mainly because Americans continue to subsidize Europe's military security. That policy was justifiable in the 1950s but is hardly so today. Arguably from the US point of view, NATO is especially anachronistic; although the United States is the dominant world power militarily, it is at the same time a declining power in terms of economic influence and willingness to bear significant military costs and risks.[46] Europeans have incentives within this structure to frustrate specific US objectives, but relatively little motivation to build an institution more suited to the present security situation and distribution of power.

Just as fundamentally, it can be argued that the very political construct of a united 'Western alliance', the core on which NATO is built, is anachronistic. The Western countries may constitute a common civilization, but that is not the same as a coherent political entity capable of acting with a unified purpose. Historically, the West has been united only in the presence of a common enemy. Without such imminent danger, the rationale for NATO's continued existence is politically weak.[47]

France's attitude toward NATO, although in flux, illustrates that point. France is working with NATO more closely now than it has in a generation, but it still refuses to reenter the unified command and has resisted otherwise useful NATO innovations such as the Combined Joint Task Forces (CJTFs) – which would allow selected groups of countries to intervene together outside of NATO's Article 5 Treaty area – because the CJTFs would give Supreme Allied Commander Europe (an American post) too much leverage over French forces. For France, as for many other Europeans, Western unity has in practice meant subordination to the United States.[48] Even if the United States will take a less assertive role in European security from now on, as the Clinton policy strongly indicates, the earlier legacy is hard to overcome, and it frustrates many practical ideas for moving forward.

A broader organization could take various institutional forms. Russia wants the CSCE to replace NATO. CSCE does have a membership that transcends Cold War divisions, but realistically it is not a military institution; CSCE's tasks are preventive diplomacy and the setting of standards for intra-national and external conduct. For that reason, assigning NATO's military missions to CSCE would be just as out of character as giving NATO mainly a political role.

A European Defense Organization (EDO), fully inclusive from the beginning, would instead be needed to guarantee existing borders from violence or the threat of force. It could comprise a fairly simple charter, based on a mutual security guarantee. That pledge could be based on troop deployments and regular exercises such as NATO has pioneered. In fact, NATO's Article 5 guarantee, if widened to the whole of Europe, could be a model.

Clearly the rationale for such a new institution is political, not military. NATO has highly developed military institutions that might take years to replicate – if that could be done at all. A new body would compensate through two political advantages. First, many regional security organizations have suffered from the exclusion of key members; the Organization of African Unity excluded South Africa, and the Association of Southeast Asian Nations historically left out Vietnam, Laos and Cambodia.[49] A new European security institution would avoid that error. Second, a new body would carry no political baggage. Neither France nor Russia would have reason to hang back from or resist its work. If one can make a functionalist argument for retaining what already exists, one could also argue that starting over is more politically efficient in terms of future tasks.

But could a new institution guarantee collective security in Europe? Whether collective security is possible at all has been controversial for decades and continues to be so today. I will not repeat that debate here.[50] Traditionally, while advocates of collective security have had a hard case to make, two fairly optimistic points can be made about contemporary Europe. First, such a system works best among democracies, which almost never attack one another. Much of Europe is evolving toward democracy, even if the transition is painfully slow. Second, collective security need not work perfectly to work at all; states can and will retain selective defense commitments to buttress the general obligation. An informal Concert mechanism of major powers would in practice have to support such a system for it to survive, and all the major powers in Europe are either democracies or becoming so.[51] There is little *a priori* reason to think that a broader European security institution would be less able than NATO to keep the peace; after all, a new institution would approximate a broader NATO, albeit with a fresh mandate and no Cold War legacy.

Yet along with these potential benefits are key risks. It would be hard to replicate NATO's integrated command structure within another institution, especially one so wide that political consensus on its form and degree of control would be problematic. That structure has helped to pacify Western Europe and is precisely what attracts many of the former pact countries to NATO. Many people also doubt that US troops would ever be redeployed in Europe during peacetime if NATO dissolved. Furthermore, as US officials often point out, NATO is America's only durable institutional link to Europe. Without it, the United States would lose perhaps irreplaceable influence and a practical way to coordinate security policy with Europeans, with the risk that Europe would become more 'insular' or even hostile to Washington's interests.[52]

Fortunately, indirect progress toward the third option can be made through the first. If the Partnerships are deepened over the long run, and Russia does evolve into a relatively benign, democratic, Eurasian power, NATO will eventually be so broad as to effectively become another institution. At that time, it would have lost most of its identity as an alliance and become a genuine collective-security institution. That has been NATO's stated aim since the Harmel Report was issued in 1967. The advantage of allowing it to happen one step at a time is that NATO's present instrumental value – the integrated command structure that allows members to act efficiently when they choose to, and closely integrated decisionmaking institutions that can help ease Eastern Europe's security dilemmas – would be preserved. If Russia does revert to authoritarianism, NATO's identity as an alliance could then re-emerge quickly.

Some Wider International Implications

Any major change in the Atlantic subsystem would have wider international implications. Choosing a policy should involve some effort to think these through.

The first option suggests a long transition period before post-Cold War security structures and alignments become clear. During that time, Europe either will or will not develop a more cohesive security identity, and America either will or will not stay militarily engaged in Europe in a meaningful, credible way. Of course, these outcomes are highly interdependent and expectations about either will affect the other. Over the short term, the European Union will probably widen its membership rather than deepen existing ties, coalitions among its members and with America will tend to be issue-specific and ad hoc, and relations with Russia will probably drift. If

Russia continues to reform, that pattern could proceed for a long time. Internationally, coalitions would be similarly fluid, since there would be no sharply defined conflict to polarize them.

The second option would repolarize much of the world, not just Europe. Although the Cold War would not return, since mutual fears would be weaker than in the 1940s, many countries outside as well as inside Europe would be pressured to choose sides. A tighter Russian sphere of influence in Central Asia, for example, would affect the security of Iran, Pakistan and the Persian Gulf states, and through them the security of India and China. It is difficult to know whether economic cooperation would be subordinated to military ties, as happened during the Cold War; now, unlike then, these ties significantly cut across political divisions.

The implications of the third option are least clear, but they would probably involve a loose major-power concert over the broader international system as large powers in other regions associated with the European group. Such a system has in fact emerged: as the decisionmaking over Bosnia indicates, joint intervention is now effectively negotiated among a group of countries that collectively have the ability to act decisively and that seek mainly to preserve stability in Europe. Widening the formal transatlantic security structure beyond NATO would simply reinforce that tendency by giving a small group of major countries more reason to direct the larger body. The 1991 Gulf War and the Bosnian conflict (albeit to a lesser extent) have shown that no European country can effectively act alone against an adversary with a sizable, modern conventional arsenal.[53] Coalitions will thus be needed, and if there is no sharp threat they will probably be subsets of a wider concert of powers.

For the United States, this may be a good outcome. US officials for years have sought a pluralistic world with open economic doors, and that is more nearly true now than it has been since the 1920s. A broad, loose European security structure, achieved by stages, is a relatively risk-free way to solidify this achievement.

NOTES

I thank Jonathan Clarke, Bob Lieber, Rob McCalla, and David Painter for their comments on an earlier draft of this essay.

1. See remarks made by NATO Deputy Secretary-General Balanzino during the visit by Russian Foreign Minister Andrei Kozyrev to sign the PFP presentation documents. NATO Integrated Data Service (electronic version, no pagination), 22 June 1994.
2. These objectives were set out in the invitation and the PFP framework document, both issued at the North Atlantic summit in Jan. 1994. They are summarized in Gerhardt von Moltke, 'Building a Partnership for Peace', *NATO Review*, June 1994, NATO Integrated Data Service, electronic version.

3. Ibid. As Moltke observes, 'This is not a kind of competition or race. . . . It simply reflects the reality that countries develop in different ways and at different rates.'

4. See Ronald D. Asmus, Richard L. Kugler, and F. Stephen Larrabee, 'Building a New NATO', *Foreign Affairs*, Vol.72 (Sept.–Oct. 1993), pp.28–40.

5. Michael R. Godfon, 'US Opposes Move to Rapidly Expand NATO Membership', *New York Times*, 2 Jan. 1994, p.A1.

6. Quoted in Craig R. Whitney, 'NATO Plight: Coping With Applicants', *New York Times*, 4 Jan. 1994, p.A4.

7. As of now, no NATO member views the conditions specified in the framework document as a checklist that, once specifically fulfilled, automatically will qualify a country for membership. Such a decision will be made on broad political grounds. See Paul E. Gallis, 'Partnership for Peace', Congressional Research Service Report no.94–351, 22 April 1994, p.2. This policy, however, has been controversial. Sen. Richard Lugar (Rep.-Indiana), who favors quicker membership for some Central European countries, viewed PFP as 'the [Clinton] Administration's lowest common denominator'. See Lugar's remarks in *The Future of NATO: Joint Hearings before the Subcommittee on European Affairs of the Senate Committee on Foreign Relations and the Subcommittee on Coalition Defense and Reinforcing Forces of the Senate Armed Services Committee*, 103rd Cong., 2d sess., 1 and 23 Feb. 1994, p.12.

8. Several US officials have made these points. See, e.g., Secretary of Defense Les Aspin, 'Partnership for Peace', remarks delivered to a forum sponsored by the Atlantic Council of the United States, 3 Dec. 1993, p.3; and Gallis, p.5.

9. Michael R. Beschloss and Strobe Talbott, *At the Highest Levels: The Inside Story of the End of the Cold War* (Boston: Little, Brown, 1993), p.185.

10. I thank Tom Hanson, Director of NATO and European Affairs at the Atlantic Council, for pointing this out to me.

11. Testimony of Frank Wisner, Under Secretary of State for Policy, in *The Future of NATO: Hearings*, pp.27–8.

12. See comments by Wisner, ibid., p.27.

13. Comments to this effect by Sen. John Warner (Rep.-Virginia), ibid., pp.6–7, have been echoed by several NATO members. Some German leaders, however, have been more receptive to the idea of quicker membership, partly as a way to extend the West's security perimeter eastward from their own borders.

14. I thank Stanley Sloan of the Congressional Research Service for pointing this out to me.

15. One defense official from a former WP country told a NATO counterpart that he did not want NATO to relax its standards for new members. Confidential briefing, June 1994.

16. This updates and expands the list found in Daniel N. Nelson, 'Not All Quiet on the Eastern Front', *Bulletin of the Atomic Scientists*, Nov. 1990, p.36.

17. See 'Hungarian Minorities in East-Central Europe', *Atlantic Council Bulletin*, 12 May 1994, p.3; and Nelson, p.36.

18. I thank Tom Hanson of the Atlantic Council for this point. See also Gallis (note 7), p.5.

19. Karl Deutsch *et al.*, *Political Community and the North Atlantic Area* (Princeton, NJ: Princeton UP, 1957), p.32.

20. Ibid., pp.33–5.

21. Ibid., p.35.

22. For a good discussion of recent developments, see John Borawksi and Bruce George, 'The CSCE Forum for Security Cooperation', *Arms Control Today*, Oct. 1993, pp.13–16.

23. Kenneth Oye argues that such institutional change in all NATO countries during the Cold War will be a major source of continuity in national policies from now on. See Kenneth Oye, 'Beyond Postwar Order and New World Order', in *Eagle in a New World: American Grand Strategy in the Post-Cold War Era*, (eds.) Kenneth Oye, Robert Lieber, and Donald Rothchild (NY: HarperCollins, 1992), p.25.

24. This has not precluded conflict between Greece and Turkey, but one could argue that joint NATO membership has made these disputes easier to manage.

25. Stephen Sestanovich, 'Giving Russia Its Due', *National Interest* 36 (Summer 1994), p.11.

26. Confidential interview with a US Defense Dept. official.

27. William S. Cohen, 'Expand NATO Step by Step', *Washington Post*, 7 Dec. 1993, p.A25.
28. 'NATO Partnership for Peace: Beyond the First Step', *Atlantic Council Special Report*, 21 March 1994, p.2.
29. Cohen (note 27).
30. Lugar, 'NATO's "Near Abroad": New Membership, New Mission', Speech to the Atlantic Council of the United States, 9 Dec. 1993, p.9.
31. Daniel Williams, 'Western Envoys Wary of Russia's Entry Into NATO', *Washington Post*, 25 June 1994, p.A18.
32. See Henry Kissinger, 'Not This Partnership', *Washington Post*, 24 Nov. 1993, p.A17; Kissinger, 'Be Realistic About Russia', *Washington Post*, 25 Jan. 1994, p.A19; Zbigniew Brzesinski, 'A Bigger – and Safer – Europe', *New York Times*, 1 Dec. 1993, p.A23; and Brzezinski, 'The Premature Partnership', *Foreign Affairs* 73/1 (March–April 1994), pp.67–82.
33. Kissinger, 'Not This Partnership'.
34. Ibid.
35. Brzezinski, 'The Premature Partnership' (note 32), pp.68–79.
36. Kissinger, 'Be Realistic About Russia' (note 32).
37. Brzezinski, 'The Premature Partnership', (note 32), p.76.
38. Jim Hoagland, 'Right on Russia', *Washington Post*, 2 June 1994, p.A23.
39. Sestanovich (note 25), passim.
40. Asmus, Kugler, and Larrabee (note 4), p.31.
41. Ibid., p.35.
42. Ibid., p.37.
43. Ibid., p.36.
44. Ibid., p.30.
45. Jonathan Clarke, 'Replacing NATO', *Foreign Policy* 33 (Winter 1993–94); pp.22–40.
46. Ibid. p.35. See also David Garnham, 'Ending Europe's Security Dependence', in this volume; and Owen Harries, 'The Collapse of "the West"', *Foreign Affairs* 72 (Sept.–Oct. 1993), p.46.
47. Harries, pp.46–9.
48. Ibid., p.47.
49. S. Neil MacFarlane and Thomas G. Weiss, 'Regional Organizations and Regional Security', *Security Studies* 2/1 (Autumn 1992), pp.6–37.
50. The contrasting positions are outlined in Charles A. Kupchan and Clifford A. Kupchan, 'Concerts, Collective Security, and the Future of Europe', in *America's Strategy in a Changing World*, (eds.) Sean M. Lynn-Jones and Steven E. Miller (Cambridge, MA: MIT Press, 1992), pp.151–98; and Richard K. Betts, 'Systems for Peace or Causes of War? Collective Security, Arms Control, and the New Europe', in ibid., pp.199–237.
51. Andrew Bennett and Joseph Lepgold, 'Reinventing Collective Security After the Cold War and Gulf Conflict', *Political Science Quarterly* 108 (Summer 1993), pp.213–37.
52. See 'The New Europe in a New Age: Insular, Itinerant, or International? Prospects for an Alliance of Values', address by Robert B. Zoellick, State Dept. Counselor, to the America-European Community Assoc. International's Conference on US/EC Relations and Europe's New Architecture, Annapolis, MD, 21 Sept. 1990. The speech was reprinted in US Dept. of State *Dispatch*, 24 Sept. 1990, pp.118–21.
53. Philip Zelikow, 'The New Concert of Europe', *Survival* 34/2 (Summer 1992), pp.25–6.

Why an Expanded NATO Must Include Russia

CORAL BELL

The old maxim 'be careful of what you wish for, because you may get it' has never been better exemplified than by the present situation of the Western powers *vis-à-vis* Russia. The West wished, reasonably enough, that the Soviet autocracy would disintegrate and give way to some more humane and acceptable form of government. To almost universal surprise, it did so in 1991, 74 years after Lenin's *coup d'état*. A struggle toward (with luck) democracy began in Russia and in at least some of the other 14 ex-Soviet republics. It was a famous victory, no doubt, and, to my mind, even a reasonably well-deserved one. The decisionmakers of the NATO powers during the 43 years of the Cold War (1946–89) should get high marks in due course from history (despite some grievous errors) for their crisis management during that long and dangerous peace.

Yet what has ultimately come of the Cold War triumph? Three years after the end of the Soviet Union, the decisionmakers in Moscow are visibly far less in control of everything, including their own tenure of power, than their predecessors ever were. That may well be a necessary price to pay for the transition from totalitarianism toward democracy; by definition the central government must lose some of its capacity to control the society concerned. The erosion of governmental dominance in Moscow's case unfortunately includes the ability to control the crime rate, which seems to be climbing even beyond Western levels. Even more crucially, it means a decrease in the ability to control political tendencies that will influence Moscow's future dealings with the rest of the society of states.

A Less Cautious Russia?

There is a Western theory (or at least a pious hope) that democracies never make war on each other,[1] which would seem to imply that the transition from communism toward democracy must improve the prospects of peace. In time that might occur, but of course democracy is not the only potential political alternative to communism. Moreover, historically the factors that preserved the peace during the 43 years of the Cold War had nothing much to do with democracy. They were prudent crisis management in a situation of alliance stability and conventional as well as nuclear deterrence. Several of the factors in that benign constellation have vanished or are vanishing. Unless they can be replaced by alternatives (and that is where NATO comes in) the crisis management of the future will probably be less prudent and less predictable than it was during the Cold War. In that event, the defenses of peace will be weaker, despite the recent and current expansion of formal democratic institutions in the world.

Moreover, the crises themselves are likely to be more frequent, especially in and around the former Soviet sphere of dominance, which the Russians now call the 'near abroad'. The Cold War had many disadvantages, but it imposed a sort of frozen calm in political and military relationships over much of the world, like the Russian landscape in mid-winter. Now that the Cold War has passed into history, the same landscape is experiencing an early thaw, with torrents of nationalism everywhere and unmapped quagmires in abundance.

Leninist doctrine, in addition, provided one of the factors that kept Moscow's decisionmaking cautious during the Cold War decades. Leninism held that there would inevitably be a series of 'frightful collisions' between the capitalist and communist worlds, but that since the 'wave of the future' was on the communist side, ultimate victory was inevitable. If a political system's official doctrine holds as an article of faith that it is bound to win in the long term, policymakers can always justify retreat in any particular crisis as merely prudential, since by definition it cannot affect the long-term outcome. From the first few crises of the Cold War (Azerbaijan in 1946 and Berlin in 1948) to the very end (the pulling down of the Berlin Wall in 1989) that assumption was a useful predictor of Soviet behavior, whoever the decisionmaker of the time happened to be. (The least cautious of them was Nikita Khrushchev, whose policies over Berlin and the Congo raised East–West tension to fever pitch, and who brought the world close to nuclear war in the Cuban missiles crisis. But even he retreated, albeit barely in time.)

That prudence-justifying, though erroneous, ideological assumption has clearly vanished along with communist doctrine in general. The decisionmakers in Moscow these days are in charge of defending not the interests of world revolution or the interests of the Soviet Union but the interests of the Russian Federation, which is at the moment a rough approximation of the Czarist Empire as of about 1696 (i.e., with Siberia and the Far Eastern territories, but without the central Asian and transcaucasian territories acquired in the nineteenth century). They have very little reason to believe that time is on their side, since every year's survival by the other 14 republics that emerged from the debris of the Soviet Union gives those polities extra standing as separate sovereignties within the society of states, and makes it the less probable that they can be reabsorbed into a new Russian empire with the old tsarist boundaries, as some Russian nationalists would wish. So one important motivation for patience and caution in crisis, as it existed for the true believers of the communist era, is no longer effective.

Worse still, the pressures of Russian nationalism on the decisionmakers in the Kremlin are much greater than during that epoch. The influence of the ultranationalist leader of the so-called Liberal Democratic party, Vladimir Zhirinovsky, demonstrates that point – although, fortunately, his influence is not as extensive as earlier believed. Some of the Russian rhetoric over Bosnia illustrates similar nationalist sentiments, albeit in less virulent form. If a more substantial and rational nationalist figure, perhaps former vice-president Alexander Rutskoi, should win the presidency in 1996, Russian nostalgia for a more glorious past could acquire a credible spokesman.

Even now, Russia is vigorously signalling a renewed ambition to resume its traditional place in world affairs.[2] It is doing so not under the banner of 'world revolution,' obviously, but under the pre-1917 Russian Orthodox great power banner. That trend has been visible since Russian intervention began in the Bosnian War: the Slav 'big brother' of the Serbs both protecting them from NATO air strikes in early 1994 and leaning on them a little to help deliver a settlement that will stand to the Russian account with the other great powers, and convince both the West Europeans and the Americans that the Russians are 'back in the game.' A similar pattern is emerging in the Middle East. 'Holy Russia' long saw itself as having a natural role in the Holy Land as the protector of Orthodox Christianity. A 'born again' Russia might aspire to that traditional role once more, which, of course, would not please the Israelis, given Moscow's successful fishing on the Arab side of those troubled waters during its Soviet incarnation, and the current stirrings of traditional Russian anti-Semitism. More justifiably, Moscow must feel it has a natural interest and an important role to play in the North Korean crisis, since there is a large Russian city, Vladivostok, only three hours' drive from what could conceivably be a nuclear theater of operations.

In summary, most of the factors that made Moscow rather a cautious and predictable adversary in many Cold War crises are less influential than they once were. It is in the interest of the West and of the preservation of peace that those factors are replaced by other incentives and constraints. And NATO may be a major instrument in that endeavor.

The New Sources of Crises

The great (and as yet relatively unexplored) difference between the Cold War decades and those for which policymakers must now begin to devise strategies is not at the level of danger and conflict. That level was, is, and is likely to remain high. But now that the Cold War is over, it is modestly encouraging to reflect that during those 43 years, despite an unparalleled arms competition between the superpowers, and despite a predominantly high level of international tension, there was only one period of truly acute nuclear danger, the Cuban Missile Crisis of 1962. A fortnight's acute danger in more than four decades of high tension is diplomatically well below the historical norm. Given adroit diplomacy, the decisionmakers of the next half century might hope to do as well or better, but only if they successfully adapt the institutions that served them well during the Cold War, especially NATO, to the radically changed requirements of the current and prospective turbulence in world politics.

The nature and dynamics of crisis are much as they were. It is the *provenance* of crisis, the source from which crises are coming, that has changed.

For the entire 74 years of the Leninist era, from 1917 to 1991, the sources of conflict and crisis in great power diplomacy were largely ideological. The West combated, successfully and in sequence, the communist project of world revolution, the sinister force of Nazi and fascist reaction, and then communist power as embodied after 1946 in the massive military capacity of the Soviet Union – and after 1949 also in the potential power of China, which seemed for a while likely to be a useful (even decisive) ally for Moscow. One might call that whole 74-year span the period of the wars of ideology.

Since 1992 the society of states seems to be back in a period of wars of identity. 'Back' is the operative word, since although the world has certainly been transformed, the change is not to something new but to something uncomfortably familiar from earlier diplomatic history and temporarily forgotten in the brief outburst of 'new world order' euphoria. These days there is a dismaying sense of *déjà vu* suffusing contemporary world politics. There are wars in the Balkans again. China is a more substantial and assertive power in world affairs than it has been since the 1840s. Above all, there is the revived, yet historically long established, persona of Russia as a confused, embittered, recently defeated, economically disadvantaged, convulsively resentful, great power. There is even a new and more complex variant of the 'Great Game' in Central Asia, where Russia, Turkey, and other powers maneuver for advantage and influence.

Such factors raise the question of whether the society of states is careening 'forward to the past' – as of about 1905–1912. If that were so, all of our diplomatic efforts would need to be concentrated on preventing another 1914 cataclysm. But there are differences, and though some of them (such as the nature of contemporary weaponry) may seem merely to make the situation more dangerous, there are others that make it more manageable.

The great irony of the West's Cold War victory is that it has produced a result in which the most vital and most endangered of Western interests for the time being is a benign evolution of events in Russia and around its periphery. That is a direct parallel to the situation in the years immediately after 1945, when a benign evolution of events in Germany and Japan was of the same vital importance to the West. Western objectives were secured, in part, by incorporating both ex-adversaries into the Western alliance system about six years after the end of hostilities (i.e., the US-Japan Security Treaty of 1951 and the beginning of German recruitment into NATO in the same year). Perhaps the latter decision marks the true moment of reconciliation with an old foe. (For France after the Napoleonic Wars it came faster, with recruitment to the concert of powers only three years after Waterloo, in 1818.)[3]

In each case it was recognized that an old challenge to the international order had disappeared and provision must be made to cope with a new one. In the current case involving Russia, NATO has a unique significance in that it has been the most formidable military instrument of Western power, and therefore it has also been the logical preoccupation and target of the Russian security elite. That security elite has suffered a traumatic loss of assets since 1989: the defensive *glacis* of Eastern Europe, the command and control structures of the Warsaw Pact, the forward deployed troops in Central Europe, the massive advantage in conventional weapons, the flow of conscripts from the other ex-Soviet republics. Above all, the elite has suffered the loss of its over-privileged share of Russian economic resources. (No doubt, the USA had a military-industrial complex, but the USSR *was* a military-industrial complex.) That same bereft security elite is still a powerful part of the political class in Moscow, and its choice of the man to back in some future domestic political crisis, like that of August 1991, may determine whether Russian society continues to evolve in directions that the West can welcome. Russia's beleaguered security elite needs reassurance that the strategic interests of Russia can be safeguarded, and membership in NATO would be the most direct way of providing that reassurance.[4]

NATO's Dual Role

The most crucial element in NATO's history – with particular relevance to the future of the Alliance – is that it has functioned, from almost its earliest days, as a security community for its own members as well as a military alliance against their common adversary. An alliance develops the additional role of a security community by not only providing reassurance but imposing restraints on its own members, *vis-à-vis* each other and the rest of the world.[5]

It is easiest to see this, for the earlier NATO years, by considering the cases of Greece and Turkey. They were long-standing adversaries when NATO recruited them in 1952, and to a large extent they still are. In Bosnia, for instance, the Greeks back the Serbs and the Turks back the Muslims. Moreover, Cyprus remains an unresolved bone of contention between them. Yet more than 42 years after they were admitted to the Alliance, they are both still members of NATO, despite practically every left-wing Greek government in the interim having threatened to quit. That durable NATO link, despite genuinely sharp clashes of national interests and a totally changed strategic context, testifies to the fact that a security community can be made to work even between sworn adversaries who remain deeply suspicious of each other and have many historic grudges.[6] In effect, neither country has quit because it would mean not only renouncing the assorted benefits the Alliance provides, but (vastly more galling) seeing the adversary continue to benefit. Their enmity towards each other is therefore, paradoxically, part of the bond holding them in the Alliance. And the Alliance, in turn, is part of the mesh of constraints which has precluded full-scale hostilities between them.

The case of Germany offers an even more direct parallel to the potential situation of Russia *vis-à-vis* NATO. The initial fight over German entry, more than 40 years ago (1951–54), is almost forgotten now except by those who lived through it, but in its time it evoked as many embittered feelings and as much impassioned controversy as potentially surrounds the case for Russian membership. After all, when the strategic need for German troops on NATO's front lines first began to be recognized in Washington, London and Paris,[7] it was only six years after German armies had occupied most of Europe, German bombs had devastated British cities, German soldiers had killed a great many Americans, and the German government had operated a policy of cold-blooded genocide, carefully organized by efficient German bureaucrats.

Yet once a diplomatic mechanism, the Western European Union (WEU), had been found for integrating Germany into NATO, all the earlier agonizing over the idea seemed to vanish like snow in summer. By the time of the next crisis with the Soviet Union (Berlin in 1958) the Germans were assumed to be predestined Western co-belligerents against the dangerous men in the Kremlin.

That kind of sea change in Western public opinion could prove even easier for Russia than it was for Germany. Americans have never actually fought the Russians, and the British and French have not done so formally since the Crimean War. For Britain, Russia has in fact been an ally against three would-be hegemonic powers in Europe (Napoleonic France, the Kaiser's Germany, and Hitler's Germany). The Cold War was expensive enough, but the decisionmakers in the Kremlin did not unleash on the world anything like the torrent of death and destruction of Hitler's war.

Against those favorable auguries, it must be conceded that whereas in 1951 NATO decisionmakers believed they saw an absolutely clear military and moral necessity for German troops to bolster the Alliance's military position to deter a possible Soviet push westward, no such clear strategic imperative is visible in the present situation. The only way a common strategic interest of equal weight and urgency could arise in the foreseeable future would be if China achieved a quantum leap in its military and diplomatic potential (perhaps by alliance with Japan?) so that it became a newly formidable adversary both to Western interests round the Pacific rim, and to Russian interests in Asia. But that seems unlikely for at least a couple of decades. (An alternative possibility would be a renewed Islamic challenge to both the West and Russia, but that seems even more remote in time.)

On the other hand, in the dispersed and intractable international turbulence most likely to generate the danger of war for the foreseeable future, the retention of Russia as a military/diplomatic ally may now be just as vital for the Western powers as the recruitment of Germany was in the mid-1950s. There is already political pressure to extend the NATO security community eastward, so that it covers the vulnerable peoples who live between the German and Russian heartlands (Poles, Czechs, Hungarians and others), whose histories have as often been blighted by the one as by the other of their powerful neighbors.

A Perilous Option: Excluding Russia

It would be immensely dangerous for the West to further encourage those legitimate hopes, however, without including Russia in the security arrangements. Otherwise, such sinister figures as Zhirinovsky would not be the only Russians likely to see initiatives to enlarge NATO as deeply threatening to Russia's traditional interests. Almost any potential contender in Russia's 1996 presidential elections, and later, could attract support by denouncing alleged Western manoeuvres against Russian security and make a case for rattling the 25,000 nuclear warheads that Moscow still has at its disposal. Russia's nuclear weapons capability should be of special concern to Americans, since the Russians no longer have the advanced deployments, satellite allies, and well-organized conventional forces that once enabled them convincingly to threaten of a rapid push westward into Germany. Consequently, they must depend more on their chief remaining strategic asset: their still efficient nuclear strike capacity, whose logical targets would be in the United States. The Strategic Arms Reduction Treaty could be vitiated by such preoccupations, and the world could suddenly find itself back in a nuclear crisis as dangerous as the Cuban Missile Crisis in 1962.

The parallels between that crisis and the potential one are striking. In 1962 Khrushchev was (rightly) charged by President John F. Kennedy with, in effect, seeking surreptitiously to extend the Soviet Union's strategic reach deep into a traditional sphere of American power, ostensibly for a client state, Cuba, which represented itself as being threatened by American invasion (and probably believed itself so threatened). In the potential parallel, the West would be charged by Russian nationalists (and perhaps by Moscow decision-makers) with seeking surreptitiously to extend its strategic reach deep into a traditional sphere of Russian power, ostensibly on behalf of a group of smaller sovereignties, which are represented as potentially threatened (and well might be). Washington is not the only capital that feels itself entitled to Monroe Doctrine-type sensitivities about its geopolitical 'backyard'.

The great powers live together peaceably, when they do, by showing a degree of prudence about such concerns. That prudence was shown, for instance, in American restraint during the East European crises of 1953 (Germany), 1956 (Hungary), 1968 (Czechoslovakia), and 1971 (Poland). Washington's strategy of prudence, hard-hearted though it seemed to many East Europeans, avoided hostilities that would have entailed enormous dangers to them as well as to the West itself. A victory over communism occurred without bloodshed ultimately. The eventual success of that diplo-macy of strategic caution will need to be remembered by both the East European leaders, who are naturally anxious for a better security environ-ment, and by NATO decisionmakers in this new and delicate phase of the long encounter between Russia and its Western neighbors. One aspect most needing to be borne always in mind is the impact of that encounter on the perennial domestic political debate within Russia, between the 'Slavophiles' and the 'Westernizers.' The current decisionmakers in Moscow generally identify with the Westernizers, and the survival in power of that strand of opinion is important to the future success of all Europe, both economically and politically. There will always be pressure on the Westernizers from the Slavophiles, especially if a genuinely representative political system survives in Russia, since most Russians are fervent nationalists. But the pro-Western strand of opinion is more likely to be able to resist pressures for dangerous diplomatic or military ploys if the West shows an adequate consciousness of Russian sensitivities.

Toward a Broader NATO

Thus the package which the diplomats and strategists of NATO will need to construct must, if it is to stand any chance of adoption and survival, rest on a three-way balance among the interests of the West, the interests of the East Europeans, and the interests of the Russians. The need for that delicate tri-partite balance, in turn, suggests that NATO itself might tend to develop a 'three pillars' structure, rather than the 'two pillars' idea, which has so long been suggested but never effectively built. It should potentially enhance rather than diminish the prospect (which has been the implicit motive for the two pillars metaphor) of developing a distinctive European security identity. Perhaps an 'EDU' (European Defence Union) rather than WEU would be appropriate. The weakness of the old scheme was that there never seemed much point (other than placating anti-American feeling) in divorcing Western Europe's strategic preoccupations from those of Washington. But the suggested change would give real substance and meaning to a European defence identity of a wider scope.

For the Alliance itself, which has appeared in some danger of diminution or loss of a clear *raison d'être* after the Soviet collapse, the change would imply a major enlargement of its area of concern. In analytical terms, its development and role since 1949 has so far been as the main security community of the status quo military alliance. The suggested expansion would make it, at least in embryo, the main security community of the whole Euro-Atlantic concert of powers. Its functions and strategies, however, would remain basically as they are: containment, deterrence, and reassurance. Containment of conflicts within the security community, deterrence of threats from outside it, and reassurance on both fronts.

That might seem an overly ambitious vision, but if one looks at how events are evolving in Bosnia, it appears already to be taking on substance. The only effective threats of military action in Bosnia have been those of NATO air strikes, which early in 1994 at least pressured the Serbs into easing the sieges of Sarajevo and Gorazde, and may eventually force them into giving up some of the territory they have seized. More tellingly, *Russian* diplomatic pressure on the Belgrade Serbs was needed to persuade the Bosnian Serbs to make even such modest concessions as they have made. That is to say, NATO has already been, in that crisis at least, the effective military face of the concert of powers, and Russia has been the most essential contributor to its diplomatic effectiveness. Policymakers in Moscow originally appeared quite ambivalent about the Bosnian conflict. Russian nationalism (expressed as pan-Slav attachment to the Serb cause) remains strong – although not as strong, luckily, as it was in 1914. The actual experience of dealing with Serbian nationalists, however, appears to have produced a useful exasperation in the chief Russian negotiator, Vitaly Churkin. He has been quoted as saying that the Serbs 'must be made to understand that Russia is a great power and not a banana republic'.[8] Churkin's annoyance is an entirely traditional reaction by an envoy of the concert of powers to a minor quasi-ally who is rocking the boat too persistently.

The old Russia was the most devoted and messianic member of the early nineteenth century concert of powers. The present day policymakers at the foreign office in Moscow have only to look through their back files to see what techniques and strategies were useful for that particular constellation of power. The parallels between Russia's situation then and its situation now *vis-à-vis* the West are strikingly close. Then as now the sprawling multi-national giant, far overshadowing in size and resources all its neighbors save China, was never quite able to get its act together or define its identity coherently. It never quite caught up economically or politically, and was beaten again and again by outsiders, as Stalin bitterly reflected in a well-known passage of a 1931 speech:

> One feature of the history of old Russia was the continual beatings she suffered from falling behind, for her backwardness. She was beaten by the Mongol khans. She was beaten by the Turkish beys. She was beaten by the Swedish feudal lords. She was beaten by the Polish and Lithuanian gentry. She was beaten by the British and French capitalists. She was beaten by the Japanese barons ...[9]

Russia has not only needed to be *at* the 'top table' (the concert of powers), it has needed the reassuring *existence* of the top table far more than smaller but more coherent sovereignties such as (originally) Britain, France, or Prussia. In that respect the wheel really does seem to have come full circle.

Of course, a workable concert of powers for the remainder of this century, and still more for the next, must be global, not merely Western (still less merely European), if only to match the globalization of the world economy and the redistribution of military power away from its traditional holders. The latter phenomenon, the redistribution of military power, which is still pro-ceeding apace, began, with neat symbolism, in the defeat of Russia by Japan in 1905 – probably the true beginning of the sequence of disasters that have afflicted Russia in the past 90 years (though the seizure of power by the Communist Party appears in retrospect clearly the worst). It is salutary to reflect that at the beginning of this century seven capitals (London, Paris, Berlin, Vienna, St Petersburg, Washington and Tokyo) more or less con-trolled the whole of the society of states, whereas by the end of the century there will probably be nearly 200 effective sovereignties, and about ten of them may be nuclear powers.

The rates of change in relative economic growth will speed up changes in military balances, so we are still in the early stages of this great trans-formation, which may more deeply affect the society of states than even the astonishing political changes of the past five years. Rapid economic change tends to induce social and political resentments and instabilities, as in the Shah's Iran during the 1970s. Combining the rising ferment of ethnic con-sciousness with the instabilities induced by rapid economic change produces quite a recipe for future international turbulence.

That does not mean that no mechanisms for managing the crises, miti-gating the conflicts, and limiting the hostilities, are possible. It means that the diplomatic strategists of the great powers need to work at strengthening those mechanisms that exist, clarifying the division of labor between them, and devising new ones where there are deficiencies.

In the Bosnian crisis, the absence of a clear division of labor between UN officials and NATO officers seems to have been responsible for much of the shambles that has characterized the peacemaking mission. The bureaucrats and the military cannot fix that problem by themselves; it is a matter for the decisionmakers of the great powers. Jonathan Eyal, Director of Studies at the Royal United Services Institute in London, has caught the circumlocutionary clumsiness of the situation as of early 1994:

> The world was asked to believe that the US, Britain and France, the main actors within NATO, were asking the US, Britain and France, the most important members of the Security Council, for an authorization which would allow the US, Britain and France to undertake air strikes in Bosnia, all on account of defending not the people of the republic but rather British and French soldiers on the ground . . .[10]

The society of states needs to do better by the time the next batch of crises arrives. And it can, if the concept of the security community, as developed in NATO, is made more inclusive (by taking in new members to the east) and parallel arrangements are developed in areas where NATO itself should not intrude. That latter point is necessary for the Alliance's own preservation, as well as for Third World sensitivities. More people were killed in a few weeks of the violence in Rwanda than in the three years of war in the former Yugoslavia, but any joint military intervention by the West in such areas would look too much like 'collective colonialism', or a rerun of the imperial scramble in the late nineteenth century. Security communities need to be regional, in Africa and elsewhere. But in NATO's case, given adequate handling of the inclusion of Russia and the East Europeans, the region (though certainly *not* the membership or rules of procedure) could more or less correspond to that of the Conference on Security and Cooperation in Europe (CSCE): Vancouver to Vladivostok. (There seems to be no agreed name as yet for this vast area. 'Northern Arc' would be at least as accurate as 'North Atlantic' ever was, and would permit the retention of the NATO acronym.)

Military alliances (as compared to such diplomatic and cultural organizations as the CSCE) have the great advantage of openly operating and being accepted as necessarily hierarchies of power. All the members may be nominally equal, but some of them are inherently and undeniably more equal than others. No one could argue that in the past 45 years that the decisions of NATO have been as much shaped by its minor members as by the United States. The Alliance has always been, and no doubt will continue to be, run by an 'inner club' of the five or so members with the most military, diplomatic, and economic clout. The other members go along because of the advantages to them of the system, and France's ostensibly 'empty chair' receives due attention.

That is why the alleged disadvantages of additional members (only Russia, Ukraine and Poland are strategically vital) do not appear decisive. Russia would, of course, necessarily become a member of the inner club, because of its military capacities. NATO traditionalists will no doubt wince at the thought, but that change in membership might even have advantages for the most delicate internal balances of the Alliance – those between Washington and the West European countries, especially Germany. The true heart of the Alliance is the transatlantic connection, and the chief foreseeable danger to that connection is the potential regrowth in the United States of the neo-isolationist sentiment that briefly showed its head above ground in Patrick Buchanan's bid for the Republican presidential nomination in 1992: the argument that the United States should shake off its external burdens, and in particular leave NATO to the Europeans. That bid might be dismissed as ephemeral as well as unsuccessful, but in a sense President Clinton's successful presentation of himself as the 'domestic policy' president was a more adroit riding of the same underlying wave of popular sentiment. Feelings among the US electorate of weariness and disenchantment with the burdens of world leadership are not only inevitable, but could readily become still more politically effective in the prospective world of dispersed, intractable turbulence than they ever could have been facing the single coherent threat of Soviet power.

On the other hand, it is difficult to believe that even the most purblind of American nationalists would argue that NATO could safely be left to the Europeans if those Europeans included the Russians. In effect, such an abdication would potentially hand the leadership of that cherished Alliance to the once and perhaps future rival superpower. Moreover, since the second most powerful military force in any such grouping would be the reintegrated Germany, the ghost of Rapallo could easily hover in the air, conjuring up a more formidable rival to the United States in the world leadership contest than either the Soviet Union or Western Europe could ever have been. That specter, in turn, would make it essential the United States retain leadership of so potent an organization in its own national interest. Thus the force of American nationalism could be enlisted to maintain the transatlantic link, instead of operating against it, as has lately been the danger. Incidentally, the interest of France in returning to full membership in NATO would also be enhanced, since otherwise French isolation from Europe's security arrangements would be almost total.

Russia as a NATO Member

Naturally, the decisionmakers of the NATO powers and those in Moscow have had to manage their *rapprochement* as porcupines do their love-making: very cautiously. As far as can be discerned from published reports, that has been the case with the negotiations over Russian membership in the Partnership for Peace.[11] The PFP is clearly a useful waiting room, but no one's temper is much sweetened by being kept too long in a waiting room. Obviously there are and will be divided opinions within the Russian political-military establishment about how close to get to the Western powers.[12] Some of the comment in Moscow on the signature of the PFP agreement was to the effect that it consolidated the Western victory in the Cold War, and to my mind that is how it should be construed in the West as well. The logical way to offset the resentments that perception could engender among Russians is to offer without too much delay the only convincing token of real acceptance of diplomatic and strategic equality: full membership in the Alliance.[13] The political crossroads of 1996 in both Moscow and Washington – with the presidential elections – may impose a deadline.

It might be objected that including Russia in the Alliance overlooks the purpose for which NATO was originally founded: to defend the interests of the West. However, the intent of a policy of inclusion is to maintain that aim. In the present circumstances the best mode of defending Western interests is to enlarge the concept of the West to include Russia and the lands that lie between it and the present NATO area. In Cold War polemics it was sometimes useful to depict the Soviet Union as a sort of 'anti-West,' but that was always quite ahistorical. Marxism was a Western heresy and a Judeo-Christian heresy. The roots of Russian culture, just as much as those of the other European powers, lie in ancient Greece and Palestine. The Iron Curtain was an unnatural barrier across a single civilization, and the fall of the Soviet tyranny has made possible the removal of the economic and political divisions that barrier imposed. Russian membership in NATO would end the strategic division that went with them.

The case for Russian membership in NATO does not depend on any illusions about a sudden advent of harmony in world politics, or of an identity of interests between Russia and the West, or of democracy and stability in the Russian political system, or prosperity in the Russian economy. Still less is it based on any particular tenderness for the current decisionmakers in Moscow (though we might have worse, and probably will have at some point). The basis of a policy of inclusion is a consciousness of the massive dangers to the interests of the West (the first of which is the preservation of peace) in the present and prospective turbulence in the great arc around the Russian heartland, in areas proximate to Russian power and susceptible to Russian influence.

If membership in NATO were extended to the East Europeans without also being extended to Russia, it would create a situation of grave danger for them as well as for the West and for the interests of peace. On the other hand, if the East Europeans were permanently excluded they would justifiably regard themselves as relegated to a 'buffer zone' or 'gray area', and that perception would exacerbate the tensions of the region as well as the political resentments among its people. The world is back in the unfinished business of the society of states before the wars of ideology began in 1917. That business includes the making and breaking of sovereignties, competing group identities and the territorial bases they claim to control, the transfer or loss of populations, and the redrawing of frontiers. Russia is a necessary partner in coping with the consequent turbulence.

NOTES

1. In so far as theories of the obsolescence of war have been based on the past wars of aggression or inadvertence between what might be called the traditional great powers of the society of states, they appear well founded. But those powers are only a handful of the nearly 200 contemporary sovereignties. Most of the current outbreaks of war are within societies outside that traditional circle. Their causation may need to be approached via political sociology rather than via international relations theory. But see Martin Van Creveld, *The Transformation of War* (NY: The Free Press, 1991); John Mueller, *Retreat from Doomsday: The Obsolescence of Major War* (NY: Basic Books, 1989); and Carl Koysen, 'Is War Obsolete? A Review Essay', *International Security* 14 (Spring 1990), pp. 61.
2. See, for instance, as regards the extreme nationalists, especially Vladimir Zhirinovsky, Kevin Fedarko, 'Rising Czar?' *Time*, 11 July 1994, p. 29. Also see Gennadi I. Chufrin, 'Russia Is Looking East with New Interest and New Flexibility', *International Herald Tribune*, 15 June 1994, p.4; and 'Imperial Nostalgia: Russia and the Slavs' *Economist*, 3 July 1994, p.49.
3. For an account of the nineteenth century concert of powers, see Henry Kissinger, *Diplomacy* (New York: Simon & Schuster, 1994), pp.78–102. For an interpretation of the re-emergence of a concert relationship between the central balance powers in the post-Cold War world, see Richard Rosecrance, 'A New Concert of Powers,' *Foreign Affairs* 7/1 (Spring 1992), pp.64–82. In my own view, the strongest evidence of the return of a somewhat disguised concert system is the current functioning of the UN Security Council. When that piece of diplomatic machinery was created in 1944–45, it was on the assumption that the wartime 'Grand Alliance' would continue, with the somewhat grudging addition of China and France, as in essence a postwar concert of powers. Hence the institution of the veto, and hence also the near-inoperability of the system for the whole Cold War period. But since 1990 the Security Council has been in almost continuous operation with practically no vetoes cast, although Moscow and Beijing have certainly not liked all the Western policies involved. Their acquiescence appears evidence that they find the concert useful enough to sacrifice marginal interests for the sake of preserving it. My reason for calling the concert 'somewhat disguised' is that the Security Council appears as its diplomatic and ideological face, and the Group of 7 industrial powers (G-7) its economic face. Since the nineteenth century society of states was much less institutionalized, the underlying power relationships were then more clearly visible.
4. That idea may at first sight appear (especially to old NATO hands) a contradiction in terms.

So it would be, if the initial purpose of an organization had to remain its final purpose. But the strength of political and military institutions like NATO lies in their capacity for flexible response to radically changed circumstances, such as, in this case, the disappearance of the threat against which NATO was originally founded. There are obviously difficulties and dangers in the course of action suggested here, but there are equal or greater dangers in most of the alternative futures proposed for NATO. Especially, to my mind, the danger of creeping irrelevance, or supercession by other organizations such as CSCE or WEU, less competent to maintain the essential 'spine' of NATO, the transatlantic connection. Of course, NATO's 'secrets' would be open to Moscow, but are we sure they are not already so? Its essential infrastructure and the armed forces of the present member powers would still be there. If tensions between Moscow and the rest rose again toward Cold War levels, Russia would presumably either make an exit (like France) or be suspended (like New Zealand from ANZUS) and the incident would be a useful warning signal for other members. For differing views, see Zbigniew Brzezinski, 'The Premature Partnership', *Foreign Affairs* 73/1 (March–April 1994), pp.67–82; Charles L. Glaser, 'Why NATO Is Still the Best: Future Security Arrangements for Europe,' *International Security* 18 (Summer 1993), pp.3–50; and Jeffrey Simon, 'Does Eastern Europe Belong in NATO?' *Orbis* 37/1 (Winter 1993), pp.21–35.

5. For an analysis of NATO's general dampening effect on security tensions between alliance members, see Josef Joffe, 'Europe's American Pacifier', *Foreign Policy* 54 (Spring 1984), pp.64–82; and Joffe, *The Limited Partnership: Europe, the United States and Burdens of Alliance* (Cambridge: Ballinger, 1987).

6. For a discussion of the many sources of friction between Greece and Turkey, see Monteagle Stearns, *Entangled Allies: U.S. Policy Toward Greece, Turkey, and Cyprus* (NY: Council on Foreign Relations Press, 1992).

7. The strongest reaction against the project for German recruitment came from France, which for a time, through the concept of the European Defense Community, seemed almost ready to sacrifice an independent French Army in a bid to prevent the creation of a new German Army and especially a new German General Staff. There were also great doubts in Britain, and in Germany itself. The crisis came to a head at the end of 1954, and was resolved in the first few weeks of 1955. For a general account of the German rearmament issue within NATO, see Gordon Craig, 'Germany and NATO: the Rearmament Debate, 1950–1958', in *NATO and American Security*, (ed.) Klaus Knorr (Princeton, NJ: Princeton UP, 1959), pp.236–59.

8. 'Bosnian Serbs Must Pull Out of Gorazde, Yeltsin Says', *International Herald Tribune*, 20 April 1994, p. 4. Also see 'Russia Should Break from Serbs,' *The Australian*, 20 April 1994, p.14.

9. *Problems of Leninism* (Moscow: FLPH, 1945), p.356.

10. Jonathan Eyal, 'The Results of Western Stupidity', *The Australian*, 20 April 1994, p.11.

11. See William Drozdiak, 'Moscow Accepts Partnership and Strategic Cooperation with NATO', *International Herald Tribune*, 11–12 June 1994, p.1.

12. See Andranik Migranyan (a member of Boris Yeltsin's presidential council), 'Partnership for Peace: No, Russia is Too Big for This Exercise', *International Herald Tribune*, 24 June 1994, p.4. Also see the interview with Russian foreign minister Andrei Kozyrev, 'You Can't Expect Angels to Appear Overnight', *Time*, 11 July 1994, p. 35. Kozyrev quotes the Russian communist leader, Gennadi Zyuganov, as drawing a parallel between the PFP and Hitler's Barbarossa plan for invading Russia.

13. Various Russian political leaders have stressed that the inclusion of their country in NATO is the indispensable final step in ending the Cold War. E.g., see Boris G. Fedorov, 'The Cold War Will End Only When Russia Joins NATO', letter to the editor, *Financial Times*, 20 Sept. 1994, p.18.

Beckoning Quagmires: NATO in Eastern Europe

JONATHAN. G. CLARKE

For nearly half a century NATO kept the peace in Europe without firing a shot in anger. With the defeat and disappearance of its erstwhile Soviet adversary, one might have expected this fortunate state of affairs to continue. Suddenly, however, within the space of three months at the beginning of 1994 the following events took place: NATO heads of government issued a declaration that linked NATO's security directly with the conflicts in post-communist Eastern Europe; NATO ambassadors agreed on an ultimatum to parties in the Bosnian conflict that fairly bristled with warlike rhetoric; NATO fighter planes shot down four 'enemy' aircraft over Bosnia; a NATO plane was itself shot down on an intended bombing mission; and NATO ground troops killed an 'enemy' soldier.

What is the explanation for such developments? Were they an aberration or did they presage far-reaching changes in NATO's posture and doctrine? In short, where is NATO headed in the post-Cold War era? These are important and troubling questions. To search for answers, it is necessary to look beyond the short-term impulses afforded by the Bosnian crisis into NATO's post-Cold War search for identity.

Finding something for NATO to do has become a cottage industry in its own right. Numerous reasons have been offered:[1] NATO retains the trans-atlantic link against the possibility of a resurgent Russia; it represents a focus of trans-European stability at a time of flagging European political integration; it inhibits the re-emergence of Germany as the dominant, potentially nuclearized European military power;[2] it permits the United States to share its security burden with trusted, militarily effective partners and prolongs American influence in Europe;[3] it represents years of investment in combined training and force interoperability, factors that will be important if, as many assert, future European and American security requirements will increasingly be met through multinational cooperation.[4]

Transcending these ideas, a widespread concern that the demise of the Warsaw Treaty Organization (WTO) might trigger instability in Eastern Europe fuelled a lively debate about a possible role for NATO. In mid-1991, both President George Bush and Secretary of State James A. Baker III made speeches emphasizing the preeminent priority they attached to stability in the emergent noncommunist Eastern Europe.[5] Those concerns were matched in Eastern Europe where Polish President Lech Walesa and Czech President Vaclav Havel took the lead in seeking membership in NATO on behalf of the Czech Republic, Poland, Hungary, and Slovakia.[6] These themes soon made their way into academic arguments to the effect that 'NATO is not an organization whose mission is over.'[7]

Those functions and concerns are not to be lightly dismissed. Is NATO, however, the right agency to address them? Do they in sum continue to provide a convincing justification for NATO's survival *as a military organization* beyond the demise of the Warsaw Pact? And if they do, what are the implications for US national security policy? What new commitments do they presage for the western democracies? In short, for what purpose are all the generals, admirals, tanks, ships and planes?

To the European members of NATO, such questions may seem overly theoretical or old fashioned. For them, the problems are close at hand and the consequences of miscalculation immediately tangible. Looking for assets with which to tackle the various security problems on the Continent, the West Europeans view NATO as the only readily available instrument. They regard the reshaping of the Alliance as a strictly practical problem.

For the United States, however, NATO's inexorable metamorphosis from an antihegemonic defensive force into a rapid-reaction unit to quell brushfire conflicts raises more principled and fundamental questions. Does the 'new' NATO portend American involvement in the type of fratricidal European quarrels from which the United States throughout its history tried to stand clear? If that is the import, what is the nature of American interests?

The New Rationale

NATO's advocates recognize the force of these questions. They know that defense alliances cannot live by good intentions alone; alliances need to have something specific to do – a military mission. As Senator Richard Lugar (Republican-Indiana) put it in a speech to the Atlantic Council in December 1993:

> A credible American commitment to an alliance focused on territorial defense against a non-existent threat . . . cannot long be politically sustained on Capitol Hill. If only for domestic political reasons, a *new rationale* . . . revolving around *new missions* . . . may be essential to halting the erosion in support for NATO in the Congress.[8]

More recently, that 'new rationale' has come to be expressed less in terms of concrete missions than in a more abstract form. In an indiscreet but revealing remark in March 1994, a senior British Army officer explained the rationale for his activities in Yugoslavia: 'Frankly, I don't care much what happens to Yugoslavia. But I care a hell of a lot what happens to NATO.' As far as that officer was concerned, the prime purpose of NATO's intervention in Bosnia is to prevent the organization from becoming what he described as 'an international laughing stock'.[9]

In the United States, the view that NATO's foremost task is to assert its own 'viability' commands support across the political spectrum. Jeane Kirkpatrick, a senior scholar at the conservative American Enterprise Institute, and Morton Abramowitz, president of the liberal-inclined Carnegie Endowment for International Peace, have jointly promoted this proposition in the *New York Times*.[10] National Security Advisor Anthony Lake spoke in the same vein in a speech about Bosnia to the School of Advanced International Studies at Johns Hopkins University, 'We have an interest in showing that NATO – history's greatest military alliance – remains a credible force for peace.'[11]

Years before Lake's speech, NATO's leaders and bureaucrats had, in fact, already initiated what proved to be a long and agonizing debate about what that mission might be. Beginning with the 1990 NATO summit in London and reaching a doctrinal high watermark at the 1991 summit in Rome, they traversed a path strewn with ambitious new notions such as the 'new strategic concept', 'out-of-area capability', and 'North Atlantic Co-operation Council'.[12]

Those proposals always seemed somewhat paperbound exercises, however. They failed to grip the public imagination as a sufficient justification for a military alliance marshalling enormous firepower and consuming huge resources. The erosion of NATO's credibility continued: the number of American troops in Europe continued to fall; budgetary constraints impelled the Canadians to announce a withdrawal of their NATO forces to Canada; in the United States, congressional support could no longer be taken for granted.[13] Even when NATO naval forces began to patrol the Adriatic in July 1992 to monitor observance of sanctions against Serbia and NATO deployed AWACS aircraft in November 1992 to enforce the UN-mandated 'no-fly-zone' over Bosnia, it did not seem to be enough. Lugar's graphic forecast that NATO must 'get out-of-area' or else it would go 'out-of-business' typifies the impatience with pious statements and ineffectual action.[14] As the Bosnia crisis intensified and reform prospects in Russia became more clouded, the fear of NATO's total irrelevance finally concentrated minds. At their summit meeting in January 1994, NATO's leaders issued a declaration designed once and for all to guarantee the Alliance's 'indispensability'.[15]

The strategy they adopted had two main components: first, an expansion of the Alliance toward the east through the 'Partnership for Peace' program under which any member of the former Warsaw Pact or European neutral nation could, after meeting certain conditions, form a partnership with NATO; and second, an agreement that NATO could offer itself as a military executor to support the peacekeeping or peacemaking activities of the United Nations, the West European Union (WEU), or the Conference on Security and Cooperation in Europe (CSCE).

A Ticking Time Bomb

NATO's leaders could be well satisfied with those 'battle plans for survival'.[16] Their focus had been on keeping the Alliance afloat, with the means being less important than the ends. In that task they were eminently successful,[17] but they have left behind a ticking time bomb. Within the text of the communiqué lie two phrases that, if they represent statements of serious intent, dramatically expand the potential for NATO involvement in crisis management far beyond the Alliance's traditional boundaries.

The first is: 'NATO will consult with any active participant in the Partnership [for Peace] if that partner perceives a direct threat to its territorial integrity, political independence or security.' The underlying philosophy for that statement may be found earlier in the declaration: 'Our own security is *inseparably* linked to that of *all* other states in Europe.' For these purposes the declaration defines 'Europe' as comprising the whole CSCE membership and, therefore, as including the former Soviet central Asian and transcaucasian republics.[18]

The practical implications of this doctrine are already under debate. Sophisticates point out that the word 'consult' means no more than that. The Alliance agreed to talk but did not enter into any new Western defense guarantees, and in particular stopped short of offering NATO membership to any of the East European countries. In setting out the initial case for the Partnership for Peace (PFP), Secretary of State Warren Christopher was careful to stress the evolutionary nature of the changes.[19]

Perhaps the sophisticates are right, but it is already clear that others harbor more expansive interpretations of the text. Many East Europeans, notably the Czechs and Poles, make no secret of the fact that they see association with NATO as the first step toward full NATO membership – in which belief they will have derived strength from President Clinton's assurances to the Polish Assembly in July 1994[20] – and as the beginnings of a system of 'all-European defense guarantees'.[21] In doing so, they echo the words of the late NATO Secretary-General Manfred Wörner, who for many years entertained a vision of NATO as the 'focal point of a pan-European security system'.[22]

The expectation of a more activist NATO posture is confirmed by the second of the Brussels summit's commitments:

In pursuit of our common transatlantic security requirements, NATO increasingly will be called upon to undertake missions in addition to the traditional and fundamental task of collective defense of its members, which remains a core function. We affirm our readiness to support, on a case by case basis in accordance with our own procedures, peacekeeping and other operations under the authority of the Security Council or the responsibility of the CSCE, including by making available Alliance resources and expertise. Participation in any such operation or mission will remain subject to decision of member states in accordance with national constitutions.[23]

Once again, the escape words may be found. Peacekeeping operations will be voluntary and national constitutions will apply. Nonetheless, the trend is clear. In 1991 Wörner spoke in terms of a NATO-led defense community that would see NATO deployments to trouble spots from the Atlantic Ocean to the Ural Mountains.[24] In a similar vein, researchers at the RAND Corporation advocate that NATO assume responsibility for what they call 'arcs of insecurity' in northern and southern Europe.[25] Most telling of all, the Brussels summit approved the American proposal to create NATO Combined Joint Task Forces (CJTF) with the specific mission of providing military intervention capabilities.[26]

It may be seen, therefore, that the Brussels declaration contains a tension between PFP, which fell short of East European aspirations for full NATO membership, and the more expansive language on continental security, which met most of the East European requirements. All in all, however, by moving the Alliance toward involvement in Eastern Europe, the Brussels summit set the seal on proposals that had been brewing for at least two years.

The New Commitments

If those proposals are taken at face value (and the CJTF initiative suggests that they are being treated seriously at the military level), they represent a dramatic expansion of both the number and nature of conflicts in which NATO may potentially become involved. The summit declaration also signaled, at least in spirit, a fundamental shift in attitude from that expressed by a NATO diplomat in 1990: 'if there's a problem with the Turkish population in Bulgaria, or trouble between the Czechs and Slovaks, you think NATO is going to send in the troops to keep the peace? Forget it.'[27] In point of fact, those may be precisely the sort of commitments that the Brussels summit accepted.

Of course, new commitments are not of themselves necessarily bad or suspect. That the West holds a major stake in the peaceful evolution of

Eastern Europe and the former Soviet Union is not in dispute. However, the very importance of this issue makes it all the more vital that we examine it seriously and with our eyes open both about the nature and the implications of those commitments. In some ways, collective defense resembles options trading: the fortunate few always manage to make profits, thus avoiding losses and the consequent margin calls. Not everyone, however, can be consistently lucky and savvy. As prudent traders, we need to remain alert to the possible downside risks and ensure that we maintain the necessary reserves of money and will. Otherwise we ought not to enter the market.

The first margin calls have, in fact, already been made. As noted earlier, in a remarkably foreshortened calendar, NATO moved from the Brussels summit to the brink of war in three months. On 28 February 1994, barely six weeks after the Brussels meeting, two American F-16 fighter aircraft flying under NATO command shot down four Bosnian Serb *Galeb* jets over Bosnia. Six weeks later, on 13 April, NATO lost its first aircraft to hostile fire when a British Royal Navy Harrier was downed over Gorazde. On 22 April the North Atlantic Council issued an ultimatum to the Bosnian Serbs to withdraw from Gorazde or face an all-out bombing campaign against targets drawn up by NATO's Allied Forces Southern Europe headquarters. On 30 April NATO forces killed a Bosnian Serb soldier.[28]

In short, what began in London in 1990 as a vaguely academic exercise to lend NATO new relevance has 'gone live' with a vengeance. Initial reaction evinced both elation and caution. Successive issues of *The Economist* showed that the same editorial committee could experience both emotions: the first cover, titled 'Serbs in their Sights', reflected the exhilaration of crusaders going to war; the second, called 'In Bosnia's Bog', expressed the anxious second thoughts of politicians who saw their careers threatened by the prospect of plane-loads of body bags.[29]

Those headlines express the dilemma well: do the measures adopted at the Brussels summit mean that NATO is headed for a glorious new chapter of renewal that will allow it to play a central role in the 'historic transformations' of Europe? Or will the contemplated new missions cause the Alliance's destruction as it sinks into the quicksand of ill-conceived meddling in quarrels of which it understands little? Or – perhaps the most likely prognosis – once the scale of its potential new commitments becomes apparent, will NATO quietly back away from its brave rhetoric and thus reveal itself as an emperor without clothes?

Alas, events to date provide scant evidence that NATO leaders have fully thought through the implications of the Alliance's projected involvement in Eastern Europe and the former Soviet Union – or at least they have yet to reveal those implications to their publics.

NATO partisans are ambivalent toward Bosnia. On the one hand, as

Catherine Kelleher of the Brookings Institution has pointed out, they recognize that the Bosnian turmoil represents a test case of the Alliance's capacity to respond to a conflict in the heart of Europe – a conflict, moreover, whose ethnic and nationalities dimensions appear to foreshadow so many other potential struggles in Eastern Europe.[30] From the earliest days of the crisis they have, therefore, looked for ways to promote NATO involvement. References to NATO's willingness to contribute to solving the crisis have filled NATO communiqués on many occasions.[31] On the other hand, Alliance leaders remain alert to the acute dangers of active involvement in unpopular wars and have tried to discourage analysts from making Bosnia a paradigmatic case.[32]

Clearly, it would not be appropriate to make the fate of NATO hostage to a single case – especially one which arose so early in NATO's post-Cold War career. Nonetheless, the starting point for any analysis of the likely shape and utility of post-Cold War NATO must be Bosnia.

As an organization, NATO has not been shy of involvement in the Bosnian maelstrom; to the contrary, it has shown an almost indecent eagerness to launch hostilities – in sharp contrast to attitudes in the Pentagon where, under both the Bush and Clinton administrations, more cautious counsels have prevailed. A vivid example of NATO's belligerent enthusiasm came on 23 April 1994, when Yasushi Akashi, the UN Representative in Bosnia, vetoed NATO proposals for air strikes on Serb positions around Gorazde. The result was a public spat between Akashi and Wörner. The latter's main argument was that failure to launch strikes would destroy the Alliance's credibility.[33]

In many ways, Woerner's argument represents the most troubling aspect of NATO's *Drang nach Krieg*. Considerations of whether forceful intervention will be useful or not appear to have assumed a subordinate importance to institutional self-preservation. This state of affairs raises the troubling possibility that we will be propelled into military confrontations simply to save NATO's reputation.

The evidence in Bosnia points in that direction. The overwhelming body of scholarly writing traces the origins of the current conflict not only to an extraordinarily complex set of events since the fall of the Yugoslav Communist party in January 1990; not only to Tito's gerrymandering of the internal borders separating the various Yugoslav republics to maintain ethnic peace; not only to the legacy of World War I, the interwar years, and World War II; but all the way back to the establishment of the Ottoman empire and the tenth century split in Christianity.[34] The consensus of military opinion is that conflicts with roots of this depth cannot possibly be addressed solely with 'surgical' air strikes – no matter how 'smart' the munitions. Chairman of the US Joint Chiefs of Staff General John M. D. Shalikashvili, has acknowledged that point on several occasions.[35] Secretary of Defense William J. Perry has written that the 'reconnaissance strike force' lessons of the 1991 Gulf War are not applicable in Yugoslavia.[36] After early resistance, most of the American political leadership has also begun to accept that view.[37]

To date, events on the ground in Bosnia have confirmed the pessimistic assessments. Far from intimidating the Serbs or bombing them back to the negotiating table, NATO's coercive measures have made a bad situation worse. Following the apparent NATO 'success' in lifting the siege of Sarajevo in February 1994, the Serbs simply shifted their attentions to the Muslim enclave of Gorazde in eastern Bosnia. When they were forced to pull back from Gorazde in April, the Serbs conducted a scorched earth policy that rendered the city nearly uninhabitable. (They also disguised some of their soldiers in police uniforms and left them in the city suburbs, rechristened as 'militia.')[38] The NATO actions seemed to have little connection to the search for peace. Indeed the Pentagon acknowledged that NATO's April ultimatum did not have a larger political or diplomatic purpose, but was aimed solely at punishing the Serbs.[39]

That sequence of events illustrates the dilemma NATO faces in accepting new commitments in Central or Eastern Europe. If setbacks occur, as they have in Bosnia, NATO will confront a difficult choice: either to follow classic deterrence theory[40] and escalate the level of violence, perhaps with wide-scale bombing or the introduction of ground combat forces or, if political reluctance to accept the risks entailed in such steps wins the day, to beat an ignominious retreat.

Much of NATO's difficulty over Bosnia results from structural deficiencies, both physical and intellectual. NATO's forces are physically designed for high-intensity conflict with the Soviet Union; intellectually, the conceptual underpinning of NATO lies in 'nation-on-nation' trans-border aggression described in Article 5 of the 1949 Washington Treaty. Neither condition applies neatly in the case of Bosnia. The Bosnian Serbs may have acquired territory, but they have not crossed any international boundaries; nor have they threatened the territorial integrity of any NATO member. Of course, the Serbs in Belgrade have played their part in the war, but it is straining reality to liken their actions to an Article 5 *casus foederis*. This is not the type of combat for which NATO has been training for the past 45 years.[41]

Given the enormous difficulties the Alliance has encountered in Yugoslavia, NATO's leaders might have been forgiven for wanting to digest the lessons from that experience before looking for new pastures on which to graze. In their Brussels declaration, however, the leaders single out the situation in southern Caucasus, specifically the conflict involving Azerbaijan and Armenia, as constituting a particular threat to stability.[42] Based on the assertion cited earlier that the security of the NATO members is 'inseparably linked to that of all other states in Europe', the implication once again is that

NATO is ready to risk its credibility in transcaucasian conflicts. There is, after all, little point in NATO's designating a situation as undesirable unless, when the chips are down, it is prepared to take action to back up its statements.

NATO's statement on the southern Caucasus grounds itself in 'respect for territorial integrity, sovereignty, and independence'.[43] In one sense, NATO is simply echoing long-established principles from the United Nations and the CSCE. But in its identity as a military alliance that possesses massive firepower to enforce its will, NATO is also raising the expectation that it will somehow *guarantee* these principles. Writing in *Foreign Affairs* in 1993, William Pfaff called for precisely that policy: 'the most important step would be for NATO to guarantee against forcible change of those political frontiers in Eastern, East-Central, and Balkan Europe that have not yet been violated but are threatened because of ethnic claims and rivalries.'[44] (One could comment ironically that, had this doctrine been in force in 1991, NATO might have been obliged to intervene on behalf of the federal Yugoslav government to prevent the secession of Slovenia, Croatia, and Bosnia.)

With encouragement like that outlined by Pfaff, it is not difficult to foresee the day when beleaguered leaders throughout Eastern Europe will appeal to NATO to make good on its promises. Indeed, that already seems to be happening. In the Baltic republics, leaders state that they are 'counting on NATO for insurance'.[45] Eduard Shevardnadze, the embattled president of Georgia, has taken the same tack – eliciting widespread sympathy (perhaps for the wrong reasons, as explained below) but few hard commitments.[46] At some point, however, the repeated appeals to NATO may become irresistible, if for no other reason than, as American *National Interest* editor Owen Harries has commented, unless NATO 'does something' to resolve ethnic or territorial conflicts once it has placed its prestige on the line, the credibility of the Alliance will be fatally impaired.[47]

People of Whom We Know Nothing

Neville Chamberlain's phrase about 'a quarrel in a far away country between people of whom we know nothing' has become infamous in history as the apotheosis of cowardice and appeasement. It is now deployed to counter anyone who argues for caution in accepting military commitments to unfamiliar places. Advocates of military activism assert that 'we live in an integrated world. A serious infection that gets out of control in one place is threatening to the whole organism.' In this sense no country or people can be dismissed as 'far away'.[48]

This is not the place to revisit the appeasement battlefield; Chamberlain's underlying question, however, remains worth asking: what do we know of those countries to which NATO is extending its promissory notes? Who, for example, among the signatories of the Brussels declaration would care to explain to their electorates which of the warring parties in Tajikistan – the Khojent, Kulab, Garm, and Pamir – merits NATO protection and which NATO air strikes? Who would care to explain the ethnic makeup of the Caucasus, which one scholar of the region notes, 'makes areas such as the Balkans and Afghanistan look simple by comparison?'[49]

These are not facile questions, nor are they meant to be cute. Throughout its near half century of existence, NATO commanded firm public support in large part because people knew what its purpose was and, in general, agreed with it. Without a similar clarity of purpose about ends and means, that firmness of support will be placed in jeopardy. We need, therefore, to look briefly at some of the potential commitments and reflect on whether, in the cold light of reason, those tasks really best fall to NATO.

A useful place to start is with the Baltic states and Russia. What does the language of the Brussels declaration in respect to 'territorial integrity, political independence or security' imply about potential NATO involvement in those countries?

It would seem to imply a good deal of involvement. The Baltic republics and Russia have a long history of sharply differing approaches to their mutual relationship.[50] Russian Foreign Minister Andrei Kozyrev has declared that the Baltic states have been a 'Russian sphere of influence' for centuries. Conversely, such Baltic leaders as former Lithuanian foreign minister Algirdas Saudargas have remarked that the 'best relations with Russia are no relations at all.' Former Lithuanian prime minister Vytautas Landsbergis has declared that 'aggression from Russia is growing fast.'[51] There are even suggestions that arrangements are in place for the Baltic governments to establish themselves as governments-in-exile in Sweden if a Russian attack takes place.

Antipathy between ethnic Balts and Russian settlers (or colonizers, as they are often called by their opponents) exacerbates the atmosphere of mutual distrust. Some 1.4 million Russians live in Latvia and Estonia, constituting 30 per cent of the population in the former and 34 per cent in the latter.[52] Both countries have contemplated restrictive citizenship laws that would have the effect of disenfranchising the Russian minority and preventing it from owning land.[53] From the Baltic point of view, those restrictions seem reasonable answers to past discrimination and to present fears of a Russian 'fifth column'. To nationalists inside Russia, however, such actions are an intolerable provocation. In other words, claims and counter-claims proliferate about the very issues of security and political independence mentioned in the Brussels declaration. Do NATO planners foresee interposing Alliance forces into these quarrels?

The situation in Ukraine also provides scope for invoking the Brussels provisions. Russians and Ukrainians (or at least those in the less Russified west of the country) differ fundamentally about the validity of the latter's independence, with one respected Russian academic stating that Ukrainian independence has an 'artificial and temporary character'.[54] Further, a powder-keg issue exists over Crimea, with, in this case, the brew spiced with nuclear weapons.[55] Commentators have been quick to describe the Crimean issue as 'the next Bosnia' and to call for Western action on the basis that, in the words of former US national security adviser Zbigniew Brzezinski, 'if we don't want the Russian empire restored, we have to have a strong Ukraine.' Roman Popaduk, Ukraine's ambassador to the United States, has called for American protection to prevent what he cryptically calls 'one state imposing its power over the others.'[56] Those urgings have already found their mark in the United States with a letter in May 1994 from Warren Christopher to the Ukrainian government pledging full American support for the Ukrainian position on Crimea.[57]

This is not the place to debate the rights and wrongs of the competing attitudes – Stephen Sestanovich of the Carnegie Endowment for International Peace has made the case for a more nuanced view of Russian intentions[58] – but to draw attention to the sort of historical and ethnic morass into which NATO's Brussels doctrine may draw the Alliance. Crimea was conveyed to Ukraine in 1954 by a casual Kremlin diktat, ironically enough to mark the 300th anniversary of the Ukrainian liberation from Polish-Lithuanian rule. Does NATO really feel confident that it is equipped to take sides, or even to mediate, in Russian-Ukrainian disputes? Or will the errors of historical fact and selective legitimation lead to a repeat of the Bosnian tragedy – only this time with more extensive and dangerous NATO involvement?[59]

However complex the historical and demographic background in the Baltic states and Ukraine may be, there is at least one benefit for NATO planners: internationally recognized states and borders are involved, the defense of which constitutes NATO's *raison d'être*. That situation does not apply, however, to the issue of the Hungarian minorities in Eastern Europe – an issue that one Western intelligence officer described to the author as the gravest, yet least understood, problem confronting policymakers in Europe. That is not surprising, perhaps, in light of Professor Norman Stone's comment that 'the history of central Europe is notoriously difficult.'[60]

The key event in the dispersal of the Hungarian population outside Hungary's borders was the 1920 Treaty of Trianon, which reapportioned the fragments of the Austro-Hungarian empire by reducing the territory of Hungary by roughly two-thirds and by assigning some 3.5 million ethnic Hungarians to foreign countries, principally Romania, Czechoslovakia, Yugoslavia, and Ukraine. Over the years some return migration has taken place, but recent figures show 1.6 million Hungarians in Romania (concentrated in Transylvania), nearly 600,000 in Slovakia, approximately 400,000 in Yugoslavia (principally in Vojvodina), and some 170,000 in the transcarpathian region of Ukraine. Hungarian governments tend to regard themselves as being responsible for all 15 million Hungarians, not just the 10.5 million who live inside Hungary.[61]

The potential for disputes (centering around a Hungarian aspiration to revisit and revise the Trianon provisions) between Hungary and its neighbors is not insignificant; if a greater Romania (see below) or a greater Serbia were to be formed, the effect on the Hungarian communities in Transylvania and Vojvodina is not easy to calculate. But it is the suspicion between Slovakia and Hungary that should most readily concentrate NATO minds. As we have seen, those countries number among the four most likely new adherents to NATO, yet their relations are subject to chronic underlying tension. Slovaks blame the Hungarian minority for their country's political and economic malaise, while on the Hungarian side, Foreign Minister Geza Jeszenszky warns that 'it is not possible to maintain good relations with neighbors who oppress minorities.'[62]

Once again, it might be thought that these problems – added to the Bosnian conflict – would have been enough for NATO to digest for the foreseeable future. In fact, however, the Brussels declaration, as we have seen, included the whole of the CSCE membership within its purview. What are the potential commitments that lie in wait in that wide region?

To take the Armenia–Azerbaijan quarrel first: in 1923 Stalin took the enclave of Nagorno-Karabakh, then populated mainly by Christian Armenians, away from the Christian majority Soviet republic of Armenia and awarded it to the Soviet Republic of Azerbaijan. His aim was to foment divisions between the Christian and Muslim populations so that he could better consolidate communist rule.[63] As Soviet control weakened, open warfare broke out in June 1988; hostilities have now claimed 15,000 lives on both sides and resulted in one million internal refugees inside Azerbaijan.[64]

This conflict possesses much of the same potential for regional war as has been ascribed to Yugoslavia: the faultlines between Christianity and Islam; the machinations of outside powers – Russia, Iran, and (NATO member) Turkey – as some observers have pointed out, if ever the latter two are to find a mutual *casus belli*, Azerbaijan is the place; covert transborder assistance from Armenia and Afghanistan; rivalries among the international oil giants; and humanitarian horrors.[65] Clearly, the sooner the conflict is mediated, the better. But where does NATO fit in? Who is aggressor and who is victim in this tragedy? Reports on the war deliver diametrically opposed interpretations, depending on whether they are filed from Yerevan or Baku. On whom would NATO's bombs fall, and to what end?

The situation in Moldova is only slightly less ominous, and once again Stalin's handiwork may be seen. On this occasion he was building on a century and a half's territorial haggling between Russia and the Ottoman Empire and, after 1939, between Russia and Romania.[66] Receiving Moldova from Romania in the infamous Molotov-Ribbentrop deal of 1939, Stalin grafted onto it a thin slice of Ukrainian territory on the east bank of the Dniester river, where the leadership was predominately Russian – despite the fact that ethnic Russians were only the third largest population group after ethnic Moldovans and Ukrainians.

With the heavy hand of Soviet imperialism now lifted, the ethnic Romanian population of Moldova has revived its Romanian culture, changing from the Cyrillic to the Latin alphabet. This move has upset the ethnic Russians, who have sought independence for a self-styled 'Trans-Dniester' Republic, and they have received support from units of Russia's 14th Army, which remain stationed in the territory.[67]

The Moldovan government has gone to great lengths to accommodate the aspirations of the Transdniestrians. The stage is set for a double dose of what NATO has condemned as 'the use of force for territorial gain'. Inflamed by nationalist propaganda from outside the country, the Romanian population may try to reunite with Romania. Conversely, the Russians may make an attempt to unite with various Russian-dominated parts of Ukraine, namely Crimea, Odessa, and the Donbass, to form a new state called Novorossia.[68] If either eventuality takes place – with or without Moscow's machinations – which side does NATO support? And how? Does NATO weigh in to sustain the boundaries established by what distinguished British historian Paul Johnson has called a 'gangster-pact?' Does the NATO airbase at Aviano, Italy become a staging area for NATO raids in support of the Stalinist status quo?

In Georgia the situation is no less complex. In essence, a fierce Georgian nationalism in favor of a unitary Georgian state is pitted against non-Georgian minorities in South Ossetia and the Muslim-inclined (though far from fundamentalist) Abkhazia region. In the resulting violence, enormous population dislocation has occurred; 100,000 South Ossetians have fled into Russia's North Ossetia Autonomous Region. Russian troops have intervened forcibly, for the most part to back the incumbent central Georgian government of Eduard Shevardnadze.[69]

As with Bosnia, there are considerable doubts whether NATO leaders have understood the nuances of the conflict in Georgia. When he visited Washington in March 1994, Shevardnadze was given a hero's welcome. That reception may in part have been a tribute to his role as Gorbachev's foreign minister and because he was a much more sympathetic figure than his predecessor, Zviad Gamsakhurdia, but there was also a noticeable sympathy for his policy in the ongoing internecine struggle. A similar attitude was evident when the UN Security Council passed a resolution condemning Abkhazian separatists and calling for the maintenance of the territorial integrity of Georgia.

In fact, the situation contains more than a little moral ambiguity. Georgia's treatment of its minorities leaves a great deal to be desired. In 1990 Gamsakhurdia unilaterally abolished South Ossetia's autonomous status within Georgia. The Abkhazians have also exploited reports of Georgian atrocities to garner considerable help from the Confederation of the Peoples of the Caucasus and from Russian sympathizers.[70]

Under such circumstances, can NATO be sure that it has made the right choice, or does the Alliance risk being 'manipulated' – as the French acknowledge themselves to have been in Rwanda?[71] In 1991 Secretary of State James Baker threw the weight of American diplomacy behind maintaining Yugoslavia as a unitary state. A case can be made that this encouraged Serbian hardliners. Is NATO certain that it is not making the same mistake in Georgia? To what end does NATO foresee any deployment of its assets? To assist Georgia's oppression of its minorities? Or, Bosnia-style, to protect a breakaway mini nation-state? Or, in general opposition to any reassertion of Russian influence? Would NATO intervention bring back a Cold War-like proxy fight between East and West for control of Georgia?[72]

The list of actual and potential conflicts may be projected almost indefinitely. The Institute of Geography at the Russian Academy of Sciences has identified 160 border disputes within the territory of the former Soviet Union, and the Stockholm International Institute for Peace has listed 30 current feuds in the Caucasus region alone.[73]

Viewing that long and somewhat traumatizing list, NATO managers may be tempted to gloat over the prospect of many years of business. Such problems, they assert, prove the proposition that in a continent of incipient chaos NATO represents a much-needed focus of stability.

Wanted: Seriousness of Purpose

There will certainly be no disagreement that these problems are dauntingly serious in character. In turn, they deserve treatment that will be equally serious. Unfortunately, there are grave doubts about NATO's attitude on precisely that point. As noted earlier, even NATO's strongest advocates do not hide the fact that the main reason for its involvement in Bosnia lies in NATO's need for 'credibility'; that is, the Alliance wants to stay in business. Similar considerations appear to underlie its intentions elsewhere in Central and Eastern Europe.

In many ways, that is the worst possible reason for NATO involvement.

All the conflicts mentioned above are extraordinarily complex and require the most sensitive handling. The common thread to all of them is that historical factors far beyond the traditional experience of NATO's battle planners are at work. Consider the example of a single Transylvanian town: Sibiu in modern Romania. The town has also experienced periods of German rule – when it was called Hermanstadt – and Hungarian rule – when it was called Nagyszeben. The German population has fluctuated between 98 per cent and 31 per cent; the Hungarian population between 0.9 per cent and 19 per cent; and the Romanian population between 2 per cent and 65 per cent.[74] In a contemporary dispute between Hungary and Romania, where would justice and fairness lie?

Only someone with extreme confidence in his grasp of the facts and assurance about his objectives would want to insert himself into that or any other of the situations described above. Solid, bankable information, however, is rarely available – the reports of the destruction in Gorazde that led to the NATO ultimatum may, for example, turn out to have been highly exaggerated, if not fabricated.[75]

Legitimate questions arise, therefore, about the wisdom of NATO's apparent eagerness to seek out opportunities to plunge into conflicts and quarrels. Notwithstanding the cautious wording of the Brussels declaration, NATO has allowed the expectation to arise in Eastern and Central Europe that NATO will be available to intervene in the problems of that region. The dangers are great. By wishing to insert itself into the picture, NATO risks upping the military ante for reasons that have nothing to do with events on the ground and everything to do with alliance politics.

NATO has much legitimate business to conduct with Eastern Europe and the former Soviet Union. The joint exercises, confidence building measures, and transparency foreseen in the Partnership for Peace program form a useful foundation for future work. These are the areas into which the Alliance should be advancing, not into loosely worded commitments, the precise status of which is concealed from the publics in the NATO member states. The last thing NATO needs to do is to prove its relevance in the post-Cold War era by starting wars or making existing wars worse. It has just concluded a supremely successful 45 years of maintaining the peace without firing a shot. NATO should not turn its back on that legacy and seek to become an armed conflict-resolution organization simply to stay in business.

NOTES

1. A succinct review may be found in David Haglund, S. Neil MacFarlane, and Joel J. Sokolsky, 'NATO and the Quest for Ongoing Viability', in *NATO's Eastern Dilemmas*, (eds.) David Haglund, S. Neil MacFarlane, and Joel J. Sokolsky (Boulder, CO: Westview,

1994), pp.11–36.

2. Anne-Marie Le Gloannec, 'Change in Germany And Future West European Security Arrangements,' and William E. Odom, 'Germany, America, the Strategic Reconfiguration of Europe,' in *The Future of Germany*, (ed.) Gary L. Geipel (Indianapolis, IN: Hudson Inst., 1991), pp.129–140 and 190–218, resp.

3. See James Schlesinger, 'An American Assessment: Hands Across the Sea, Less Firmly Clasped,' in *In Search of a New World Order* (Washington, DC: Brookings Instn., 1992), pp.139–56; and Joseph S. Nye, 'The United States and International Institutions in Europe after the Cold War,' in *After the Cold War*, (eds.) Robert Keohane, Joseph Nye, and Stanley Hoffmann (Cambridge, Mass.: Harvard UP, 1993), pp.104–26.

4. See, e.g., *Global Engagement: Co-operation and Security in the 21st Century*, (ed.) Janne E. Nolan (Washington: Brookings Instn., 1994) for a comprehensive discussion of the issues involved in cooperative security, esp. pp.3–17.

5. At the time, it was clear that both Bush and Baker placed stability ahead of self-determination in their list of priorities. In a speech to the Supreme Soviet of the Ukrainian Soviet Socialist Republic on 1 Aug. 1991, Bush warned of a 'suicidal nationalism.' In June Baker had advocated the continuing territorial integrity of Yugoslavia. US Dep. of State *Dispatch*, 1 July 1991, p. 463.

6. Vaclav Havel, 'New Democracies for Old Europe', *New York Times*, 17 Oct. 1993, p. E17; and Ruth Marcus, 'Clinton Assures Poles of NATO Membership, Eventually', *Washington Post*, 8 July 1994, p. A16.

7. See, e.g., Charles L. Glaser, 'Why NATO is Still the Best: Future Security Arrangements for Europe', *International Security* 18/1 (Summer 1993), p.18; and Jeffrey Simon, 'Does Eastern Europe belong in NATO?' *Orbis* 37/1 (Winter 1993), p.21. Others have proposed the formation of a 'NATO-European' nuclear-equipped expeditionary force to counter instability in Eastern Europe. See Marco Carnovale, 'Why NATO-Europe Needs a Nuclear Trigger', *Orbis* 35/2 (Spring 1991), pp.223–33.

8. Richard G. Lugar, 'NATO's Near Abroad: New Membership, New Missions', speech to the Atlantic Council, 9 Dec. 1993, p. 18 (emphasis added).

9. Quoted in Noel Malcolm, 'Furiously in All Directions', *National Review*, 7 March 1994, p.49.

10. Jeane Kirkpatrick and Morton Abramowitz, 'Lift the Embargo', *New York Times*, 20 April 1994, p. A19.

11. Quoted in Daniel Williams, 'Unlike the West, Serbs Adhered to Strategic Goals,' *Washington Post*, 17 April 1994, p. A10.

12. A description of these developments agreed to at the November 1991 NATO summit in Rome may be found in 'Statement on the Defense Estimates 1992', Cmnd. 1981, London, HMSO, 1992. In essence, the 'new strategic concept' implies a shift in NATO's emphasis toward a more mobile force, capable of rapid reaction; 'out-of-area' refers to the agreement in principle that NATO forces may on a case by case basis be deployed outside the original NATO territory as defined in the 1949 Washington treaty. The North Atlantic Co-operation Council was founded in 1991 on the initiative of then-German foreign minister Hans-Dietrich Genscher and US Secretary of State James Baker to facilitate political-military discussions between NATO and the Warsaw Pact members. The evolution of NATO attitudes toward Yugoslavia is detailed by James B. Steinberg in 'International Involvement in the Yugoslav Conflict' in *Enforcing Restraint: Collective Intervention in Internal Conflicts*, (ed.) Lori Fisler Damrosh (NY: Council on Foreign Relations, 1993), pp.27–79.

13. A good example of congressional anxiety may be found in the support given by the House of Representatives in passing on 19 May 1994 an amendment to the Defense Authorization Act for Fiscal Year 1995 proposed by Rep. Barney Frank (D-Mass.) calling for phased reductions in US forces in Europe unless the Europeans paid for more of the cost of those forces. *Congressional Record*, 19 May 1994, pp.H3735–46.

14. Quoted in Stephen S. Rosenfeld, 'NATO's Last Chance', *Washington Post*, 2 July 1993, p.A19.

15. 'Declaration of the Heads of State and Government participating in the Meeting of the North Atlantic Council held at NATO Headquarters, Brussels on 10–11 January 1994', NATO

press service M-1(94) 3, p.1. (Hereafter cited as Brussels Declaration.) The same language appeared in the communiqué of the foreign ministers meeting in Istanbul on 9 June 1994. NATO press service M-NAC-1(94) 46, p.1.

16. 'NATO's Battle Plans for Survival', *Economist*, 15 Jan. 1994, pp.49–50.
17. Some critics have attacked the PFP concept, but they have made little headway. E.g., see Henry Kissinger, 'It's an Alliance, Not a Relic', *Washington Post*, 16 Aug. 1994, p A19.
18. See Brussels Declaration, pp.4–5 (emphasis added).
19. Warren Christopher, 'NATO Plus', *Washington Post*, 9 Jan. 1994, p.C7.
20. Clinton affirmed, 'I have always stated my support for the idea that NATO will expand.' Quoted in 'No Commitment to NATO', *New York Times*, 7 July 1994, p.A12.
21. See Howard E. Frost, 'Eastern Europe's Search for Security,' *Orbis* 37 (Winter 1993), pp.37–53; and Jane Perlez, 'Poles Will Press Clinton on NATO Membership', *New York Times*, 5 July 1994, p.A5.
22. William Drozdiak, 'NATO Seeks New Identity in Europe', *Washington Post*, 4 Oct. 1991, p.A19.
23. Brussels Declaration, p. 3. Much of the declaration's language reflected earlier discussion in the Alliance, particularly at the June 1992 foreign ministers meeting in Oslo.
24. Ted Galen Carpenter, *A Search for Enemies: America's Alliances after the Cold War* (Washington, DC.: Cato Inst., 1992), p.16.
25. Ronald D. Asmus, Richard L. Kugler, and F. Stephen Larrabee, 'Building a New NATO', *Foreign Affairs* 72/4 (Sept.–Oct. 1993), p.30.
26. Stanley R. Sloan, 'Combined Joint Task Forces and New Missions for NATO', *Congressional Research Service Report* no. 94–249 F, 17 March 1994, p.1. The June 1994 Istanbul NATO foreign ministers meeting confirmed this concept. Military planning for the task forces is proceeding, although wrangling over political authority for them bedevils progress.
27. Quoted in Richard Weitz, 'Pursuing Military Security in Eastern Europe', in *After the Cold War*, p.344.
28. John Lancaster, 'Tentative Plan Favors Wide Bombing', *Washington Post*, 22 April 1994, p. A41. The text of the NAC statement in *New York Times*, 23 April 1994, p.A6.
29. See *Economist* of 16 April and 23 April 1994.
30. Catherine McArdle Kelleher, 'Co-operative Security in Europe', in *Global Engagement*, pp.293–352.
31. See, e.g., the communiqué of the NATO foreign ministers meeting in Athens, 10 June 1993: 'We are determined, individually and as an alliance to support the efforts of the United Nations and other institutions to end this war.' NATO Press Service, M-NAC-7 (93) 38, p.7. Similar comments were included in the communique of the North Atlantic Council meeting on 9 June 1994 in Istanbul: 'The alliance reiterates its determination to carry out the necessary action under the authority of the UN Security Council . . . to enforce UN Security Council resolutions.' NATO Press Service M-NAC-7 (94) 41, p.5.
32. Jonathan G. Clarke, 'Replacing NATO', *Foreign Policy* 93 (Winter 1993–94), p.30.
33. Michael R. Gordon, 'NATO and the UN in Dispute Over Strikes Against the Serbs', *New York Times*, 24 April 1994, p.A12.
34. See, e.g., Robert D. Kaplan, *Balkan Ghosts: A Journey through History* (NY: St. Martin's, 1993); Michael Ignatieff *Blood and Belonging: Journeys in the New Nationalism* (NY: Farrar, Straus, and Giroux, 1994); Lenard Cohen, *Broken Bonds: the Disintegration of Yugoslavia* (Boulder, CO.: Westview, 1993); Misha Glenny, *The Fall of Yugoslavia: The Third Balkan War* (NY: Penguin, 1994; and Alex N. Dragnich, *Serbs and Croats: the Struggle in Yugoslavia* (NY: Harcourt Brace Jovanovich, 1992).
35. Michael Gordon, 'NATO Plans to Hurt Serbs', *New York Times*, 23 April 1994, p.A7.
36. William J. Perry, 'Military Action: When to Use It and How to Ensure Its Effectiveness', in *Global Engagement* (note 4), p.236.
37. See the remarks of US Ambassador to the United Nations Madeleine Albright, quoted in Julia Preston, 'UN Security Council to Boost Forces in Bosnia', *Washington Post*, 28 April 1994, p.A20.
38. Roger Cohen, 'Serbs Hold Part of Gorazde', *New York Times*, 29 April 1994, p. A1; and

John Pomfret, 'Serbs Move Guns from Gorazde', *Washington Post*, 28 April 1994, p. A20.

39. Gordon (note 35).
40. See, e.g., William R. Van Cleave, 'Strategic Deterrence, Defense, and Arms Control', in *Thinking About America*, (eds). Annelise Anderson and Dennis L. Bark (Stanford, CA.: Hoover Instn., 1988), p. 35.
41. For an interesting discussion of the need to adapt NATO structures from high intensity to low intensity fighting, see Bernard MacMahon, 'Low Intensity Conflict: the Pentagon's Foible', *Orbis* 34/1 (Winter 1990), pp.3–16.
42. Brussels Declaration, p. 6.
43. Ibid.
44. William Pfaff, 'Invitation to War', *Foreign Affairs* 72/3 (Summer 1993), p.97.
45. Victoria Page and Douglas Stanglin, 'Too Close for Comfort', *US News and World Report*, 7 Feb. 1994, p.41.
46. Shevardnadze made this appeal in a speech to the National Press Club, Washington, DC, on 8 March 1994.
47. Owen Harries, 'An Anti-Interventionist No More: America's Credibility Is at Stake', *Washington Post*, 21 April 1994, p. A31.
48. Chamberlain's remark quoted in Telford Taylor, *Munich: the Price of Peace* (NY: Doubleday, 1979), p. 8. On interdependence see Stephen Engelberg, 'If and When', *New York Times*, 1 May 1994, p. E1.
49. Paul B. Henze, 'Conflict in the Caucasus', unpubl. MS Washington, DC, 4 Feb. 1993, p.2.
50. For documentation of differing statements by Baltic and Russian leaders, see Jan Arveds Trapans, 'Averting Moscow's Baltic Coup', *Orbis* 35 (Summer 1991).,pp.427–35.
51. Quoted in 'Nearly Abroad', *Economist*, 5 February 1994, p. 51; and Pope and Stanglin, p. 41. See also Malcolm Grey, 'Danger Zones', *Maclean's*, 11 Feb. 1991, pp.16–18; and Robert Cullen, 'Cleansing Ethnic Hatred', *Atlantic*, Aug. 1993, pp.30–36, for accounts of the long-standing resentments arising from the Soviet occupation of the Baltic states.
52. On the general problem of the Russian diaspora, see 'The 25 Million of the Russian Diaspora', *Economist*, 10 July 1993, p. 39.
53. 'Russians, Nyet', *Economist*, 25 June 1994, p. 51.
54. 'Imperial Nostalgia', *Economist*, 2 June 1994, p. 47.
55. For concise accounts of Ukraine's tense relations with Russia, see Chrystyna Lapychak, 'Ukraine's Troubled Rebirth', *Current History*, Oct. 1993, pp.337–41; and Paula Dobriansky, 'Ukraine: A Question of Survival', *National Interest* 36 (Summer 1994), pp.65–72. On the Crimea dispute, see Claudia Rosett, 'Yearnings in Crimea Threaten to Set Off Ukrainian Powder-Keg', *Wall Street Journal*, 14 Feb. 1994, p. 1.
56. David Sneider and Igor Torkakov, 'Crimea – the Next Bosnia', *National Review*, 9 September 1993, pp.26–28. Brzezinski's comment quoted in Jane Perlez, 'Fear of Russia Is a Way of Life in Ukraine', *New York Times*, 8 Jan. 1994, p.E3. Brzezinski develops this view at length in 'The Premature Partnership', *Foreign Affairs* 73 (March–April 1994), pp.67–82. Ambassador Popaduk's comment appears in 'Ukraine: Challenge From a Former Soviet Republic', *Presidential Studies Quarterly* 23 (Spring 1993), pp.229–33. Susan Clark, 'Security Issues and the Eastern Slavic States', *World Today*, Oct. 1993, pp.84–93, also advocates Western intervention to prevent conflict between Ukraine and Russia.
57. Daniel Williams, 'Christopher Supports Ukraine in Feud over Crimea', *Washington Post*, 24 May 1994, p. A14.
58. Stephen Sestanovich, 'Giving Russia Its Due', *National Interest* 36 (Summer 1994), pp.3–13.
59. For an account of how inconsistent Western, particularly US, policy regarded certain borders in the former Yugoslavia as legitimate while disregarding others, see Robert W. Tucker and David C. Hendrickson, 'America and Bosnia', *National Interest* 33 (Fall 1993), pp.14–27.
60. Norman Stone, 'The Hungarians: History makes a Comeback', *National Interest* 36 (Summer 1994), pp.58–64. On the Hungarian problem generally, see Bennet Kovrig, 'Hungarian Minorities in East-Central Europe', The Atlantic Council of the United States, March 1994, pp.1–50.
61. John Chipman, 'Managing the Politics of Parochialism', in *Ethnic Conflict and International*

Security, (ed.) Michael Brown (Princeton, NJ: Princeton UP, 1994), p. 249.

62. 'Slovakia: Iron in the Soul', *Economist*, 12 March 1994, p.56.

63. Much useful background is contained in William Ward Maggs, 'Armenia and Azerbaijan: Looking toward the Middle East', *Current History*, Jan. 1993, pp.6–11. See also 'Europe's Forgotten War', *Maclean's*, 30 Aug. 1993, pp.26–7.

64. Steve LeVine, 'Azerbaijan Throws Raw Recruits into Battle', *Washington Post*, 21 April 1994, p.A20.

65. See Kenneth MacKenzie, 'Azerbaijan and Its Neighbors', *World Today*, Jan. 1992, pp.1–2; and 'Russia's Interest in the Transcaucasus', *Economist*, 11 Dec. 1993, p.62.

66. An excellent account of this problem may be found in Charles King, 'Moldova and the New Bessarabian Questions', *The World Today*, July 1993, pp.135–39.

67. 'Bessarabian Homesick Blues', *Economist*, 30 Oct. 1993, p.62; and Malcolm Gray, 'Moldova's Dirty War', *Maclean's*, 27 July 1992, pp.20–1.

68. 'Russians Abroad: Pawns or Knights?' *Economist*, 10 July 1993, p.39.

69. See Kathleen Newland, 'Ethnic Conflict and Refugees', in *Ethnic Conflict and International Security*, pp.143–64; and John Chipman, 'Managing the Politics of Parochialism', in ibid., pp.237–64.

70. The background to the Georgian conflict may be found in 'Nationalism in the Former Soviet Empire', *Problems of Communism*, Jan. 1992, pp.121–33; and Richard Clogg, 'Turmoil in Transcaucasia,' *The World Today*, Jan. 1994, pp.3–5.

71. Raymond Bonner, 'As French Aid the Tutsi, Backlash Grows', *New York Times*, 2 July 1994, p. 5.

72. On the dangers inherent in the Georgian situation, see Elizabeth Fuller, 'Georgia since Independence: Plus Ça Change . . .' *Current History*, Oct. 1993, pp.342–6. It is of note that she describes the Abkhazians as 'Muslim', whereas Clogg rejects that label. If experts on ethnicity disagree, it is difficult to see how NATO policymakers can be confident that they have read the situation correctly.

73. Jacques Attali, 'An Age of Yugoslavias', *Harper's*, Jan. 1993, pp.20–22.

74. Istvan Deak, 'Uncovering Eastern Europe's Dark History', *Orbis* 34 (Winter 1990), pp.57–65.

75. Roger Cohen, 'UN Military Aide Says Plight of Gorazde Is Exaggerated', *New York Times*, 30 April 1994, p.3. For an interesting discussion of how false TV images can distort policy making, see Nik Gowing, *Real Time Television Coverage of Armed Conflicts and Diplomatic Crises*, Working Papers Series 94–1, Kennedy School of Government, Harvard Univ., 1994, p.13.

Romancing NATO: Partnership for Peace and East European Stability

HUGH DE SANTIS*

If one is to believe official statements, NATO is transforming itself from a military alliance into an extended political-security family that will embrace not only the ex-Warsaw Pact states but also the republics of the former Soviet Union. Whatever their innermost thoughts, neither the current nor the prospective members of the Alliance harbor public doubts about NATO's enduring importance for European peace and order. In fact, there is a remarkable uniformity of views among those who are nurturing NATO, a 'circle-the-wagons' mentality that is impervious to opposing logic or reality.

One might have expected the collapse of the Warsaw Pact and the disintegration of the Soviet Union to invite discussions of NATO's eventual disestablishment. Instead, those developments have served to justify NATO's perpetuation – indeed, rejuvenation – as a bastion of stability in a potentially disorderly Europe. Much like the United States, which has historically behaved as though it were in but not of this world, NATO seems to be somehow suspended above the swirl of social and political change that has buffeted Europe since the democratic revolutions of 1989–90.

The almost religious devotion to NATO stems from many factors, including the incontestable assertion that there is at present no other institution that can perform its security function.[1] At least as important, however, are the social-psychological sources of NATO-philia. One can not participate in the ruminations about NATO without becoming immersed in a process of 'adaptive cooptation,' the socialization in the larger policy community's *a priori* faith that it is the one and only reliable framework of European security. To dissent from that belief is to invite charges of heresy and alienation from one's community of peers. To compound the problem, the huge NATO bureaucracy – in the member countries as well as in Brussels – unavoidably produces a narrowly defined division of labor that compartmentalizes one's participation in the policy process. The bureaucratic division of labor creates a natural tendency to generalize about the present and future effectiveness of NATO on the basis of one's parochial concerns and to assume the whole is simply the happy sum of its parts.

* The views expressed are solely those of the author and do not necessarily reflect the views of the Department of Defense or any other agency of the United States government.

Unfortunately, such unswerving commitment to NATO does not bode well for European stability. In the case of NATO and the embryonic organisms it has spawned since the end of the Cold War, notably the Partnership for Peace (PFP), the United States and Europe – both East and West – are not only weaving unrealizable dreams, they are weakening the bonds of political and economic continental cooperation and, in so doing, creating conditions that presage a redivided Europe rather than a Europe whole and free.[2]

This is not to imply that Europe is headed back to the ideological *status quo ante*. Communism has been thoroughly discredited, and there is scant chance that it will be revived. But political authoritarianism of one form or another could reemerge in Eastern Europe, where fledgling democracies are only beginning to resume the nation-building on which they tentatively embarked after World War I. Moreover, the possibility cannot be precluded that they will gravitate economically and politically toward Russia – Moscow's recent decision to join the PFP notwithstanding – as those states struggle to redefine their relationship with the Western half of Europe that persists in keeping them at arm's length. Initially, at least, the redivision of Europe will probably breathe new life into NATO. That will only last, however, until it becomes clear that the Alliance retards rather than reinforces European unity; that it is part of the problem of rather than the solution to regional integration.

The Evolution of The Partnership for Peace

Ever since the democratic revolutions of 1989–90 brought the World War II era to an end, NATO has been laboring to infuse meaning into its existence, on whose continuation, the Alliance's adherents devoutly believe, the future of European stability rests. NATO's frantic effort to keep pace with the dizzying pace of change in Eastern Europe and in the former Soviet Union has produced a purportedly new strategic concept that emphasizes, in addition to the stale rhetorical sops to its 'European pillar,' quick-reaction forces and two political-military initiatives to extend the Alliance's security umbrella as far east as the Urals.[3]

The North Atlantic Cooperation Council (NACC) was NATO's first organizational attempt to incorporate the former Soviet Union and its Warsaw Pact allies into a European security framework. Announced amid great fanfare at the Rome summit of the North Atlantic Council in November 1991, the NACC formalized the loose diplomatic linkages that had formed between NATO and its erstwhile adversaries during the previous year and the growing level of contacts between East European military officials on a host of issues from arms control to the industrial conversion of defense industries. The NACC institutionalized annual ministerial meetings as well as regular consultations between Eastern and Western representatives of NATO's political, economic, and military committees. The objective was to intensify relations between East and West, thereby contributing to regional political-military stability.[4]

For all the attention NATO lavished on it, the NACC was little more than a *beau geste* designed to temper the former Warsaw Pact states' impetuous expectations of rapid assimilation into Western institutions. It created the appearance of an evolving security framework, when, in reality, NATO was organizationally unprepared and politically disinclined to do any more than display its good intentions. This became readily apparent to the East Europeans following the collapse of the Soviet Union at the end of 1991 and NATO's subsequent decision to extend NACC membership to all former Soviet republics, three of which were engaged in warfare, either with each other (Armenia and Azerbaijan), or with secessionist groups (Georgia).[5]

NATO's inability to fill the strategic vacuum created by the end of the Cold War became more visible in March and April 1992 after the onset of fighting in Bosnia (which continues to threaten the security of the Alliance's southern flank). Constant bickering between the United States and the European allies, France and the United Kingdom in particular, precluded a coordinated response to the festering crisis. NATO did dispatch warships to the Adriatic in support of the United Nations embargo on Serbia and, in April 1993, it began operations to enforce the 'no-fly zone' over Bosnia-Herzegovina. But these measures proved to be more symbolic than real; the carnage in former Yugoslavia continued all the same.

Despite having failed to preserve order in its own back yard, NATO nonetheless offered its services to the Conference on Security and Cooperation in Europe (CSCE) at the Oslo ministerial meeting in June 1992. Mindful of the CSCE's lack of any coercive mechanism to enforce policy decisions, NATO announced its willingness to undertake regional peacekeeping operations on an ad hoc basis. Six months later in Brussels, NATO extended its peacekeeping umbrella to the United Nations, where it unabashedly promised to do for the world what it could not do for the former Yugoslavia. 'We confirm today', the communiqué solemnly declared, 'the preparedness of our alliance to support, on a case-by-case basis, in accordance with our procedures, peacekeeping operations under the authority of the UN Security Council'.[6]

At the same time, NATO invited discussion in the NACC to broaden its peacekeeping efforts. By the second half of 1993, however, the East European states had grown weary of the ceaseless consultation and were increasingly concerned about the ambiguity of their security relationship with the Alliance. Originally conceived to include the Soviet Union and the five former Warsaw Pact states, the NACC had ballooned to 36 members of considerable geographic, economic, and cultural diversity. More important, in

light of the unremitting turbulence in the former Yugoslavia, the rising
tensions in Russia that preceded the coup attempt in October 1993, and the
Czech-Slovak divorce, the NACC's deliberations offered little in the way of
tangible support to comfort the East European states.

To be sure, East European governments were content to bide their time
in the NACC so long as Soviet troops remained in their countries. As the
Soviet military presence receded, however, officials such as Jerzy Milewski,
national security adviser to Polish President Lech Walesa, began to express
interest in NATO membership, both publicly and privately. Still, East
European leaders advocated a gradual process of integration during which the
Visegrad arrangement (the association linking Poland, Hungary, and Czechoslovakia) could be buttressed by some accord with NATO that exceeded the
'passive' character of the NACC, or what Walesa referred to as 'NATO 2'.[7]

East European exhortations for closer ties with NATO intensified in the
winter of 1992–93. The breakup of Czechoslovakia and the emergence of
such new states as Croatia and Ukraine undermined East European confidence in the NACC, Visegrad, and other appurtenances of the security
status quo. On the eve of the collapse of Czechoslovakia, Foreign Minister
Milan Knacko appealed for the 'urgent' creation of a security structure that
would facilitate cooperation with NATO 'on all levels.' NATO, Polish
Foreign Minister Krzystof Skubiszewski told *La Libre Belgique*, must affirm
that 'threats to the security of any country in Central or Eastern Europe will
involve the Alliance: Security in Europe must be viewed as a whole.'

More disturbing still were the political aftershocks of the attempt to depose
Russian President Boris Yeltsin – the emergence of a nationalist-communist
bloc, the growing irritation with Ukraine's political assertiveness, and
Moscow's covetous gaze on the former Soviet territories in the 'near abroad.'
Mindful of the presence of Russia's 14th Army in Moldova, Romanian
Foreign Minister Teodor Melescanu volunteered the wish at the end of 1992
that the coming year would promise more than NATO's 'mere glance of
sympathy.'[8]

Through the spring and summer of 1993, East European leaders
accelerated their lobbying of NATO capitals.[9] Although they sought a
security guarantee that would lead ultimately to full membership in the
Alliance, they remained wary of actions that might alarm Russia and thus
resume the Cold War confrontation. They consequently began to press the
United States and its allies for some loose association with the West that
would bridge the gap between NATO membership and *de facto* neutrality.

Up to this point, the United States had carefully avoided discussions of
NATO enlargement to avoid arousing renewed fears of encirclement in
Russia. Contradictory statements by Boris Yeltsin reinforced American
caution. During his visit to Prague and Warsaw on 25–26 August 1993

Yeltsin accepted the expansion of NATO, only to reverse his position upon returning to Moscow. Caught between the diplomatic pincers of East European appeals for closer security cooperation and Russian unpredictability, American and West European officials met at the end of October to thrash out the matter. Unlike some European allies, notably the Germans, who favored the full admission of the new democracies to NATO within some predetermined time frame, the United States preferred a partial association on the basis of bilateral treaties of military cooperation, which would defer the automatic military guarantees under Article 5 of the Washington Treaty and, equally important, preserve the possibility that Russia would eventually join the West in strategic partnership. That position, which crystallized in the fall of 1993, was felicitously called the Partnership for Peace (PFP).[10]

NATO unveiled the PFP in January 1994 at its meeting in Brussels. In contrast to NACC, PFP was hailed as the cornerstone of a new security relationship between NATO and the newly democratic states in the East. In accepting membership in PFP, subscribing states consented to uphold the obligations of democratic societies and to affirm their commitment to the Charter of the United Nations and the Helsinki Final Act. They also agreed to ensure the accessibility of their national defense planning and budgeting processes to the Alliance and develop the capability to contribute to NATO's peacekeeping, search and rescue, and humanitarian operations. To develop the interoperability of NATO-PFP military forces, the signatories further agreed to submit 'presentation documents' to NATO that would identify the political and military measures they planned to take in pursuit of their objectives. On the basis of the input from joint peacekeeping field exercises, these documents would be refined into 'individual partnership programs' to promote military cooperation within the Partnership framework.[11]

The PFP has greatly extended the scope of contact between NATO and Eastern Europe; the East European states now participate in some NATO exercises and receive certain technical military information. Ostensibly, the creation of a combined joint task force (CJTF) for peacekeeping provides a framework for Europe-wide security cooperation, much as the European security and defense identity (ESDI) establishes closer military ties between the Alliance and the Western European Union. NATO officials further believe that the PFP gives some structure to East European security concerns, reduces political competition among the fledgling democracies, and offers instructive experience in the way democracies work.[12] On the other hand, PFP falls considerably short of a security guarantee; it assures the East European states only of consultations if their security is threatened. Worse, it is likely to accelerate competitive tensions in the East, thereby weakening the development of regional stability and European integration.[13]

In the first place, the PFP provides neither the criteria nor a timetable for bringing the Eastern states into NATO. True, NATO's 'security partners' will actively participate in political and military discussions in Brussels and at Supreme Headquarters Allied Forces Europe (SHAPE). But according to the framework document, such activities are expressly designed to implement the partnership program rather than to integrate the fledgling democracies into NATO. The NATO policy community, echoing the views of President Bill Clinton, maintains that membership in the Alliance remains the ultimate objective of PFP. The Partnership for Peace, Clinton told the Polish parliament in July 1994, is only a beginning. 'Bringing new members into NATO . . . is no longer a question of whether, but when and how.' Some NATO officials contend that the vague linkage between PFP and NATO is quite purposeful; it permits prospective partners to coordinate their military activities with NATO at their own pace rather that at the insistence of Alliance authorities. As a US State Department official put it, PFP is 'positively self-differentiating.'[14]

In insecure Eastern Europe, however, encouraging political differentiation is a risky proposition. Lest one forget, political differentiation led to the *sauve qui peut* policies of the 1930s that helped to seal Eastern Europe's political fate for more than a half century. The race for admission to NATO has already eroded the cooperation between the East Central European signatories of the Visegrad agreement of 1991, which pledged the member states to work toward mutual political, economic, and security cooperation.

Clearly, the Czech-Slovak divorce in January 1993 undermined the integrity of the Visegrad arrangement long before the PFP initiative appeared. The disintegration of Czechoslovakia has increased tensions between Hungary and Slovakia over territorial and minority rights issues; it has also removed the common border between the Czech lands and Hungary. But PFP has accelerated the process by exacerbating the competition for incorporation into NATO. In January 1994, on the eve of Clinton's visit to Prague to celebrate the Partnership program, the Czech defense minister failed to attend a previously arranged Visegrad meeting, much to the chagrin of his colleagues. Since then, joint political and defense discussions have been sporadic, in large part, American officials concede, because Czech Prime Minister Vaclav Klaus has opposed any further institutionalization of Visegrad cooperation lest it might impede his country's accession to NATO.[15]

For all intents and purposes, multilateralism in Central Europe is now confined to economic issues, including the creation of a free trade association. Even in the economic realm cooperation is fragile; Hungary and Poland have applied for membership to the European Union independently. Although political as well as economic consultations continue among the Visegrad states, cooperation has become a formality, in the view of a State Department official. 'Visegrad,' a Czech general bluntly stated, 'is a question of the past.'[16]

By focusing its attention on military cooperation with the East, the PFP may also unwittingly inhibit the emergence of civilian control over national defense. As Jeffrey Simon has pointed out, the transfer of control over military affairs to civilian authorities is embryonic throughout Eastern Europe. Yet, the PFP program places emphasis on military cooperation, albeit in peacekeeping activities, at the expense of closer political relations, without which, the East European states cannot hope to enter NATO. Pentagon officials dismiss such concerns on grounds that whatever military requirements are recommended at SHAPE are subject to political approval in Brussels. Presumably, the hope is that East European military officials will intuitively comprehend the role that civilian authorities play in the decision-making process. Perhaps; but if military exercises are allowed to dominate the PFP-NATO relationship, the transfer of authority in the emerging East European democracies may not take place as cooperatively as the Western allies think, if at all.[17]

Furthermore, the Partnership program may be imperceptibly reproducing conditions that led to the Cold War. To be sure, the opacity of the PFP and the emphasis on peacekeeping reflect the West's concerns about alienating Russia from Europe. Indeed, PFP's very existence is a concession to Russian sensibilities. Were the United States and its European allies indifferent to Russia, or were they to perceive Russia as a renewed security threat, NATO probably would have already expanded. The West's task, Senator Richard Lugar (Republican-Indiana) has observed, is to make NATO expansion 'more palatable for Russia'. But what may appear to be prudent to the West tends to be viewed in Eastern Europe as 'a lack of vision,' in Polish Foreign Minister Andrzej Olechowski's words. Brussels must still decide, a Czech journalist pointed out, 'whether it wants to have Central and Eastern Europe as its buffer zone against Moscow or whether it really considers us to be partners worthy of protection'.[18]

For their part, the Russians, particularly those in the military, perceive the PFP as a potential security threat. Since NATO was directed against the former Soviet Union, they reason, and since PFP is an extension of NATO, then PFP is likewise directed against Russia. That reasoning, and the historic fear of encirclement, explain why Boris Yeltsin reversed his initial acquiescence in East European membership to PFP and why Defense Minister General Pavel Grachev and Foreign Minister Andrei Kozyrev have engaged Brussels officials in discussions on a special strategic relationship within the NATO-PFP framework that takes into account Russia's size and power, including its nuclear presence on the Continent. It may also explain why Russia ultimately decided to join PFP.[19]

As it turned out, Russia received no inducements to join PFP, and certainly no veto over NATO's security options *vis-à-vis* Eastern Europe and the former Soviet republics. However, it would be naive to believe that Moscow has abandoned its quest for a special relationship in NATO or, if that proves to be unattainable, for a revitalized CSCE (which was originally a Soviet initiative) that would supersede NATO's security role. Nationalist figures such as former vice-president Alexander Rutskoi, who vilified the Yeltsin government's acceptance of PFP as a 'national betrayal,' have already begun to press their case. Even some NATO members seem sympathetic to Russia's desire for a special status. Security, German Foreign Minister Klaus Kinkel stated, cannot be created 'in confrontation with Russia'.[20]

Russia's security objectives, however, are incompatible with those of its former Warsaw Pact allies. Even though Russia has joined the PFP without conditions or reservations, the East Europeans, and some Western diplomats as well, remain suspicious that a second Yalta accord may still result from Moscow's aim of a broader understanding on post-Cold War security outside PFP. Moreover, as Lugar observed, NATO attempted to sweeten Russia's participation in PFP by issuing a statement that referred to its 'unique consultation' with the Alliance. At the very least, Olechowski has pointed out, such arrangements would lead to 'the marginalization of smaller states in the region'.[21]

Given the ambivalence that underlies the Clinton administration's simultaneous efforts to expand NATO and integrate Russia into a united Europe, East European anxieties are hardly surprising. Such anxieties motivate Eastern governments to warn the West about the reimperialization of Russia and, in so doing, to stoke the embers of Cold War thinking that continues to burn in NATO. The West is asked to believe that the Russians, for all the confusion, indecision, and bureaucratic bungling that impedes economic reform, are proceeding systematically to reimpose tyrannical control over their former dominions in Georgia, Tajikistan, Belarus, Moldova, and eventually Ukraine and Eastern Europe. In contrast to the cautious, uncertain, improvisational path the United States and its allies are following in establishing closer links to Eastern Europe, Russia is supposedly preparing methodically to reabsorb the region.

To avoid alienating the East Europeans, the United States has stressed that Russia's legitimate security concerns cannot be satisfied by undermining the sovereignty and independence of its neighbors. Secretary of Defense William J. Perry went so far as to say that PFP is a hedge against the possibility that the old Soviet practice of intimidation and domination may be revived in nationalistic guise. On the other hand, neither Perry nor Deputy Secretary of State Strobe Talbott are presently prepared to extend security guarantees to the East European states that might be viewed in Moscow as a return of the strategy of containment.[22]

This approach of leaving it up to the Russians to embrace or reject the framework and conditions of a US-defined European security architecture is reminiscent of the take-it-or-leave-it manner in which the Soviet Union was invited to participate in the Marshall Plan. Stalin's rejection of the West's disingenuous offer, it may be useful to remember, helped to solidify the division of Europe at the expense of Eastern Europe. No wonder officials in the region are troubled by the prospect that history may be repeating itself.[23]

All the diplomatic tergiversation has left East European governments in a quandary. Having found fault with the NACC for being a consultative structure without a process, they are now beginning to conclude that PFP is a process without a structure. 'Without specific guidelines on how PFP relates to the NACC and to NATO membership', a Bulgarian diplomat lamented, 'the final goal is undefined, to put it mildly.' The expansion of the PFP eastward has compounded the problem for the former Warsaw Pact states. 'PFP is meaningless', a frustrated Polish diplomat fumed. 'If you want Turkmenistan and Azerbaijan in PFP, then why not Russia? Then maybe you should invite North Korea. Why not?'[24]

Fearful of being abandoned again by the West, the Poles and some of their neighbors have quickly submitted their so-called presentation documents to Brussels. In some cases – Poland's, for example – the partnership documents have been accompanied by requests for American aid to accelerate the process of military integration. In response, Clinton has called for legislation to appropriate $100 million in assistance to the Partnership program, $25 million of which he plans to earmark for Poland. While Congress may support the president's request, it will probably do so grudgingly. Given the preoccupation with domestic cost-cutting, many legislators are likely to worry that American assistance to Poland will invite similar requests from other PFP signatories, thereby leading to a European entitlement program.

With or without American aid, the next phase of the PFP agenda, according to the framework document, is to translate these proposals into actual work plans, or individual partnership programs. How long it will take the 21 PFP members to complete this phase and how soon thereafter they can expect to enter NATO is unclear. NATO does not appear to be in any hurry to accelerate the process. 'We can muddle through indefinitely', a Pentagon official confidently remarked.[25]

Images and Assumptions

The condition of policy stasis or, to put it less generously, psychological immobility that characterizes the relationship of the United States and

Europe, both East and West, on NATO expansion is likely to persist as long as the assumptions that govern the behavior of the actors remain impervious to reality. Influenced by its political and cultural mythology, the United States, the dominant voice in the European security debate, seems to believe that the future will be a linear extrapolation of the past. Just as NATO preserved Europe's security during the Cold War, so too will it safeguard the Continent's stability during political and economic integration. Now that the former Soviet allies have thrown off the shackles of communism in favor of democracy, it is only a matter of time before emerging hardcore capitalists and yeoman farmers will reflect the Jeffersonian values and beliefs that the United States has been historically beaming to the world. In the meantime, NATO will be necessary.

Contradictorily, however, the United States also assumes that the Europeans, left to their own devices, are incapable of managing their own security, the 'European pillar' rhetoric notwithstanding. Certainly they have proved unequal to the task in former Yugoslavia, where political parochialism and lingering mutual mistrust among Germany, France, and Britain prevented a unified response to the crisis from the outset. Moreover, as European officials are quick to point out, NATO – that is, the US military presence in Europe – is needed to counter the potential remilitarization of Russia, which maintains a substantial nuclear arsenal. Until such time that Europe, with or without Russia, can be integrated, the United States, acting through NATO, must remain a vigilant protector of its post-Cold War wards of democracy, East and West.

Europe harbors a different, but equally contradictory, set of assumptions about the future that reinforces America's NATO-centered approach to post-Cold War security. Unlike the United States, West Europeans fear that further political turbulence in the region could plunge the continent into endless paroxysms of violence. Despite the diminution of nationalistic rhetoric from the new coalition government in Budapest, European governments remain wary that ethnic tensions between Hungarians and Slovaks and between Hungarians and Romanians could erupt into military hostilities. More discomfiting still is the possibility of a Russian-Ukrainian clash.[26]

Selfish and short-sighted, however, they continue to assume that the United States will preserve European stability. Except for Germany, which geographically and culturally straddles East and West, they are loathe to become economically and politically involved in 'the other Europe', much less Russia, which remains part of the outliers of the *orbis romanus*. PFP is the perfect instrument for the faint of heart: it keeps the United States engaged in Europe, makes no commitments to the new democracies, and provides the allies with the comforting anonymity of consensus.

At the same time, the West Europeans wish to assert political primacy over their security affairs. Even though they continue to count on America's military guarantee, they paradoxically refuse to defer to Washington on security matters, as they did during the Cold War. The result is the mutual recrimination and political stalemate that has afflicted Alliance policy on Bosnia.

East Europeans, meanwhile, fret that other Yugoslavias loom ahead. Some maintain, as a Polish diplomat contended, that territorial and ethnic conflict is just as likely to erupt in the West as in the East. But they believe that the United States, if not the West Europeans, will contain the spread of future hostilities and that NATO would intervene if Russia were to threaten their security. They assume that PFP will eventually lead to NATO membership because they are now democracies, because such security linkages will foster Western, especially American, investment in Eastern Europe, and because Russia is intent on resuming its historic imperialist course. Besides, they maintain that they have no alternative.[27]

Such views are at least problematic and, in some cases, inconsistent with reality. In the case of the United States, the assumption that NATO can be the same cohesive force for European security in the future as it has been in the past is a tenuous one. Like some aging beauty, tucks here and there may perpetuate the appearance of another time; but the reality of time's toll is nonetheless unmistakable. Without a clear military threat, the Alliance *qua* alliance cannot be sustained. NACC, PFP, ESDI, and other face-lifts may extend its bureaucratic life, but it will no longer command the political cohesion induced by a common military threat. The inability to achieve an Alliance policy consensus regarding the former Yugoslavia is instructive. So are the diverging perceptions of threat within the Alliance. The French, Italians, and Spanish want to shift NATO's center of gravity southward to defend against potential security risks in North Africa and the Middle East. For their Scandinavian allies, however, instability in the neighboring Baltic states and the Russian military presence on the Kola peninsula are far more worrisome.

Leaving aside intra-NATO differences, it is unlikely that Congress and the American public will endorse the presence of 100,000 US troops in Europe for long. An amendment sponsored by Representative Barney Frank (Democrat-Massachusetts) to devolve three-fourths of the cost of protecting Europe to the allies and eventually to reduce the American troop level to 25,000 was included in the House version of the defense authorization bill. Although that amendment did not survive the congressional conference on the bill, it is certain to be revived in some form in the future.[28]

Furthermore, American expectations of democracy in Eastern Europe reflect an ignorance of the history of that region and a worrisome complacency about the implications of current political developments. In good Wilsonian fashion, Clinton seemed to be both preacher and prisoner of idealistic abstraction when he warned the French National Assembly last June about the 'disease of militant nationalism'.[29] Democracy, alas, is not a well-travelled road in Eastern Europe. Except for the Czechs, the efforts of the East European peoples to establish democratic institutions after World War I were quickly aborted in favor of authoritarianism, monarchism, and quasi-fascism. There is no reason to believe that the path to democratic government will be any smoother in the post-Cold War period. While the repudiation of communism has unleashed the forces of economic and political pluralism, it has also given rise to a recrudescence of nationalism that may stifle its growth.[30]

Implicit in the success of the former communists in elections in Lithuania (late 1992), Poland, and Hungary (both 1994) is the popular support for state welfarism – reform with a human face – rather than free-market competition. Although all of these governments have continued to endorse the reformist agendas of their conservative predecessors, one should not be surprised by the return to statist alternatives, if not authoritarianism, if their efforts do not translate into improved economic conditions for the majority of the electorate.

Despite the lack of Alliance policy cohesion and the growing tendency to challenge Washington's leadership (France and Britain in Bosnia, Italy in Somalia) when they disagree with US policies, the allies find it inconceivable, as French Foreign Minister Alain Juppé remarked in May 1994, that the United States would abandon the world – that is, Europe.[31] Precisely what the post-Cold War American international presence means, however, is fuzzy even to West Europeans. Neither the continued reduction of US military forces nor the self-absorbed mood of the public and Congress instills confidence that the United States will respond more assertively to the next Yugoslavia. What Washington's NATO partners choose to ignore is that unilateralism is America's historic foreign affairs orientation. NATO, after all, was only possible because of America's ideological crusade against the communist infidel. *Realpolitik* was the means to achieve a decidedly moral end.

East Europeans may want to keep another aspect of the culture of foreign policy in mind. As new democracies, the former Warsaw Pact states anticipate that they will eventually join NATO. Somehow they fail to see that national interests also define American foreign policy. Historically, the United States has never had much interest in Eastern Europe, and there is little to indicate that the modest flow of post-Cold War American investment into their region will dramatically alter historic patterns. East Europeans like to believe that investment will follow security. For the West, however, it is the other way around. The Poles, Hungarians, Czechs, and Slovaks may be on firmer ground in assuming that NATO will come to their defense in the event they are threatened by Russia. Perhaps; but the reluctance of NATO to enlarge its membership may be an implicit recognition, at least by the West Europeans, of an informal Russian sphere of influence in the region.

Policy Options

NATO-centered assumptions aside, the policy options available to decision-makers to achieve the goals of a Europe whole and free are likely to produce the opposite effects. One option is to accelerate the integration of Europe by extending NATO membership to all PFP signatories, including Russia, as soon as possible, say, before the end of the century.[32] The influx of some 20-odd new states into NATO is obviously impracticable, both operationally and politically. It defies credulity to expect Kazakhstan or Tajikistan to enter the Alliance. Assuming all the states to which membership has been nominally extended were assimilable, NATO would begin to look like CSCE, the elephantine size of which nullifies its peacemaking, if not its peacekeeping, utility. Besides, including newly independent states from Central Asia and the Caucasus, not to mention Russia, would vitiate NATO's *raison d'être* as a *European* security organization. NATO might even become subsumed under the CSCE.

A more realistic variant of the expansion option would initially confine membership invitations to the East European states, or to what the Western European Union, which is also contemplating enlargement, refers to as the '6 plus 3' – Moscow's former Warsaw Pact allies plus the Baltic states. Operationally, however, those states would not easily integrate their forces with those of NATO. Data-sharing remains a problem for the Poles and others, as do civil-military roles. In addition, the composition and quality of the military assets in the Visegrad group is not yet conducive to integration.[33] More important, both the United States and the West Europeans would be reluctant to provide security guarantees to either the Balkan states, which might envelop the allies in the spread of hostilities from the former Yugoslavia, or the Baltic states, which could alarm the Russians.

By excluding Russia, this variant entails significant risks. The extension of security guarantees to the former Warsaw Pact states might provoke historic Russian fears of encirclement, possibly leading to the reabsorption of Belarus and Ukraine and renewed East-West confrontation. Furthermore, bringing the former Warsaw Pact and Baltic states into NATO would force the issue of economic integration, which the West Europeans would prefer to defer, either to accommodate domestic constituencies or to placate poorer states, such as Portugal and Greece, that fear the dilution of economic aid from the European Union (EU).

Some of these problems would probably be avoided if Eastern Europe were invited to join NATO piecemeal rather than en masse; given their greater economic development, preference would be given to the Visegrad states. But that approach is certain to divide Eastern Europe, exacerbating the trends that have already led to the practical dissolution of the Visegrad accord.

More destabilizing consequences could follow from the limited expansion of NATO. In the East Central European region, it is likely that Slovakia would not enter in the first tranche. This could provoke a nationalist reaction, especially if Hungary sought to use political leverage in the Alliance to demand improvements in Slovakia's treatment of its Hungarian minority as a condition of membership. In the case of the Balkans and Baltic states, the limited-enlargement option would be tantamount to consigning those peoples to second-class status. Such a perception would be a stimulus to revived authoritarianism, and it could aggravate tensions between have and have-not states – Hungary, say, and those states on its non-Germanic borders, which would implicate NATO.

Moreover, Russia may view the inclusion of the Visegrad Three as the first phase of eventual encirclement, thereby prompting it to reestablish ties with the buffer states on its northern and southern flanks that, having been bypassed by the West, are likely to find it in their interest to comply. Interestingly, bilateral economic ties between Russia and Bulgaria have increased since 1993, and Sofia and Moscow are discussing the prospects for military-industrial cooperation.[34]

This leaves PFP and the sons of PFP that may follow, as the least conflictual and thus the most viable option for NATO expansion and European integration. In a way, the PFP has become a kind of NATO surrogate, a good-faith warrant that may later be redeemable into shares of the Alliance without exposing NATO or its member states to spending any political or economic capital in the meantime. But that is tantamount to closing one's eyes in childlike fashion and making a wish in the hope that it will come true. By waiting for fate to resolve the uncertainties of human choice, the United States and Europe alike inevitably become fate's hostages, for better or worse.

Faute de mieux, East European governments formally value their participation in PFP, as they do their peripheral attachments to the EU, WEU, OECD, CSCE, and other institutions that connect them to the West. 'We seek membership in all European organizations', a Polish diplomat observed, 'to avoid the curse of being between Germany and Russia.' Below the surface, however, East European anxieties are mounting, and the thought of being left to drift yet again by the West may produce responses that will alienate the fledgling democracies from each other and consequently from NATO and the West. At minimum, PFP and its promise of a secure future have removed the incentive for cooperation in Eastern Europe. Whatever officials say to the contrary, the former Warsaw Pact states are climbing over each other to beat the competition to Brussels. Privately, some Czechs have self-servingly scoffed at neighbors who request American military assistance and who approach the partnership plan as an aid program rather than as a business arrangement. In the same spirit, some Poles have dismissed the conflict in the Balkans as 'marginal' to European interests, in contrast, say, to Russian-Ukrainian tensions.[35]

In addition, the PFP initiative has slowly shifted the focus of attention in Eastern Europe from political-economic to military-security integration. Granted, the 25-member Organization for Economic Cooperation and Development (OECD) has opened membership negotiations with the Visegrad states, and the United States is pressing Western Europe to open its markets to Eastern goods. But these moves, which may yield little in the way of substance, cannot compare to membership in NATO. It is not that Eastern governments would not welcome access to EU markets, but rather that they have invested their hopes and energies in membership in NATO as the conduit to economic stability and military security.

In the long run, the combination of political competition and the diminution of regional economic cooperation will not be conducive to stability, particularly if the perceived courtship with NATO turns out to be a mere flirtation. It is implicitly understood in Eastern Europe that economic pluralism is a precondition of NATO membership. But while the emergence of free-market strategies is predictably encouraged by the West, the pain and insecurity it has wrought is simultaneously fostering renewed interest in state welfarism, if not economic *dirigisme*.

Public disenchantment with the social effects of a 20 per cent drop in GDP during the past four years and the government's inability to spread the benefits of foreign investment to the populace resulted in the sweeping victory of the Socialist Party in the May 1994 elections in Hungary. In Poland, where 16 per cent of the working population is unemployed, the Democratic Left Alliance and the Polish Peasant Party – the coalition that ruled throughout the Cold War – similarly rode the wave of public disillusionment with economic shock therapy to power. Mainly because of the political skill of Prime Minister Vaclav Klaus and the use of public works to create jobs, the Czech Republic has thus far avoided the social tensions that have beset its neighbors. But this is likely to change once the government privatizes labor-intensive industries.[36]

The political consequences of economic insecurity and social despair are political authoritarianism and regional conflict of the sort we have witnessed in the former Yugoslavia. Prudently, officials in the United States and Europe have cautioned against overreaction to the shifting electoral sentiment in Lithuania, Poland, and Hungary. To be sure, recent political developments in

Hungary and Slovakia give no cause for alarm. Gyula Horn, the leader of the Socialist Party that decisively won the May 1994 elections in Hungary and the new prime minister, has publicly affirmed his government's commitment to improve relations with its neighbors. In contrast to the late prime minister Jozsef Antall, who declared that he was the representative of all 15 million Hungarians – including the 5 million living outside their homeland – Horn has called for a historical reconciliation with neighboring states. In Slovakia, too, newly elected Prime Minister Jozef Moravcik has taken steps to improve relations with the Hungarian minority in his country and thus with Budapest, including passage of a law that permits the official registration of names in one's mother tongue.[37]

Nevertheless, the combination of economic turmoil, political passivity on the part of the West, and the absence of localized structures and relationships that might contain nationalistic exuberance could quickly submerge these hopeful signs of cooperation in a raging sea of recrimination and revenge for past wrongs. One can catch a glimpse into the ethnic and territorial divisions that smolder below the political surface of the new democracies in the prickly reaction of some East Europeans to the so-called Stability Pact on 'good neighborliness' initiated by French Prime Minister Edouard Balladur under EU auspices. Reluctant to expose their dirty laundry in a public setting, East Europeans governments have criticized the West's ignorance of their historically rooted prejudices and its facile 'Cartesian' tendency to compare problems in Central Europe or the Black Sea region to former Yugoslavia. Rather than help to stabilize Eastern Europe, some fear that the stability talks, like the Locarno Treaty of 1925 with which it is frequently compared, could lead to the 'opening of [a] new Pandora's box'.[38]

The more the states of East Europe deviate from Western standards of democratic governance, the less likely they are to be acceptable for membership in NATO. In this eventuality, one should not be surprised to hear the East Europeans denounce PFP and other NATO blandishments as cynical ploys by the West to distance itself from the East. This, as Lech Walesa told Italian journalists in May 1994, 'may mean placing the whole of Europe in jeopardy'.[39]

Walesa's admonition is instructive. Nature abhors a vacuum. Bereft of hope of their eventual integration in the West and, due to PFP and the siren song of NATO enlargement, deprived of any effective institutionalized means to contain national differences in shared regional associations, the East Europeans will seek other means to avoid isolation and safeguard their security. Some will try to draw closer to Germany, as the Czechs appear to be doing economically and as Hungary and Poland would doubtless like to duplicate, in the reconstruction of *Mitteleuropa*. Others may establish new political and economic linkages with Moscow, as Bulgaria (analogous to the

Czech-German relationship) is already doing and as Romania and the Baltic states will probably be forced to do, which is likely to extend an informal Russian sphere of influence over those states on its frontiers. As Marie Mendras points out, both Yeltsin and Kozyrev have already implicitly or explicitly affirmed a *droit de regard* over the Baltic states and Ukraine to defend their security interests and the rights of Russian minorities. Some states will try to harmonize relations with Germany and Russia, as the Poles, who have renewed trade ties with Moscow, appear to be doing.[40]

After Partnership for Peace

In this by no means implausible concatenation of events, NATO is likely to be given a new lease on life. Perversely, the redivision of Europe would ensure the perpetuation of NATO, at least for a while. In the end, however, NATO's longevity, at least its functional longevity, is still likely to be circumscribed. Assuming that Russia does not attempt to reimpose its military dominance over the East European states, and that German *ostpolitik* is essentially economic in nature, strains and stresses within NATO and probable recriminations over 'the loss of Europe' will take their toll on Alliance cohesion.

The decline of NATO's vitality, however, may lead to the revitalization of Europe. With any luck, the East Europeans will discover sooner than later that nationalistic forms of government are no more likely to promote social and economic development than communism did. At some point, East and West may in their own interests finally recognize that they need each other. Without the infusion of capital, technology, and management expertise, Eastern Europe will not be able to develop the economic productivity that sustains democracy and social order. Without the markets and low-cost labor of the East, Western Europe will not be able to expand and the EU will find it difficult to compete with the regional trade combinations in the Western Hemisphere and East Asia.

The same convergence of interests is likely to take place in the security context. For Europe to enjoy the fruits of economic integration, it must also maintain political cooperation, hence, preserve a stable security environment. Unfortunately, Europeans continue to view the United States as the guarantor of their security, a perception that Washington self-servingly encourages. Such thinking is illusory. Clinton's problems with Bosnia, Haiti, and North Korea aside, the political priorities in the United States have shifted from foreign to domestic affairs. Moreover, the demise of the Soviet empire and the retreat of communism have deprived the United States of the moral justification for the military stewardship of the world. At the very least, Europeans should be hedging their bets. Alain Juppé told *Les Echo* in June

1994 that 'it is the destiny of the WEU to merge with the EU.' The sooner
Europeans transform their rhetoric into reality the easier it will be to build
regional security arrangements. The expansion of the Franco-German
Eurocorps, the creation of a Baltic peacekeeping battalion, and the planned
military exercises between NATO countries and Eastern Europe, among
other developments, provide bases for integration.[41]

The United States can help. It can begin by accepting that the world is in
the process of historic change and that institutions like NATO that were
relevant in the past are anachronisms in post-Cold War Europe. Rather than
try to breathe new life into NATO, the United States should be encouraging
its European allies and friends to assume the responsibility for their own
security. Whether the Europeans are up to the task is arguable, but they will
never be truly independent if Washington persists in treating them as security
dependents.

This is not to say that the United States should abandon Europe. American
interests clearly dictate otherwise. To buttress the foundation of a European
security structure, and, in so doing, to stifle anxieties about neo-isolationism,
the United States should continue to extend its strategic umbrella to Europe
to offset Russia and to inhibit others from developing nuclear forces. In addition, it should deploy a skeleton force and prepositioned equipment on the
Continent, maintain adequate lift capability to respond to major crises, and
participate in regional security consultations.

As the emerging future becomes more palpable, it may become clearer to
everyone that a 'common European home', as Mikhail Gorbachev used to
call it, can only be constructed by local craftsmen from Europeanized structures, primarily the EU and the WEU. For this to occur, the Europeans will
have to overcome their parochialism and collectively assume responsibility
for their affairs. The United States, for its part, will have to accept, not simply
decree, that the Cold War is over and assist rather than resist the development
of an independent, integrated Europe by gradually devolving security responsibility to its allies. This may be wishful thinking, too. If so, it is at least
animated by the realities of the evolving future than by the illusions of an
irretrievable past.

NOTES

1. Such views appear routinely in the institution's house organs. See, as examples, Gen. John
   M. D. Shalikashvili, 'A New NATO in a New Era', *NATO's Sixteen Nations* 38/1 (Jan./
   Feb.1993), pp.6–8; and Manfred Wörner, 'The Alliance in the New European Security
   Environment', *NATO's Sixteen Nations* 38/3 (May/June 1993), pp.8–11. See also Stanley R.
   Sloan, 'Transatlantic Relations in the Wake of the Brussels Summit', *NATO Review* 42/2
   (April 1994), pp.27–31.
2. For an early exposition of this view and an alternative Eurocentric security framework, see

Hugh De Santis, 'The Graying of NATO', *Washington Quarterly* 14/1 (Autumn 1991), pp.51–65. This bottom-up approach to European security may be contrasted conceptually with the CSCE-centered framework found in Jonathan Clarke, 'Replacing NATO', *Foreign Policy* 93 (Winter 1993–94), pp.22–40.

3. On the evolution of NATO in the post-Cold War period, see, e.g. Stephen J. Flanagan, 'NATO and Central and Eastern Europe: From Liaison to Security Partnership', *Washington Quarterly* (Spring 1992), pp.141–51; and the series of essays in *The Search for Peace in Europe: Perspectives from NATO and Eastern Europe*, (ed.) Charles L. Barry (Washington, DC: National Defense Univ., 1993).

4. For the texts of both the new strategic doctrine and the Rome Declaration of Peace and Cooperation, see NATO, Press Communiqués S-1 (91) 85 and 86, 7 Nov. 1991, Brussels, Belgium.

5. Stefan Frohlich, 'Needed: A Framework for European Security', *SAIS Review* (Winter–Spring 1994), pp.36–39.

6. For more on NATO and CSCE, see Emilio Colombo, 'European Security at a Time of Radical Change', *NATO Review* 40/3 (June 1992), pp.3–7. Colombo traces the evolution of the complementarity of NATO and CSCE to the initiative he and Hans-Dietrich Genscher, then respective foreign ministers of Italy and the Federal Republic of Germany, launched in 1981. He especially points out the lack of confidence among East Europeans in the CSCE's enforcement capabilities. The 17 Dec. 1992 communiqué on UN peacekeeping is reprinted in *NATO Review*, Dec. 1992, pp.28–31.

7. The Milewski interview with *Rzeczpospolita* appears in *Foreign Broadcast Information Service Daily Report: Eastern Europe* (hereafter cited as *FBIS: Eastern Europe*), 11 Sept. 1992, pp.14–16.

8. See the Knacko interview with Vienna's *Die Presse* in *FBIS: Eastern Europe*, 21 Dec. 1992, p.6. Skubiszewski's interview appears in *FBIS: Eastern Europe*, 31 Dec. 1992, pp.21–23. Such views were reinforced by some West European parliamentarians, who privately urged the Poles, Czechs, and Hungarians to make immediate application for NATO membership. See the discussions, e.g., between Germany's Hans Stecken, chair of the Bundestag Foreign Affairs Committee, with Hungarian officials, *FBIS: Eastern Europe*, 9 Dec. 1992, p.16. Melescanu is quoted in *FBIS: Eastern Europe*, 21 Dec. 1992, p.21.

9. See the representations of then Czech, Polish, and Hungarian defense ministers (Antonin Baudys, Janusz Onyskiewicz, and Lajos Fur) in *FBIS: Eastern Europe*, 2 June 1993, pp.17–20, 1 June 1993, p.10, and 24 May 1993, p.12–13, resp. The East European press also became more active. See, e.g., the editorial in the Hungarian *Pesti Hirlap*, quoted in *FBIS: Eastern Europe*, 21 May 1993, pp.11–12.

10. For background, see Thomas W. Lippman, 'Christopher Talks of `Partnership' in East', *New York Times*, 29 Aug. 1993, p.A6; and article by Jiri Payne in *Lidove Noviny*, repr. in *FBIS: Eastern Europe*, 12 Nov. 1993, pp.12–14.

11. NATO, Press Communiqué M–1 (94) 2, 10 Jan. 1994, Brussels, Belgium. A host of bilateral and multilateral exercises between NATO and Eastern Europe are already in process and more are planned for the future.

12. Interview with official in the Office of the Secretary of Defense, 6 June 1994, Washington, DC. All interviews have been conducted on background to protect the confidentiality of the sources.

13. Jeffrey Simon has also pointed to the Partnership's potentially destabilizing consequences, although he remains optimistic that, if properly implemented, it can still simultaneously serve as the tool for East European security cooperation and NATO's continued viability. See 'NATO's New Strategic Task: Stabilizing the East', *Joint Forces Quarterly* 2 (Summer 1994), pp.40–3.

14. Clinton address to Polish parliament, Federal News Service transcript, 7 July 1994, p.6. Interview, Dept. of State, 11 June 1994.

15. Julie Kim provides some background to the deterioration of Visegrad cooperation in her updated brief, 'Poland, the Czech Republic, Slovakia, and Hungary: Recent Developments', Congressional Research Service Report, 19 July 1994, p.4. Officials at the State Department and Defense Department with whom I met uniformly acknowledged that Klaus had lost

interest in the Visegrad process during 1994.

16. Interview, Dept. of State, 11 June 1994; discussion with Czech general, Washington, DC, 20 June 1994. Also see the interviews with Klaus and Walesa in the Czech and Austrian press, *FBIS: Eastern Europe*, 31 May 1994, pp.10–12, and 36–37, resp.

17. Simon (note 13), p.43; interview with Pentagon official, Washington, DC, 6 June 1994.

18. Lugar's comments about Russia and NATO enlargement in his speech to the Overseas Writers Club, 'European Security Revisited: The State of the Alliance and U.S. Vital Interests in 1994', Washington, D.C., 28 June 1994, pp.7–8. Olechowski's remarks appear in an interview with *Le Figaro*, 14 June 1994, repr. in *FBIS: Eastern Europe*, 15 June 1994, pp.17–18. Also see Pavel Posusta, 'An Alarming Signal Is Resounding from Moscow', in *Mlada Fronta Dnes*, reprinted in *FBIS: Eastern Europe*, 16 Dec. 1993, p.11.

19. Discussions with officers on the Joint Chiefs of Staff, Washington, DC, 22 May 1994. Andrei Kozyrev has stressed the importance of a special relationship to keep Russia on its westward track. See Andrei Kozyrev, 'The Lagging Partnership', *Foreign Affairs* 73 (May–June 1994): 59–71. Also see Pavel Grachev's comments to Agence France Presse in *FBIS: Eastern Europe*, 26 May 1994, p.2.

20. Rutskoi vented his frustration in an interview with *L'Espresso*, reprinted in *FBIS: Central Eurasia*, 15 July 1994, pp.6–7. Also see the article by Mia Doorhaert, 'No Special Status in PFP for Russia', in Holland's *De Standaard*, repr. in *FBIS: Western Europe*, 14 June 1994, p.10; and Kinkel's comments on European security in ibid., 13 June 1994, pp.20–21.

21. William Drozdiak, 'Russia Vows to Sign NATO Partnership Plan', *Washington Post*, 11 June 1994, p.A17; and Daniel Williams, 'Western Envoys Wary of Russia's Entry into NATO, *Washington Post*, 25 June 1994, p.A18. Also see the comments of Slovak prime minister Jozef Moravcik, Czech foreign minister Josef Zieleniec, and Petre Roman, president of the Democratic Party of the Romanian National Salvation Front, in *FBIS: Eastern Europe*, 23 May 1994, p.10, 20 May 1994, p.4, and 31 May 1994, pp.2–3, respectively. Lugar, p.8.

22. Thomas W. Lippman, 'NATO Peace Partnership's New Look: A Protective Shield Against Moscow', *Washington Post*, 8 Feb. 1994, p.A11.

23. On the possible resumption of East–West tensions, see Georgi Arbatov, 'Eurasia Letter: A New Cold War?' *Foreign Policy* 95 (Summer 1994), pp.90–103.

24. Interviews with Bulgarian and Polish diplomats, Washington, DC, 3 June and 9 June 1994, respectively, and with Pentagon official, 6 June 1994.

25. Interview with Pentagon official, 6 June 1994.

26. Daniel Benjamin, 'Hungary's Leaders Mull Reconciling with Neighbors', *Wall Street Journal*, 18 July 1994, p.A8; also see the comments of Hungarian Foreign Minister Laszlo Kovacs in *FBIS: Eastern Europe*, 13 July 1994, pp.13–14. Interview with Professor Lawrence Freedman, King's College, London, 11 April 1994.

27. Interview with Polish diplomat, 9 June 1994; discussion with Czech general and Ministry of Defense officials, 20 June 1994.

28. *Congressional Record*, House of Representatives, 19 May 1994, pp.H3736–3746.

29. Clinton's remarks to the French National Assembly quoted in Maureen Dowd, 'Clinton Warns of Violent Nationalism', *New York Times*, 8 June 1994, p.A16.

30. Craig R. Whitney, 'Leaders Back Free Hungary Plus Stability', *New York Times*, 26 June 1994, p.4.

31. Alain Juppé, 'French Foreign Policy and the Challenges of the Post-Cold War World', speech delivered to Johns Hopkins School of Advanced International Studies, Washington, DC, 11 May 1994.

32. Jeane Kirkpatrick has called for an inclusivist NATO that would include Russian as well as European pillars. See 'A Pillar for Democracies', *Washington Post*, 6 Dec. 1993, p.A23. Former secretary of state James A. Baker III has advocated a phased incorporation of Russia as well as its former Warsaw Pact allies in NATO. See 'Expanding to the East: A New NATO', *Los Angeles Times*, 5 Dec. 1993, pp.M2, M6.

33. Interview with Pentagon official, 6 June 1994.

34. See 'Defense Cooperation Agreement Signed', *FBIS: Eastern Europe*, 24 June 1994, p.6.

35. Discussions with Polish diplomat, 6 June 1994, and Czech Ministry of Defense officials, 20

June 1994.

36. See Robert McIntyre, 'Lenin's Boom: Why Capitalism Falters in Eastern Europe', *Washington Post*, 12 June 1994, p.C3; and David B. Ottaway, 'Socialists Win Decisively in Hungarian Elections', *Washington Post*, 30 May 1994, p.A12. Also see 'Poland: Souls in a New Machine', *Economist* 16 April 1994, pp.1–22; 'Out of Work in Eastern Europe', ibid., 9 July 1994, p.48; and Ferdinand Protzman, 'Czech Republic Doing Well, for Now', *New York Times*, 22 June 1994, p.D4.

37. See Horn's remarks on relations with Hungary's neighbors and Slovak developments in *FBIS: Eastern Europe*, 19 May 1994, p.6; 29 May 1994, p.4; 31 May 1994, pp.33–4; and 2 June 1994, pp.8–9.

38. See Alan Riding, '9 East European Nations Join Round Table Talks', *New York Times*, 28 May 1994, p.8; 'Havel Advisor Interviewed on Stability Conference', *FBIS: Eastern Europe*, 26 May 1994, pp.4–5; 'Russia Gives Stability Pact Cool Reception', ibid., 31 May 1994, pp.6–7; 'Czechs Offer to Help Strengthen Stability', ibid., 31 May 1994, pp.2–3; 'Czechs Not to Link Agreements to Pact', ibid., p.3; and '[Hungarian] Ministry Official Views Balladur Plan, Conference', ibid., 2 June 1994, pp.10–11.

39. See 'Walesa Admonishes West Over Selfish Policies', *FBIS: Eastern Europe*, 19 May 1994, pp.15–16.

40. Marie Mendras attributes Russia's desire to reestablish a sphere of influence over the newly independent states on its borders to its imperialist history. Given its history, she points out, it is difficult for Russia to relate to Lithuania or Ukraine, much less Georgia or Kazakhstan, as independent nations rather than as part of its imperial patrimony. See 'La Russie cherche-t-elle a reconquérir l'europe?' *Rélations Internationales et Stratégiques* (Spring 1994): 70–5. Also see 'Poland to Seek Closer Ties with Russia', *New York Times*, 9 June 1994, p.A6. The security dimension of this policy reorientation is implicit.

41. Juppé's comments appear in *FBIS: Western Europe*, 10 June 1994, pp.23–5. Reliance on the American military guarantee is not confined to Western Europe. See, e.g., Romanian Foreign Minister Teodor Melescanu's interview with the Dutch paper *De Standaard* in *FBIS: Eastern Europe*, 9 Nov. 1993, pp.30–1.

'Cold War' Continuities: US Economic and Security Strategy Towards Europe

BENJAMIN C. SCHWARZ

With the end of the Cold War, the American foreign policy community has been avid to try something new. Having spent decades evaluating the drab minutiae of arms control and in other ways attempting to manage the seemingly eternal US–Soviet rivalry, members of that community have eagerly answered the call to refashion America's national security strategy. The flood of recent reports, articles and books, however, is disappointing. After promising bold new thinking on America's grand strategy, these writings boldly call for the status quo. Some take a nip here: the United States can reduce its troop strength in Europe to 100,000 ('although not below that'). Others take a tuck there: 'not all Third World states are equally important to the United States' (although it would be 'a mistake to ignore the spillover effects' of Third World instability 'on international order and on American interests'). In short, when these alterations are finished, the essentials of America's 'Cold War' strategy remain inviolate.

The Clinton administration's 'Bottom-Up Review' of US defense policy, released in September 1993, illustrates this stasis. Having promised a fundamental reassessment of America's national security requirements, Pentagon planners concluded after six months of analysis that US security demands military spending of more than $1.3 trillion over the next five years and the permanent commitment of 200,000 US troops in Europe and East Asia – in other words, a strategy remarkably similar to that of the Cold War. Moreover, rather than relinquish America's costly and risky responsibilities by dissolving Cold War alliances, the administration now plans to *expand* NATO's responsibilities eastward. Those who call for a more modest US defense policy argue that American defense plans are extravagance born of paranoia or of a defense establishment's anxiety to protect its budget. In fact, however, given the way the United States has defined its interests since World War II, the plans are quite prudent. And that is the problem.

The demand for new strategies for a new world springs from the assumption that the Soviet 'threat' fundamentally determined US diplomacy from 1945 until the end of the Cold War. Now that the USSR has disappeared, it would seem reasonable that American security policy would change profoundly. But this view presupposes that Washington's Cold War grand strategy was – and that foreign policy in general is – a response to the pressures of other states. If, however, US security policy has been primarily determined not by external threats but by the apparent demands of America's economy, it would follow that, despite the collapse of the Berlin Wall, Washington's global strategy must remain largely unaltered. Persuasively, albeit unwittingly, this is the argument that the foreign policy community advances today in its post-Cold War strategic reassessments. To appreciate the dilemma that arises when the United States seeks its domestic well-being in sources beyond its borders, we must examine those internal imperatives that dictate foreign policy. In other words, we must explore that policy from the inside out.

The US Role in Cold War Europe

Diplomatic historians fall into two general categories. The tradition of *innen-politik* argues that internal pressures mainly determine foreign policy. In con-trast, the scholarship of *aussenpolitik* views relations among states as a realm apart from domestic politics and holds that a state's foreign policy is deter-mined mostly by the pressures of the international system. In assessing the forces that shape a country's foreign policy, therefore, the *aussenpolitik* approach stresses strategic considerations and perceptions of external threats. This approach dominates the interpretation of American strategy since World War II. The history of US national security policy after 1945 is thus under-stood as the story of America's response – sometimes paranoid, sometimes clumsy, occasionally prudent – to the threat of a superpower rival.

That such a view is misleading becomes apparent through the critique of US Cold War strategy produced by the school of foreign policy known as 'political realism.' Realism, which holds that gaining power and security are the primary foreign policy objectives of states (in contrast, say, to furthering an ideology or pursuing profits) is, of course, an expression of *aussenpolitik*. Believing that external pressures determined strategy, many realists – including such penetrating American foreign policy thinkers as George Kennan and Walter Lippmann – were convinced that much of America's Cold War security policy was irrational. Neither Kennan nor Lippmann, for example, could understand the US commitment in Vietnam, an area of no intrinsic strategic value. Nor, more important, could they understand why America's foreign policy elite met their suggestions for a mutual superpower disengagement from Europe with such hostility.

Kennan and Lippmann's goals in Europe were limited and specific. Defining America's interest there as preventing the continent's military domi-nation by a single power, they perceived American policy in strategic, rather than ideological or 'world order' terms. 'It is to the Red Army in Europe and not to ideologies, elections, forms of government, to socialism, to communism, to free enterprise, that a correctly conceived and soundly planned policy should be directed,' Lippmann argued in 1947.[1] Similarly, Kennan saw America's European interests in narrow, geopolitical terms.[2] While most of his government colleagues were inspired by the idea of a *Pax Americana*, Kennan had a far more modest view of America's future European – and global – role. He looked to the restoration of a plural world in which other powers – the major European states in particular – would dilute the nascent US-Soviet confrontation.[3]

Disengaging the United States and the Soviet Union from Europe (a proposal that most historians now believe would have stood a good chance of success)[4] and thereby restoring a multipolar balance of power would be, Kennan and Lippmann reasoned, in America's long term interest, for it would free the United States from its crushing responsibilities for others' security and would reduce tensions between the superpowers. As it happens, the foreign policy community had very clear reasons for wishing to maintain those responsibilities, but Kennan, Lippmann, and other realists blamed America's seeming refusal to act realistically on what they saw as its penchant for viewing foreign policy as a moral crusade.

That realist assumption was wrong. Throughout the post-World War II era, American interests and security commitments (at least the major ones) have been pursued deliberately and for consistent – if recondite – reasons, reasons not obvious to the public nor fully appreciated by the realist viewpoint. If well informed Americans had been asked 10 years ago why US troops were deployed in Europe (and East Asia), they would have answered: to keep the Soviets out. They may have wondered, however, why the United States persisted in its strategy even after Western Europe (and Japan and South Korea) had become capable of defending themselves. Today, they are thoroughly bewildered. Now that the USSR itself has disappeared, why does Washington continue to insist that an American-led NATO and the US defense commitments to East Asia are still indispensable to America's security?

If, on the other hand, National Security Council staffers, think tank analysts, or State Department policy planners were asked about America's globe-girdling security commitments, 40 years ago, 10 years ago, or now, their answers would be consistent – and noticeably different from those of educated laymen. They would justify American deployments overseas by invoking such terms as 'shaping a favorable international environment', 'reassurance of allies', and the on-going need for 'leadership', 'stability' and 'continuing engagement'. Even during the Cold War, the 'Soviet threat' might not have been mentioned. The question this begs, however, is why has the awesome task of building a stable world been deemed so crucial to

America; why have 'stability' and 'reassurance' been for nearly 50 years the mantra of the foreign policy cognoscenti?

America's Economically-Driven Cold War Policy

To understand the forces that have motivated US foreign policy since 1945, we must look not to the Soviet Union, but to ourselves; not primarily to the superpower's geopolitical rivalry, but to the ascendancy of a vision that saw new requirements for America's prosperity. From the end of World War I through the 1930s, the American political economy was changing dramatically. The most rapidly growing and profitable sector comprised large, capital-intensive, advanced-technology corporations, investment banks, and internationally-oriented commercial banks, all of which took the world market for their target. The international economy was America's future – or so it seemed to the architects of America's post-World War II foreign policy elite, who were themselves drawn almost exclusively from the world of east coast international business and finance.[5]

These men had great hope for the future, for they believed that the United States could, using such implements as the General Agreement on Tariffs and Trade and the international monetary arrangements negotiated at Bretton Woods, build and manage a new, liberal, global political economy in which trade and capital flowed across national boundaries in response to the laws of supply and demand. Of course, in such a world, the United States, which dominated the international economy, would benefit enormously, but the rest of the world would benefit as well. America's power at the close of World War II made US policymakers believe that they could translate their vision into a reality.

Such hopes were coupled with an uncomfortable recollection of the Great Depression. Fear of a return to depression fueled the drive toward a postwar international order that might guarantee America's economic health. To Secretary of State Dean Acheson and the other designers of America's Cold War foreign policy, there was only one solution. Summarily dismissing schemes to achieve national self-sufficiency through state planning, Acheson declared: 'We cannot have full employment and prosperity in the United States without foreign markets.'[6] American foreign policy generally, and America's interests in Europe specifically, since World War II cannot be understood except within the context of the project to maintain an open global economy. National policymakers knew that such a goal dictated that the United States fundamentally alter international politics.

The greatest danger to American democracy and prosperity, as US policymakers saw it, came not primarily from the Soviet Union but from Germany and Japan, since their strength was both necessary and potentially disastrous for the multinational capitalist community the United States was intent on constructing. An industrialized Germany, for instance, would be Europe's most cost competitive producer and its most effective consumer. Without full German participation in the European economy, there could be no revitalization of an international economy and that, as Under Secretary of State for Economic Affairs Will Clayton warned in 1949, would spell the beginning of the end for 'our democratic free enterprise system'.[7] But, as future Secretary of State John Foster Dulles explained in a closed Senate hearing in 1949, while Germany's integration with Western Europe was imperative, Western Europeans were 'afraid to bring that strong, powerful, highly concentrated group of people into unity with them'.[8] Similarly, a strong Japan was at once essential to Asia's economy and intolerable to its neighbors.[9] The problem lay in the inherent contradiction between capitalist economies and international politics.

Capitalist economies prosper most when labor, technology and capital are fluid, so they are driven toward international integration and interdependence. But while all states benefit absolutely in an open international economy, some states benefit more than others. In the normal course of world politics, in which states are driven to compete for their security, this relative distribution of power is a country's principal concern, and it discourages interdependence. In efforts to ensure that power is distributed in its favor at the expense of its actual or potential rivals, a state will 'nationalize,' that is, pursue autarkic policies – practicing capitalism only within its borders or among countries in a trading bloc. That action restricts both production factors and markets, thereby fragmenting an international economy.

In the normal course of world politics, therefore, international economic interdependence is impossible to achieve. As political economist Robert Gilpin remarks, 'what today we call international economic interdependence runs so counter to the great bulk of human experience that only extraordinary changes and novel circumstances could have led to its innovation and triumph over other means of economic exchange'.[10] In fact, as historians Immanuel Wallerstein and Thomas McCormick point out, international capitalism has enjoyed only two golden ages: the periods following the Napoleonic Wars and the two World Wars.[11] The key to both of these episodes of peace and prosperity has been the same: the ability and will of a single state to play the role of hegemonic power. The only way to overcome the dangers inherent to international capitalism is for a preponderant power to take care of other states' security problems for them, so that they need not pursue autarkic policies or form trading blocs in attempts to improve their relative positions. This suspension of international politics through hegemony has been the fundamental aim of US foreign policy since 1945; the real story of that policy is not the thwarting of the Soviet 'threat,' but rather the effort to impose a specific economic vision on a recalcitrant world.

After World War II Washington policymakers recognized that only the United States could achieve the prerequisite for an open world economy – ensuring that Germany and Japan were revitalized as engines of world economic growth, while simultaneously assuaging Western Europe's and Asia's fears about German and Japanese economic, military and political dominance. Thus, Washington committed itself to building and maintaining an international political order based upon an American 'preponderance of power'. By providing for Germany's and Japan's security and by enmeshing their military and foreign policies into alliances that it dominated, the United States contained its erstwhile enemies, preventing its 'partners' from embarking upon independent policies. This stabilized relations among the states of Western Europe and East Asia, for by controlling Germany and Japan, the United States 'reassured' their neighbors that these most powerful allies would remain pacific. NATO and the US-Japan Alliance, by banishing power politics and nationalist rivalries, protected the states of Western Europe and East Asia from themselves.[12]

Freed from the fears and competitions that had for centuries kept them nervously looking over their shoulders, the West Europeans (and East Asians) were able to cooperate politically and economically. As Secretary of State Dean Rusk argued in 1967: 'The presence of our forces in Europe under NATO has also contributed to the development of intra-European cooperation . . . But without the visible assurance of a sizeable American contingent, old frictions may revive, and Europe could become unstable once more.'[13] From that perspective, restoring Europe to its prewar status risked destroying America's grand design. What Kennan saw as the return to the normal power balance on the Continent seemed to most other American statesmen to be a return to the international political and economic fragmentation of the 1930s. It was, after all, an independent Western Europe that had toppled the *Pax Britannica* and its beneficent global economic order. Recognizing that Europe and East Asia could not be left to their own devices in the post-Cold War world, Washington pursued not Kennan's vision of balance and diversity, but hegemony. This preponderance ensured the tranquil world environment in which an open economic system could operate.

Thus, America's foreign policy has been 'imperialist' in the non-pejorative sense of the extension of great power influence for economic purposes. In this sense, Lenin was right. Imperialism is (or allows for) 'the highest stage of capitalism' – an open economy among the industrialized nations.

The fundamental purpose behind America's 'Cold War' policy had little to do with containing the Soviet Union, even though the Soviet threat was used to justify that policy to a nationalist public and Congress (a strategy described by Senator Arthur Vandenberg as 'scaring hell out of the American people' to secure an internationalist agenda).[14] The Kremlin's irrelevance to America's postwar planning was acknowledged in NSC-68, the National Security Council's 1950 blueprint for America's Cold War strategy, which defined the security policy it advocated 'as one designed to foster a world environment in which the American system can survive and flourish.' This 'policy of attempting to develop a healthy international community', NSC-68's authors went on to assert, was 'a policy which we would probably pursue even if there was no Soviet threat'.[15] In fact, America's 'Cold War' alliances, organized ostensibly to contain the USSR, were formed at a time when US statesmen 'did not expect and were not worried about Soviet aggression', as historian Melvyn Leffler, author of the most comprehensive study of the origins of the Cold War, concludes.[16]

Moreover, US officials recognized that their Cold War strategy actually exacerbated Washington–Moscow tensions. Arguing against Kennan's proposal for the neutralization of Germany and the consequent disengagement of the superpowers from the Continent, the Central Intelligence Agency insisted, 'The real issue is not the settlement of Germany [i.e., relaxing tensions with the Soviets] but the long term control of German power.'[17] By 1957 Kennan, grappling with why his ideas for withdrawing US and Soviet troops from Europe 'appear[ed] so dangerous and heretical' to official Washington, was forced to conclude that American statesmen 'would not have considered the withdrawal of a single American battalion from Western Germany even if the Russians had been willing to evacuate all of Eastern Germany and Poland by way of compensation'.[18] While Kennan had long believed that America's European policy was motivated by an ill-considered ideological reaction to the Soviets, he now came to realize that US preponderance in Europe served aspirations that were unrelated to the Soviet Union.

American Hegemony and the World Economy

The conviction that America's prosperity depends upon international economic interdependence and that the precondition for economic interdependence is the geopolitical stability and reassurance that flow from America's security commitments continues to animate America's national security strategy. Secretary of State James Byrnes's 1945 explanation of the motive behind American foreign policy – 'Our international policies and our domestic policies are inseparable; our foreign relations inevitably affect employment in the United States'[19] – remains the formula Washington follows today.[20] In fact, according to this reasoning, the weaker the US economy grows, the more energetically America must pursue world stability.

As Senator Richard Lugar (Republican-Indiana), explained in August 1993 when he called for American leadership to revive NATO:

> Trading within our own borders is insufficient to lead us out of economic difficulty; sustained economic growth requires an ability to export vigorously abroad. Full participation in the international market place requires a degree of stability and security in the international environment that only American power and leadership can provide.[21]

The apparent connections among the requirements of an international capitalist economy, America's economic well-being, and its defense commitments have been repeated so often that Anthony Lake, President Clinton's National Security Advisor, conflated the supposed dictates of prosperity with those of national security in announcing the administration's new foreign policy doctrine in September 1993. Explaining that 'the expansion of market-based economies abroad helps expand our exports and create American jobs', Lake declared that America's new 'security mission' is the 'enlargement of the world's community of market democracies'.[22]

The now infamous draft of the Pentagon's classified 'post-Cold War' Defense Planning Guidance (DPG), which gave the public an unprecedented glimpse into the thinking that informs America's defense strategy when it was leaked in March 1992, merely restates in somewhat undiplomatic language the logic behind America's 'Cold War' reassurance strategy. Arguing that American preponderance as a security blanket is essential for stability in Europe and East Asia, the DPG stated that the United States must therefore 'discourage the advanced industrialized nations from challenging our leadership or even aspiring to a larger global or regional role'. To accomplish this, America must do nothing less than 'retain the pre-eminent responsibility for addressing . . . those wrongs which threaten not only our interests, but those of our allies or friends, or which could seriously unsettle international relations'.[23] The United States, in other words, must provide what one of the DPG's authors termed 'adult supervision'.[24] It must protect the interests of virtually all potential great powers for them so that they need not acquire the capabilities to protect themselves, that is, so that they need not act like great powers. The very existence of truly independent actors would be intolerable to the United States, for it would disrupt American hegemony, the key to a stable world.

The draft DPG's 'post-Cold War' strategy of preponderance, then, reflects what Leffler defines as an imperative of America's *Cold War* national security policy: that 'neither an integrated Europe, nor a united Germany nor an independent Japan must be permitted to emerge as a third force'.[25] America's 'allies' were understandably troubled by the impolitic language of the draft DPG, so the Pentagon issued a sanitized, unclassified version in

January 1993. While the revised DPG may give less offense, its underlying message is the same and its economically-based arguments are even stronger. America's Cold War alliances, it asserts, ensure 'a prosperous, largely democratic, market-oriented zone of peace and prosperity that encompasses more than two-thirds of the world's economy.' This makes maintaining these alliances America's 'most vital' foreign policy priority.[26]

In 1993 President Clinton stated (echoing Byrnes's argument 48 years earlier) that 'a global economy has changed the linkages between our domestic and foreign policies and, I would argue, has made them indivisible.'[27] If this reasoning is accepted, America's security strategy seems to inexorably follow. Economic interdependence, apparently, dictates security commitments.[28] As long as world politics remain what they have always been, Europe and – East Asia – will be potentially unstable. And as long as US prosperity is understood to depend upon the stability of those regions, the United States must pacify them, employing the most prominent – and costly – feature of its present security strategy: the military power that ensures America's preeminent place in its Cold War alliances. This leads to a dismal conclusion. America's worldwide security commitments are a truly permanent burden. They amount to taking the wolf by the ears: how could America ever let go? Arguing in 1992 for the maintenance of the US reassurance strategy in Asia and Europe, a high ranking Pentagon official asked 'if we pull out, who knows what nervousness will result?'[29] The problem, of course, is that the United States can never know and, therefore, according to the assumptions underpinning its security policy, it must always stay.

Post-Cold War NATO and US Economic Renewal

Today's realists, who assume that others view national security policy through a narrow strategic lens rather than through a wider economic and political one, and who therefore argue that conflict in the former Yugoslavia is no danger to the United States, must look again to understand why foreign policy establishment figures as different as Jeane Kirkpatrick and Cyrus Vance agree that vital American interests are ultimately imperiled by Balkan turmoil. Ludicrous as it may seem at first glance, the fighting in the former Yugoslavia worries policymakers not so much for the humanitarian reasons that have received so much attention, but largely because they fear that instability in the Balkans will ultimately damage the global economy.

The interventionists' argument that America must lead efforts to pacify the former Yugoslavia merely extends the argument that America must lead in European security affairs, generally. In a memorandum written before his appointment, Deputy Assistant Secretary of Defense David Ochmanek urged

US military action in Bosnia, explaining that since American 'prosperity is intimately tied to that of the Europeans', the United States must 'maintain its capacity to influence decisionmaking in Europe.' Because NATO is 'an essential source of US influence', Washington must continue to lead European security efforts – including undertakings to stanch instability in the Balkans. 'If we want a seat at the table when the Europeans make decisions about trade and financial policy', Ochmanek reasoned, 'we can't pretend that messy security problems in Europe are not our concern as well.' If the US-dominated NATO demonstrates that it cannot or will not address Europe's post-Cold War security problems, then the Alliance will be impotent. Atlanticists maintain that without an effective NATO – that is, without the Americans providing 'adult supervision' – post-Cold War Europe will lapse into those same old bad habits that the Alliance was supposed to suppress – power politics.[30]

What would be the result of this scenario? The United States will be greatly harmed *economically*. As General William Odom, former director of the National Security Agency, argues:

> Only a strong NATO with the US centrally involved can prevent Western Europe from drifting into national parochialism and eventual regression from its present level of economic and political cooperation. Failure to act effectively in Yugoslavia will accelerate this drift. That trend toward disorder will not only affect US security interests but also US economic interests. Our economic interdependency with Western Europe creates large numbers of American jobs.[31]

This appreciation of the disastrous consequences regional instability might have for America's hegemonic position and consequently for international political cooperation and, ultimately, for international economic integration is the missing link that connects instability in the Balkans to American national interests. Unfortunately, there are many other situations in which the same connections can very plausibly be made.

According to the logic of Washington's global strategy, while the end of the superpower rivalry has reduced US security risks and commitments in some respects, it has in other ways expanded the frontiers of America's insecurity. During the Cold War, stability in Europe could be assured by Washington and Moscow smothering their respective clients. In fact, this superpower condominium, while crushing to the Europeans, was probably the best means of insuring America's overriding economic and political interest in the stability of the continent, as American statesmen have often privately acknowledged.[32] With the Soviet Union gone, however, its former charges have become free to make trouble for each other and for Western Europe. As former deputy assistant secretary of defense Zalmay Khalilzad, one of the main architects of the Bush administration's 'new world order' policy, asserts, 'Western and East Central European stability are becoming increasingly intertwined' and thus Western Europe's prosperity, upon which America's own economic health depends, is increasingly tied to economic relations with Eastern Europe. Moreover, Khalilzad argues, direct US economic interests in the region have also grown considerably, since 'East Central Europe offers new and potentially expansive markets for US goods, investments and services.'[33]

Even more important, American strategists fear that if the newly independent states of Eastern and Central Europe are not enmeshed in multilateral security arrangements under US 'leadership', the region could once again become a political-military tinderbox as it was in the 1920s and 1930s, with the Baltic countries, Russia, Ukraine, Poland, the Czech and Slovak republics, Hungary and Romania worrying about each other and with all of them worrying about Germany. And, the argument goes, as in the past, Germany's involvement in Eastern Europe's rivalries could alarm its Western neighbors as well, threatening the stability of the entire Continent.[34]

So America's responsibilities multiply. The Clinton administration and a growing number of the foreign policy elite have joined Khalilzad in asserting that these conditions dictate that the US-led NATO must be 'transformed'.[35] As Lugar argues, since European stability 'is a *precondition* for American domestic renewal' and since that stability is now threatened by 'those areas in the east and south where the seeds of future conflict in Europe lie',[36] the US-led NATO must now stabilize both halves of the Continent by extending security guarantees to all of Europe, including, possibly, to Ukraine. In other words, the United States must be prepared to go to war to defend the territorial integrity of states in regions riven by ethnic, religious and nationalist animosities, regions in which nearly all borders are in dispute. Khalilzad and other proponents of this policy acknowledge that spreading America's security blanket over so inhospitable an area demands that the United States retain a substantial number of troops in Europe.[37] Indeed, this view of threats to America leads inevitably to Cold War-era military budgets. Therefore, it is not surprising that NATO's defense ministers declared in May 1993 that despite the dissolution of the very enemy that NATO was ostensibly formed to contain, cuts in military spending had to be immediately halted, for otherwise the alliance would be unable to fulfill what NATO's Secretary-General termed its 'expanded range of missions'.[38]

Since the late 1940s, the United States has, in essence, defined its vital interests in Europe as forestalling normal patterns of economic and security competition among the states of the region. This has required an unprecedented extension of America's overseas responsibilities and commitments. So, while current proposals to extend NATO eastward are characterized by their proponents and detractors alike as radical and bold initiatives, those initiatives are in fact merely an additional payment, made necessary by changing geopolitical circumstances, on what is called America's original 'transatlantic bargain'.[39]

Realists, the foreign policy community maintains, can argue all they want that the plethora of potential hot spots in Eastern Europe and the former Soviet Union have no immediate strategic importance to the United States, but instability in these regions is intrinsically insidious to America's interests. So America must take the lead in attempts to impose stability. The liberal foreign policy commentator Walter Russell Mead, who in the past has favored reducing America's commitments abroad, says that he favors the United States having a cooperative, rather than a dominant, relationship with its allies. But Mead, reflecting the dilemma of American security policy, is unable to reconcile America's need to lighten its international burdens with his recognition of the dangerous economic consequences of America's abdicating its leadership role. The United States, Mead asserts, cannot even allow its 'partners' to assume primary responsibility for quelling the instability that, after all, most affects them. Maintaining that an '[economically] closed Europe is a gun pointed at America's head', Mead argues:

> In a well-intentioned effort to stabilize Eastern Europe, Western Europe, led by Germany, could establish something like Napoleon's projected Continental System. Eastern Europe and North Africa would supply the raw materials, certain agricultural products, and low-wage industrial labor. Western Europe would provide capital and host the high-value-added and high-tech industries...A Europe of this kind would inevitably put most of its capital into its own backyard, and it would close its markets to competitors from the rest of the world. It would produce its VCRs in Poland, not China; it would buy its wheat from Ukraine, rather than the Dakotas.[40]

Given that the actions Washington's allies would take to forestall instability without American leadership would apparently lead to US economic disaster, it seems that the United States must forever remain – in former President Bush's words – the world's 'sole superpower'.[41]

That line of reasoning – that if a hegemon must ensure the stability of a region on which it apparently depends, it must also secure those areas on which that region depends – nicely illustrates what historian Paul Kennedy calls 'imperial overstretch'. If America must guarantee the stability of a potentially unstable Europe, then logic seemingly dictates that it must guard against instability that could infect Europe.[42]

This thinking, so reminiscent of the Cold War domino theory, suggests that the logic of economic interdependence leads to a proliferation of American 'security' commitments in an unstable new world order. An imperial strategy is necessarily expansive. With awkward syntax, the authors of NSC-68 asserted in 1950 that America's freedom and welfare can only be secured through 'the virtual abandonment by the United States of trying to distinguish national from global security' and that, therefore, 'it is not an adequate objective merely to seek to check the Kremlin design, for the absence of order among nations is becoming less and less tolerable. This fact imposes on us, in our own interests, the responsibility of World leadership.'[43] In 1993 the same logic compelled Lugar to argue that the United States must make itself responsible for the stability of all of Eurasia, since 'there can be no lasting security at the center without security at the periphery.' While such assessments sound excessive, they in fact reflect the imperial thinking upon which America's security strategy – during and after the Cold War – rests.[44]

Sustaining the Unsustainable? The High Cost of *Pax Americana*

While this strategy fulfills one set of America's perceived economic needs, it is not viable. For one thing, the United States is in a deep fiscal crisis that has been gathering for a long time and will damage the country profoundly, if not resolved. Nearly 50 years of world leadership have taken their toll. The links among heavy military spending, the weakening of the economy, and fiscal imbalance are too clear to ignore. America is overconsuming and under-investing. Too much consumption is still devoted to defense, depriving the productive sectors of the economy of urgently needed resources. To be sure, the military budget is now a smaller portion of federal spending than in the 1950s and 1960s. But in constant dollars defense spending is still at Cold War levels: 18 per cent of the federal budget – $263.8 billion in fiscal year 1995 – is a substantial share to spend on defense, and America continues to spend a far higher portion of its GDP on national security needs than do other major industrial countries. Compounding this fiscal crisis, America faces social and structural economic problems (high rates of infant mortality, illiteracy, malnutrition, and poverty) of a magnitude unknown to other economically advanced states.[45]

To maintain that America can continue at anything like its current level of defense spending without damaging its economy is incorrect and irresponsible. Yet to suggest that the United States can afford to reduce that spending significantly is, given the assumptions underlying the past half century of US strategy, simply wrong. Most foreign policy reformers assert that America's enormous defense costs are the product of globalist over-extension. America's strategic dilemma, they argue, can be resolved by simply balancing its commitments and resources. But criticizing US policy for overextension fails to take America's security considerations seriously.

To argue that America's defense spending is the result of its being over-committed begs the question: what commitments involving significant amounts of military spending can be jettisoned?

The driving force behind the US defense posture is the perceived need to ensure order by, in effect, exercising hegemony in regions composed of wealthy and technologically sophisticated states and to take care of such nuisances as Saddam Hussein, Slobodan Milosevic, and Kim Jong Il so that potential great powers need not acquire the means to take care of those problems themselves. While retrenchment from these positions may seem economically attractive, it would, following the logic of US security strategy, carry enormous risks. 'The United States, as a great power, has essentially taken on the task of sustaining the world order', former defense secretary James Schlesinger concisely explained. 'And any abandonment of major commitments is difficult to reconcile with that task.'[46]

'Shaping the strategic environment', to use post-Cold War Pentagon jargon, requires today, as it has for the past 45 years, the maintenance and deployment of large and technologically advanced armed forces. American defense planners appreciate that to guard against the apparent disaster of political and economic 're-nationalization', US defense commitments must be operationally meaningful. America must convince others not only that it is committed to the security of their regions, but that it is capable of *acting* on that commitment. Imposing a protectorate over the world economy means that the United States must spend more on national security than the rest of the world's countries combined. Reassuring Western Europe, even without a military threat to the continent, is costing the United States $100 billion this year. Stabilizing East Asia is taking another $47 billion. In defense you get what you pay for, and America's 'adult supervision' strategy means that the United States – if it is lucky and nothing disastrous happens – must pay for-ever.

The United States is caught in a dilemma that eventually ensnares all hegemons. Stabilizing the international system is a wasting proposition. While other states benefit from the stability the predominant power provides, they have little incentive to pay their 'fair share' of the costs of protection since the hegemon will defend the status quo in its own interests, regardless of what these lesser states contribute. Just as Britain, as the guarantor of world stability in the nineteenth century, spent more than twice as much on defense as France or Germany, even though the latter countries' neigh-borhood was more perilous, so the United States today spends vastly more on defense than either Japan or Germany, though both countries are less secure than America.

Forced to place such importance on 'security', the hegemon directs capital, creativity and attention from the civilian sector, even as its economic rivals, freed from onerous spending for security, add resources to economically productive investments. This leads over time to the erosion of the preponderant power's relative economic strength.[47] As economic, and hence military, capabilities deteriorate, so does the very comparative advantage over other powers upon which hegemony is founded. And as its relative power declines, the international stability that the hegemon assured is, perforce, unsettled.

Thus, even without the burden of high defense spending the United States is simply less and less able to order and pacify the world. The *Pax Americana* depended upon America's preponderant strength in the decades following World War II; probably never in history did one state so dominate the international system. Yet history affords no more remarkable reversal of fortune in a relatively short time than the erosion of US hegemony in the late twentieth century. The worldwide economic system that America has fostered has, itself, largely determined the country's relative decline, even as it has contributed to America's prosperity. For those concerned with maintaining American predominance, the problem with economic interdependence is that it has worked all too well. Through trade, foreign investment and the spread of technology and managerial expertise, economic power has diffused from the United States to new centers of economic growth, thus rapidly closing the industrial and technological gap between the United States and its global partners.

These developments are not 'bad' for America economically. Almost everyone – including US consumers – benefits absolutely from the most efficient production of industrial goods in an open world economy. But with a shift in the international distribution of economic strength, American hegemony, of necessity, has been undermined. Thus, a global economy bites the hegemon that feeds it. America, then, is in a bind. The international open economic system that it believes is necessary for its prosperity weakens the very condition – American preeminence – that makes that system viable. And attempts to maintain its hegemony through security leadership only further weakens its position in the long run.

The United States has defined a very difficult role for itself. Its foreign policy, in fact, is dedicated to sustaining the unsustainable. To be sure, some optimists hold that America can escape this quandary by reaping the reward of hegemony – a global economy – without paying for it. According to that argument, America can 'lead' but in 'partnership' with other like-minded states.[48] That is an illusion. Multilateral enterprises, from juries to UN police actions, require a leader. The indispensable foundation of cooperation and integration in the Western security and economic systems was – and remains – American hegemony. The rather strident assertions of every American president since Truman of the need for American preeminence in European security affairs stems less from an overbearing chauvinism than from a

realization that, as Acheson wrote in 1952, arguing for the necessity of the
NATO alliance, 'unity in Europe requires the continuing association and
support of the United States; without it, [Western] Europe would split
apart.'[49] To hold that America can safely relinquish its hegemony because
the political, economic and military cooperation among the great powers
now ensures stability and peace is to put the cart before the horse. Stability
in Western Europe and East Asia, guaranteed by American preponderance,
was the precondition for cooperation, not vice versa. There is no reason
to believe that, without this guarantor, stability will take on a life of its
own.

The nature of international politics will not change to solve America's
security quandary. In fact, given the inevitable rise of other great powers
and trends toward greater regional instability, the wolf the United States
is now holding by the ears is likely to grow increasingly feisty, making
America's strategy of preponderance more problematic and expensive.[50]

Superpower Hegemony and the Capitalist System

Discussion of US 'post-Cold War' foreign policy has revolved around stale
generalizations about morality and foreign policy, self-satisfied assertions of
the need for America to 'remain engaged abroad' and the familiar tactical
arguments about when, where, and how to intervene militarily in foreign
quarrels. Such a dialogue fails to illuminate the important questions. It is time
for Americans to stop debating what is and is not America's 'mission' in the
world and instead to assess the viability, costs, and benefits of attempting to
maintain the international requirements of the US economy. Americans must
acknowledge, as did Kennan 40 years ago, the dilemma inherent in defining
their prosperity in terms of economic security abroad. Despairing over the
implications of the new doctrine of 'national security,' Kennan noted: 'To
what end – security? For the continuation of our economic expansion? But
our economic expansion cannot proceed much further without . . . creating
new problems of national security much more rapidly than we can ever hope
to solve them.'[51]

But while America's national security policy may be dangerous and
damaging, any significant change in that policy necessarily demands radical
change in the US economy, since that strategy, as its makers acknowledge,
grows out of the structural requirements of American capitalism. Such
changes may – and in anything but the long run will – present as many difficulties as they eliminate.

The late historian Christopher Lasch made what is at first glance the astonishing assertion that any fundamental critique of American foreign policy
must 'simultaneously take the form of an indictment of capitalism itself'.[52]

Surely a basic change in security policy can be affected without jettisoning the basis of the US economy.

In fact, economist John Maynard Keynes and historian Charles Beard proposed programs in the 1930s that tried to reconcile capitalism with non-interventionist foreign policies by proposing autarkic capitalism – what Keynes called 'national self-sufficiency'. They embraced that 'solution' even more for what they believed would be the welcome changes it would permit in foreign policy than for what they saw as its enormous domestic social benefits. As Keynes stated, 'the progress of economic imperialism' – that is, 'a great concentration of national effort on the capture of foreign trade and the . . . protection of foreign [economic] interests' was 'a scarcely avoidable part' of economic internationalism. Both Keynes and Beard hoped, therefore, that the domestic economic restructuring each proposed would allow for a more circumscribed and less expensive national security policy.[53]

But plans to alter fundamentally the domestic political economy in the name of national self-sufficiency are even more unthinkable now than they were 50 years ago, when Acheson dismissed them out of hand. Moreover, Keynes's and Beard's schemes originated when the advanced economies were far less interdependent than they are now. National self-sufficiency is not an option at this late date – at least not one that would be freely chosen. America cast its economic lot with liberal internationalism long ago, and it has succeeded in making the internationalists' dream – a world economy – a reality. A global economy is addictive: In embracing a system permeated by international market pressures, a state's economy is perforce restructured profoundly and it becomes bound to the world market by complicated patterns of trade, production, and capital flows. Having lost its economic autonomy, the United States would find a break from the global economy extraordinarily disruptive, requiring years of economic readjustment and, given the strength of international market forces, severe political measures to sustain.

Still, while the price of reversing course, of forsaking economic internationalism, is prohibitively high, the social costs of continuing to depend on the international economy may well be enormous. As Keynes and Beard understood, the more open a state is to the world market, the more vulnerable its population is to international market forces. And, in an increasingly open global economy, a state will be less and less able to modulate, let alone manage or control, the domestic effects of those forces. A state committed to economic internationalism will grow economically, but significant sectors of its population will suffer labor dislocation and a decline in income and will be plagued by economic insecurity, as the domestic economy constantly responds to the global economy's changing demands and accelerating shifts in comparative advantage.

Adhering to America's present political economy and its concomitant national security policy may nevertheless seem the best of bad alternatives. But not only is America's current policy risky and expensive, it is also unsustainable. Therefore, while it may be inconceivable that the United States would choose a non-capitalist 'solution' to its foreign policy conundrum, such a 'solution' may nevertheless be imposed upon it, as the demands of international capitalism collide with the realities of international politics. As capitalism becomes more complex and 'advanced,' it becomes more fragile. For instance, today the emergent high technology industries are the most powerful engines of world economic growth, but they require a level of specialization and a breadth of markets that is possible only in an integrated world economy.

Such a global economy is easily threatened in that disruptions – wars, for example, or reversion to competitive mercantilist policies – within or among any significant national participants send damaging shock waves throughout the entire system. As American hegemony – the political condition that holds such disruptions in check, weakens, 'renationalized' foreign and economic policies among, say, the states of Northeast Asia or Western Europe, would destroy the global economy. Capitalism, certainly as it has developed over the last 50 years, cannot survive without an open world economy. It is difficult to see, therefore, how it can survive the decline of the *Pax Americana*, as the fragmented and discordant nature of international politics reasserts itself over an illusory unity forged by an ephemeral preponderance.

Seventy-seven years ago, Lenin argued that international capitalism would be economically successful but, by growing in a world of competitive states, it would plant the seeds of its own destruction.[54] Although the empire he built is in ruins and his revolution discredited, Lenin may have the last laugh.

The US foreign policy community's definition of America's legitimate interests in Europe cannot be adequately understood if seen through the narrow prism of threats to America's physical security. America's thinking about its interests in Europe rests on a set of interrelated assumptions concerning international politics, international capitalism and national prosperity and democracy that have driven Washington policymakers since at least the turn of the century. These assumptions dictate that America pursue an imperial policy, albeit perhaps a benign one. The same assumptions have also informed every grand strategic assessment the United States government has undertaken since the end of World War II. It is no accident, then, that these assessments have concluded that, in essence, American national security policy is what it should be. To arrive at a fundamentally different conception of American interests in Europe – and hence a meaningful change in US security policy toward the Continent – either America's assumptions concerning the requirements of international stability in Europe, or the assumptions concerning the requirements of American prosperity, must change radically.

NOTES

1. Walter Lippmann, *The Cold War: A Study in US Foreign Policy* (NY: Harper, 1947), p.19.
2. In what he admitted was an oversimplification, Kennan argued in 1948 that there were 'only five centers of industrial and military power in the world which are important to us from the standpoint of national security.' These were the US, Britain, Germany and Central Europe, the Soviet Union, and Japan. Quoted in John Lewis Gaddis, *Strategies of Containment* (NY: OUP, 1982), p.30. See also George Kennan, *Memoirs: 1925-1950* (Boston: Little, Brown, 1967), p.359. Only one of these power centers was, at the time, in the hands of the Soviet Union; to Kennan, the primary security interest of the US, therefore, was to see to it that no other area fell under Soviet sway. Kennan did not believe, however, that containing the Soviet Union required America's security leadership in Europe. Memorandum from Kennan to the Undersecretary of State, 'Policy with Respect to American Aid to Western Europe', in US Dept. of State, *Foreign Relations of the United States 1947*, Vol.3, (Washington, DC: US GPO, 1974), pp.224–225; memo. from Kennan, 'North Atlantic Security Pact,' ibid., p.285; memo. from Kennan to the Secretary of State, 'Policy Questions Concerning a Possible German Settlement,' US Dept. of State, *Foreign Relations of the United States 1948*, vol. 2, (Washington, DC: US GPO, 1974), pp.1287-97. See also, Kennan, *Memoirs*, pp.406–7.

      Kennan strongly believed that NATO would, in fact, be inimical to American interests. A formal military alliance, he argued, would militarize Europe around a superpower confrontation, thus preventing the political and diplomatic flexibility needed for later European settlement. Once European territory came to be seen in a confrontational military perspective, Kennan reasoned, the Soviets could never withdraw from positions they might otherwise view as undesirably overextended. Kennan, 'Policy Questions Concerning a Possible German Settlement' and 'North Atlantic Security Pact'.
3. Kennan, 'North Atlantic Security Pact'. See also Anders Stephanson, *Kennan and the Art of Foreign Policy* (Cambridge, MA: Harvard UP, 1989), pp.145–7.
4. Ibid., p.155.
5. On this transformation of the American political economy and its influence on US foreign policy, see Thomas Ferguson, 'From Normalcy to New Deal: Industrial Structure, Party Competition and American Public Policy in the Great Depression', *International Organization* 38 (Winter 1984), pp.41–94; Lynn Eden, 'The Diplomacy of Force: Interests, the State, and the Making of American Military Policy in 1948', PhD diss., Univ. of Michigan, 1985; James R. Kurth, 'Travels Between Europe and America: The Rise and Decline of the New York Foreign Policy Elite', in *The Capital of the American Century*, (ed.) Martin Schefter (NY: Russell Sage Foundation, 1993); Franz Schurmann, *The Logic of World Power: An Inquiry into the Origins, Currents and Contradictions of World Politics*, (NY: Pantheon Books, 1974); and Bruce Cumings, *The Origins of the Korean War, Volume II: The Roaring of the Cataract, 1947-1950* (Princeton, NJ: Princeton UP, 1990), Chs.1–5, 22.
6. Quoted in Fred Block, 'Economic Instability and Military Strength: Paradoxes of the 1950 Rearmament Decision', *Politics and Society* 10 (1980), pp.35–58.
7. Quoted in Thomas McCormick, *America's Half Century* (Baltimore, MD: Johns Hopkins UP, 1986), p.81. See the similar comments by Secretary of State George Marshall in Nov. 1947, Lloyd C. Gardner, *Architects of Illusion: Men and Ideas in American Foreign Policy, 1941–1949* (Chicago: Quadrangle Books, 1971), p.231.
8. US Congress, *North Atlantic Treaty: Hearings Before the Senate Foreign Relations Committee on Executive L*, 81st Cong., 1st sess., April-May 1949, pp.355–6.
9. On the central importance of Japan in the US vision of a postwar international capitalist order, see William S. Borden, *The Pacific Alliance: United States Foreign Economic Policy*

and Japanese Trade Recovery, 1947–1955 (Madison, WI: Univ. of Wisconsin Press, 1984); Ronald L. McGlothlen, *Controlling the Waves: Dean Acheson and US Foreign Policy in Asia* (NY: Norton, 1993); Bruce Cumings, 'The Origins and Development of the Northeast Asian Political Economy: Industrial Sectors, Product Cycles, and Political Consequences', *International Organization* 38 (Winter 1984), pp.1–40; Bruce Cumings, 'Power and Plenty in Northeast Asia: The Evolution of US Policy', *World Policy Journal* 5 (Winter 1987-88), pp.79-106; and Cumings, *Origins of the Korean War* (note 5).

10. Robert Gilpin, *War and Change in World Politics* (Cambridge, MA: Cambridge UP, 1981), p.130.

11. Immanuel Wallerstein, *The Modern World System: Capitalist Agriculture and the Origins of the European World Economy in the Sixteenth Century* (NY: Academic Press, 1974); Immanuel Wallerstein, *Historical Capitalism* (London: Verso, 1983); and McCormick (note 7).

12. On America's role as Western Europe's and East Asia's 'adult supervisor,' see the comments of current and former officials cited below and Lawrence Kaplan, *The United States and NATO: The Formative Years* (Lexington, KY: Univ. of Kentucky Press, 1984); Josef Joffe, 'Europe's American Pacifier,' *Foreign Policy* 14 (Spring 1984), pp. 64-82; John Mearsheimer, 'Back to the Future: Instability in Europe after the Cold War,' *International Security* 15 (Summer 1990), pp.5–56; Bruce Cumings, 'Trilateralism and the New World Order,' *World Policy Journal* 8 (Spring 1991), pp.195–222.

13. Lyndon B. Johnson Library, National Security File, Box 51, 'The Trilateral Negotiations and NATO 1966–1967,' Tabs 43–63, Memo 153b.

14. That same year, Vandenberg's colleague, the fervently anti-communist Robert Taft, strongly suspected that the supposed dangers to the nation from the USSR failed to explain America's new foreign policy when he complained that he was 'more than a bit tired of having the Soviet menace invoked as a reason for doing any- and every-thing that might or might not be desirable or necessary on its own merits.' Quoted in William Appleman Williams, *The Tragedy of American Diplomacy*, (NY: Dell Publishing Company, 1972) p.240. For the argument that the Soviet Union served as a 'convenient adversary': as an instrument to justify at home and abroad America's world order strategy – see Christopher Layne and Benjamin C. Schwarz, 'American Hegemony – Without an Enemy,' *Foreign Policy* 92 (Fall 1993), pp.20–1.

15. See Layne and Schwarz (note 14); and Block (note 6).

16. Melvyn Leffler, *A Preponderance of Power: National Security, the Truman Administration and the Cold War*, (Stanford, CA: Stanford UP, 1992). Although Leffler's book has emerged as the central work of Cold War 'post-revisionists,' the preponderance of its evidence and conclusions reinforces the 'revisionist' critique of US Cold War policy. On this point, see the review article by Bruce Cumings, ''Revising Post Revisionism', or the Poverty of Theory in Diplomatic History,' *Diplomatic History* 17 (Fall 1993), pp.539–69.

17. Quoted in Leffler, p.284. On this point, generally, see ibid, pp.277–85, 453–63, and 500–1.

18. Kennan, *Memoirs* (note 2), p.260.

19. Quoted in Walter LaFeber, *America, Russia, and the Cold War, 1945-1966* (NY: John Wiley, 1967), p.6.

20. For examples of such reasoning, see the comments of former secretary of defense Dick Cheney and former national security adviser Brent Scowcroft. Dick Cheney, 'The Military We Need in the Future: American Leadership and Security Requirements', 4 Sept.1992, in *Vital Speeches of the Day*, Sept.–Oct. 1992, pp.13–14; and Brent Scowcroft, 'Who Can Harness History? Only the US,' *New York Times*, 2 July 1993, p.A15.

21. Richard Lugar, 'NATO: Out of Area or Out of Business. A Call for US Leadership to Revise and Redefine the Alliance', Remarks Delivered to the Open Forum of the US State Department, 2 Aug. 1993. Lugar's foreign policy philosophy is nicely encapsulated in his assertion that America's 'domestic well-being' is 'heavily dependent on stability, economic reform and the growth of market economic and democratic institutions abroad', p.6.

22. Anthony Lake, 'From Containment to Enlargement', Speech to the Johns Hopkins Univ. School of Adv. Int. Studies, 21 Sept. 1993.

23. 'Excerpts from Pentagon Plan: "Prevent the Re-emergence of a New Rival," *New York*

Times, 8 March 1992, p.A1.

24. Interview, former Defense Dept. official, Sept. 1993.

25. Leffler (note 16), p.17

26. In a similar vein, see the comments in 1990 by Dep. Asst. Secretary of State for European Affairs James Dobbins, who applied the DPG's reasoning to America's post-Cold War role in Europe specifically. US Congress, CSCE, *Implementation of the Helsinki Accords: Hearings*, 101st Cong., 2d sess., 3 April 1990, pp.8, 18; and US Congress, *The Future of NATO: Hearings Before the Senate Foreign Relations Committee*, 101st Cong. 2d sess., 9 Feb. 1990, p.19. Dep. Asst. Secretary of Defense Alberto Coll's elaboration of that argument in terms of US policy toward East Asia revealed the degree to which Washington sees its national security strategy as serving domestic economic imperatives. See Alberto Coll, 'Power, Principles and a Cooperative World Order', *Washington Quarterly* 16/1 (Winter 1993), p.8.

   Even America's nuclear preponderance serves this country's economic needs, according to a classified Pentagon report on the strategic importance of America's nuclear superiority in the post-Cold War era, leaked in 1991. Rejecting the notion that the only purpose of nuclear arms is to deter nuclear attack, the report explained that America's nuclear preponderance helps 'sustain the nation's prestige and deter Germany and Japan from developing nuclear arsenals of their own'. If Washington's former enemies were to acquire nuclear weapons, the report argued, the concomitant political and military 're-nationalization' in Europe and East Asia would close the world economy, upon which America's prosperity depends. Thus, the report concluded with the seemingly bizarre assertion that America 'must keep nuclear weapons to protect . . . a healthy and growing US economy'. Quoted in R. Jeffrey Smith, 'US Urged to Cut 50 per cent of A-Arms', *Washington Post*, 6 Jan. 1992, p.A1.

27. White House, Office of the Press Secretary, Prepared Remarks of President Clinton to The American Society of Newspaper Editors, 'A Strategic Alliance with Russian Reform,' 1 April 1993.

28. Since American prosperity presumably hinges 'on achieving and maintaining open markets for international trade and investment,' as former assist. secretary of the treasury and senior adviser to the NSC C. Fred Bergsten argues, then 'the containment of the risk of conflict among the economic superpowers' must be 'a primary purpose of US foreign policy.' C. Fred Bergsten, 'The Primacy of Economics,' *Foreign Policy* 87 (Summer 1992), pp.8–11.

29. Quoted in Morton Kondracke, 'The Aspin Papers', *New Republic*, 27 April 1992, p.12. The 'wolf by the ears', of course, was Thomas Jefferson's apt phrase describing the dilemma of slavery in America. See Benjamin Schwarz, 'From a Founding Father, an Imperfect Vision of America', *Los Angeles Times*, 4 July 1994, p.B7.

30. 'Yugoslavia and the Need to Live Up to Our Responsibilities', Memo. by David Ochmanek, RAND Corp., 9 June 1992. Copy in author's files.

31. William E. Odom, 'Yugoslavia: Quagmire or Strategic Challenge?' Hudson Inst. Briefing Paper, Nov. 1992. In the same vein, Lugar explains that fundamental American interests are greatly endangered in Bosnia because the 'devastating' economic effects in Europe of the spread of Balkan instability would mean a 'loss of jobs and loss of income in this country as we try to base a recovery upon our export potential.' MacNeil/Lehrer Newshour, 6 May 1993. Electronic version; no pagination. Sen. Dennis DeConcini (D-Ariz.) also argues that 'crucial American interests are on the line in Bosnia.' The US through NATO, he asserted, must bomb Serbian targets to pacify the former Yugoslavia because 'Europe represents America's largest trading partner. An unstable Europe would damage our own economy.' Dennis DeConcini, 'Bomb the Serbs. Now,' *New York Times*, 18 May 1993, p.A21.

32. The American public, for instance, was puzzled by State Dept. Counselor Helmut Sonnenfeldt's assertion that a Soviet-US condominium in Europe was actually in America's interest. Sonnenfeldt's thinking reflected that of the US foreign policy community, although it was clearly at variance with America's official position. See US Congress, *United States National Security Policy vis à vis Eastern Europe (The 'Sonnenfeldt Doctrine'): Hearings Before the Subcommittee on International Security and Scientific Affairs of the House Committee on International Relations*, 94th Cong., 2d sess., 12 April 1976.

33. See Zalmay Khalilzad, 'Extending the Western Alliance to East Central Europe: A New Strategy for NATO', RAND Issue Paper, May 1993.

34. Ibid.

35. The Clinton administration's Partnership for Peace initiative, designed to increase significantly the military ties between NATO and the states of Eastern Europe, stopped short of providing those states with ironclad security guarantees. Its purpose, however, is to 'reassure' those countries by enmeshing them in the NATO military system to such a degree that they become Alliance members in fact, if not in word. Moreover, formal NATO membership for Poland, Hungary, the Czech Republic, and Slovakia, President Clinton declared in July 1994, 'is not a question of if, but of when and how'. White House, Office of the Press Secretary, Remarks of the President to the Sejm, 7 July 1994, p.4.

36. Lugar (note 21), p.6. Emphasis in original.

37. Khalilzad (note 33), p.6.

38. 'Arms Cuts Worry NATO,' New York Times, 27 May 1993, p.A6.

39. See Benjamin C. Schwarz, 'NATO at the Crossroads: Re-Examining America's Role in Europe,' RAND Issue Paper, Jan. 1994.

40. Walter Russell Mead, 'An American Grand Strategy: The Quest for Order in a Disordered World,' World Policy Journal 10 (Spring 1993), p.21. Mead's argument echoes Asst. Secretary of State Breckinridge Long's May 1940 picture of the economic implications to the US of the subordination of Europe to German control. See The War Diary of Breckinridge Long, (ed.) Fred L. Israel (Lincoln, NB: Univ. of Nebraska Press, 1966), p.98.

41. The foreign policy establishment's anxiety concerning the effects of regional instability on the European political situation and ultimately on international economic interdependence extends to unstable regions far from Europe. Concern about the potential psychological and political effects of turmoil in the Persian Gulf on Western Europe and Japan was a major factor underlying James Baker's assertion that the US had to counter Iraq's invasion of Kuwait to save American jobs. His comment reflects, if oversimplifies, official opinion on the importance of Persian Gulf security to the United States. Believing that tranquility and democracy in Germany and Japan are fragile, US officials fear that a sudden economic downturn in these states could cause a repeat of the 1930s: recession and unemployment would bring extreme nationalist forces to the fore, which in turn would intensify regional political tensions and lead to the 'renationalization' of foreign and economic policies. According to that reasoning, the open economic system would slam shut and the world crash into depression. Consequently, Germany and Japan must have unhampered access to Persian Gulf oil – and not be tempted to develop forces capable of power projection to secure those supplies. Author's conversations and interviews with current and former State and Defense Dept. and NSC officials, 1991–93.

42. Hence, the foreign policy establishment's recent spate of reports on what is termed America's 'post-Cold War security agenda' argues that NATO must not only extend security guarantees to Central and Eastern Europe and the European states of the former Soviet Union, but that it also must ensure stability in the Central Asian states of the former Soviet Union (since instability there could spread to Turkey, which could, in turn, spur massive immigration to Western Europe, destabilizing that region) and in North Africa (again because of the supposed harm to US interests that would result from the potential political effects of a wave of immigration in Western Europe). See, e.g., Rethinking American Security: Beyond Cold War to the New World Order, (eds.) Graham Allison and Gregory Treverton (NY: Norton, 1992); and Carnegie Endowment for Int. Peace, Changing Our Ways (Washington, DC: 1992).

43. Quoted in William Appleman Williams, Empire as a Way of Life (NY: OUP, 1980) p.186; and Lloyd Gardner, 'Response to John Lewis Gaddis,' Diplomatic History 7 (Summer 1983), p.192.

44. Anyone familiar with the historiography of American foreign relations will find it difficult to read the arguments used by members of the foreign policy establishment to define America's post-Cold War security strategy without being struck by their ironic consonance with the views of the 'open door school' – a quasi-Marxist interpretation of American diplomacy. Led by the late socialist historian William Appleman Williams in the 1950s and early 1960s,

the open door school was the most important attempt to apply the *innenpolitik* approach to the study of American foreign policy. The open door school characterized the imperatives dictating America's global strategy in terms remarkably similar to those used by the statesmen who currently implement that strategy. To both, America's global pacification policy is pursued not simply because it 'pays', but because US policymakers believe that the economy demands it. Most important, both the leftist scholars and current officials believe that America's worldwide defense commitments are not the product of an indiscriminate and ideologically motivated globalism, but of careful thought.

45. Jonathan Peterson, 'Life in US Graded on the Curve', *Los Angeles Times*, 11 April 1993, p.A1.
46. Cited in Layne and Schwarz (note 14), p.19.
47. These arguments are made in Paul Kennedy, *The Rise and Fall of the Great Powers: Economic Change and Military Conflict From 1500 to 2000* (NY: Random House, 1987); David Calleo, *The Imperious Economy* (Cambridge, MA: Harvard UP, 1982); and Gilpin (note 10).
48. Richard Gardner, 'The Return of Internationalism,' *Washington Quarterly* 13 (Summer 1990), pp.23–39; Allison and Treverton; Carnegie Endowment for International Peace; Robert Art, 'A US Military Strategy for the 1990s: Reassurance Without Dominance,' *Survival* 34 (Winter 1992–93), pp.3–23.
49. Quoted in Gardner (note 48), p.227.
50. For the argument that the ascendancy of new great powers is inevitable, see Christopher Layne's seminal article, 'The Unipolar Illusion: Why New Great Powers Will Arise', *International Security* 17 (Spring 1993), pp.5–51.
51. Quoted in Anders Stephanson, 'Ideology and Neorealist Mirrors', *Diplomatic History* 17 (Spring 1993), p.289, note 10.
52. Christopher Lasch, 'William Appleman Williams on American History', *Marxist Perspectives* 7 (Fall 1978), p.126.
53. See John Maynard Keynes, 'National Self-Sufficiency', *Yale Review*, 26 (Spring 1933), pp.755–69; Charles Beard, *The Open Door at Home: A Trial Philosophy of the National Interest* (NY: MacMillan, 1935); and Beard, *America in Midpassage* (NY: Macmillan, 1939), p.453.
54. V. I. Lenin, *Imperialism: The Highest Stage of Capitalism* (NY: Int. Publishers), 1939 [orig. pub. 1917].

America and Collective Security in Europe

DANIEL N. NELSON

As leaders of Conference on Security and Cooperation in Europe (CSCE) members assembled for photo opportunities and ponderous statements during their July 1992 Helsinki II summit, Bosnian Foreign Minister Haris Silajdzic noted poignantly that 'This is what is killing us'.[1] Two hundred thousand deaths later, the horrors of post-Cold War armed struggles are all too clear. From the Adriatic to the Caucasus, devastating conflicts have raged in Europe largely unaffected by international action. Similar tragedies are taking place on other continents, as illustrated by the genocidal slaughter in Rwanda. Meanwhile, the world imagines worst-case scenarios of nuclear war on the Korean peninsula.

At the same time, Europe is beset by West Europeans' 'second thoughts about consummating a political union implied by their Maastricht marriage, a right wing and neo-fascist victory in Italian elections, the return of ex-communists to power in most of Eastern and erstwhile Soviet Europe via open and fair elections, and America's abandonment of leadership in the Euro-Atlantic alliance.

This troubling time, coming only five years after declarations of Cold War victory and four years after the 'euphoria, optimism, [and] confidence' at the November 1990 summit in Paris,[2] requires a wrenching shift in our hopes, expectations and preparations for the twenty-first century. At issue are no less than our most deeply felt and long-standing assumptions about international politics and global affairs.

To some observers, these conditions of a 'new world disorder' require a return to *realpolitik* – the so-called 'realism' of states pursuing national interests through the application of power. Such engagement eschews multilateral commitments, while implying a calculus of when, where, and how to use force rooted in the vagaries of state interests – *staatsrason* or *raison d'état*.[3] In its crudest form, such a position for the United States is nothing less than 'America first'; in a more sophisticated expression, it is a *weltanschauung* wherein international affairs is a game of great powers, concerts and alliances – even to the point where the only alternative to creeping systemic disorder is a purposeful spread of nuclear weaponry to other great powers so that geopolitical and geostrategic balances are maintained.[4]

Alternative voices advocate a policy of global disengagement for the United States – a minimalist foreign presence whereby little that happens abroad is of consequence unless an attack on the United States itself or its core security interests is imminent. The principal danger to American interests, according to the minimalist view, is to become enmeshed in European (or other regions') squabbles and turmoil because of alliance obligations. Such a proactive isolationism, suggesting that the United States 'design strategies that will insulate America from the economic and political consequences of future European rivalries',[5] has garnered little enthusiasm. In large part, that response is because disengagement contradicts the obvious – that the world extant when George Washington and other Founders warned against 'entangling alliances' cannot be recreated. In an environment of transnational threats and global communications, ours is no longer a choice between engagement or disengagement; aggression, genocide, 'ethnic cleansing' and other barbarous acts harm us by their presence, not only when they reach our borders.

A third path, often disparaged, is that of collective security. Seen as a radical or utopian departure by some, and alleged to have a historical record of failure, few analysts have explored the means by which Euro-Atlantic or global security could be pursued collectively.[6] But most criticisms, including 1992 commentaries by Josef Joffe and Richard K. Betts, address caricatures of collective security – straw men, rather than sensible alternatives that could be the product of diplomacy informed by both principles and 'real world' threat assessments.

Collective security ought not be viewed as a system in lieu of alliances for common defense but, rather, as a robust companion. Collective security 'failures' repeated by critics of the concept, for example, the oft-cited League of Nations debacle when confronted by Fascism and Nazism, were less a failure than a misapplication of the concept. Collective security and common defense can and should reinforce each other at every step; *security*, as an indivisible commodity, must be sought both by abating threats through all non-lethal means and by heightening capacities to defeat aggression if it nonetheless occurs. When a security threat is unequivocal and originates from one principal source – as for decades of the Cold War – NATO was an adequate means by which to meet communist and Soviet dangers. Through NATO, the United States and its allies made assiduous efforts to deter aggression and meet threat with counter-threat. Now, when the sources of threat become more ambiguous and numerous, the same counter-threat is ineffective; armored regiments, aircraft carriers or even special forces have little effect against ethnic strife, human rights violations, terrorism, mass migration, and other destabilizing developments. While we need to retain a capacity to project force, we also need a capability to inject monitors, observers, negotiators, and peacekeepers into volatile situations. In the broadest sense, Europe and other continents need a regional capability to reduce threats at the earliest opportunity.

Collective security, then, is neither an unnecessary appendage to other structures nor a naive 'feel good' remnant of idealism. Empirical studies, indeed, have found suggestive evidence to the contrary – that 'states [practicing] collective security can expect to fare better [i.e., are more likely to survive] than states adhering to any of a number of realist strategies'.[7]

The Failure at Helsinki II

The leaders of 51 states came to Helsinki in mid-1992 for only the third such high-level CSCE (otherwise known as the Helsinki Process) meeting. But that gathering, unlike the Paris summit of November 1990, had no upbeat script. Instead, the pallor of warfare from the Adriatic to the Caucasus hung ominously over the agenda.

In fairness, Euro-Atlantic security did not leave Helsinki completely empty-handed. The summit, for example, declared that CSCE is a regional arrangement under Chapter 8 of the UN Charter, inaugurated a steering-group arrangement whereby the whole CSCE membership need not convene in a crisis, used for the first time CSCE's 'consensus-minus-one' decision mechanism to suspend the rump 'Yugoslavia' (Serbia and Montenegro), approved the creation of a CSCE commissioner for minorities, and agreed that Western military force could be deployed in Bosnia to ensure deliveries of humanitarian relief.[8]

Subsequently, some of these actions – particularly those undertaken by the High Commissioner for National Minorities – have proven to be extremely valuable. With a shoestring budget and a staff of volunteers and people seconded from foreign ministries and nongovernment organizations (NGOs) such modest initiatives have become one of the best bargains for European security.

But these were not measures generated by the strategic assessments of statesmen. Instead, as television vividly depicted intense suffering in Sarajevo, Western leaders were forced to recognize that they could not remain aloof. The United States, which had sought to confine CSCE to a role 'principally as a consultative framework for promoting stability in Europe,' was pushed by the unconscionable acts of Serbian President Slobodan Milosevic and his allies to reassess its position.[9]

As tragedies arising from their previous inaction dawned on Western leaders, the Helsinki II summit did give CSCE an enlarged portfolio. Unfortunately, those small steps were desultory and belated, failing to move toward genuine collective security with an unequivocal political endorsement or adequate resources. The Western powers took a second look at collective security during the Helsinki II meeting, but they then turned away from the tasks that would have required political will and the commitment of resources.

While people die and principles are trampled, political fears blind leaders and analysts to the palpable need for a strategic shift towards truly collective security. Helsinki II still tinkered when tragic events demanded large scale construction of security architecture. None of the temporizing steps taken in July 1992 provided anything more than heightened visibility for a still impotent forum.

Nearly three years later, such lost opportunities have left the West with a terrible choice – to endorse the gains of aggression by approving a territorial division of Bosnia, thereby inviting a future rekindling of war, or to acknowledge that punitive military action is necessary to enforce UN resolutions and to exhibit resolve against genocide and aggression.

The Concept of Collective Security

Collective security differs fundamentally from common defense. In the latter, dominant or hegemonic powers gather allies around them, sharing not values but opposition to a clear and ominous adversary. Alliances for common defense implement strategies of containment and deterrence, and attempt to prevent war by balancing military capacities, not by reducing threats.

By contrast, collective security begins with the premise that threats may arise from within, and that avoiding them is at least as critical as countering those external threats with military capacities. Collective security arrangements are bound to include, not exclude, concern for the peace, stability and well-being of all participants.

Techniques for non-offensive defense, studies of conflict reduction by joint academic/policy centers, mediation via crisis resolution organs, collective and binding economic sanctions, and peacekeeping forces to separate disputants are all examples of collective efforts that avoid resorting to military coercion. Collective security does not deny the right of self-defense, but by dampening threats, it also seeks to minimize the need to exercise that right.

Both the League of Nations and the United Nations charters invoked images of global commitments to mediation, conflict resolution, and peacekeeping. Carrying out the UN's potential collective security role proved impossible during the Cold War. The veto power vested in five permanent members of the Security Council usually precluded action; indeed, the Security Council chamber frequently became merely another arena for the US–Soviet rivalry. Despite the end of the Cold War, the veto power may still prevent effective action, especially in Eurasian conflicts. Chinese intransigence may, for instance, block forceful UN sanctions against North Korea.

The continuing obstructionist potential of the veto power is only one source of trouble. Another problem is the rising financial burden. The deployment of truce observers/peacekeepers in Cambodia, Rwanda, Somalia and other locales has virtually exhausted UN resources.

Secretary-General Boutros Boutros-Ghali has reported to the Security Council on suggestions for a substantially enhanced UN capacity for military operations along the lines originally considered by Articles 42 and 43 of the Charter. But the UN's role is unlikely to expand into the vast global security role projected in 1945 – not, at least, if the states having vetoes may be parties to disputes (as Russia is likely to be), and if peace-keeping operations cannot be financed through other means. Regional organizations such as the CSCE may offer greater potential.

CSCE: Instrument or Obstacle?

CSCE originated in 1973 during the diplomatic endeavors to reduce East–West confrontation. Delegates from 35 states – all European nations, except Albania, plus Canada and the United States – met for more than two years to draft the Helsinki Accords (formally, the 'Helsinki Final Act').

Signed on 1 August 1975, the Final Act added significantly to the claim that all states must behave in ways consistent with higher standards – toward their own citizens and toward each other. Three principal areas, or 'baskets,' of agreements enunciated principles on (1) relations between states, including mutual security assurances, (2) economic, scientific and environmental cooperation, and (3) human contacts and exchanges.

Basket 1 incorporated ten principles guiding relations between participating states, 'including respect for human rights . . ., equal rights and self-determination of peoples, territorial integrity of states, peaceful settlement of disputes, [the] inviolability of frontiers . . . and military security'.[10]
Basket 2 detailed the elements of cooperation outside the realm of security, plus reciprocal assistance in 'transport, tourism, migrant workers . . . and personnel training,' while Basket 3 concerned family reunification and visits across the erstwhile Cold War divide in Europe plus the 'free flow of information, cultural cooperation and educational exchanges'.[11]

Until the late 1980s the CSCE process remained an instrument of Cold War competition. Periodic follow-up sessions to gauge implementation of the 1975 Accord – in Belgrade (1977–78) and Madrid (1980–83) – were confrontational, affected by worsening Soviet-American relations. Additional inter-sessional meetings on more specific topics were begun in the late 1970s as well, although most were beset by East–West intransigence. For the West,

CSCE was a cudgel with which to strike blows against human rights abuses committed by Soviet and East European communist regimes.

Human rights monitoring formed a large part of CSCE's endeavors in the 1970s and early 1980s, and the courageous activities of Helsinki-related groups within communist states drove a wedge of conscience into Leninist authoritarian systems. But not until Mikhail Gorbachev's 'new thinking' on foreign policy, coincident with the third principal follow-up session of CSCE held in Vienna from November 1986 through January 1989, did CSCE's movement into the realm of security have a chance to quicken.

Vienna could have set the Helsinki Process on track toward becoming the Euro-Atlantic security architecture for the twenty-first century. That potential for CSCE development was not, however, achieved.

No one can doubt that the mandate produced by the Vienna follow-up meeting substantially expanded CSCE activities in the realm of confidence and security-building measures and conventional arms reductions, moving beyond the Stockholm agreements of 1986. Variously described as a 'watershed in the CSCE process' and a 'prelude to revolution', the Vienna meeting undoubtedly helped by its very existence to accelerate the disintegration of authoritarianism in Europe's eastern half.[12] Those evaluations are particularly relevant in the domains of confidence-building and conventional arms reductions, where the 1975 Helsinki commitments were 'elevated . . . to a higher level of ambition', with calls for 'additional work on CSBMs,' and a mandate for negotiations in the CSCE framework 'between the Warsaw Pact and NATO. . . on conventional armed forces in Europe (CFE)'.[13]

Yet for all that the Vienna follow-up meeting might have been, it proved to be the beginning of a disastrous foreign policy blunder. At the Vienna meetings, the democratic West lost a chance to transform CSCE into a vigorous institution. Had major Western powers been sufficiently far-sighted, there could have emerged in early 1989 a security architecture more advanced than CSCE is today, even after Helsinki II – a Euro-Atlantic security organization that could have ameliorated the threats that led inexorably to the full-scale wars now underway in both the Balkans and the Caucasus. An absence of strategic vision led, instead, to a wasteful and indecisive 1989–90 debate in which the United States was joined by Britain and other 'Atlanticists' in opposing the strengthening of CSCE.

During that two-year period of far-reaching change, Germany's foreign minister, Hans Dietrich Genscher, argued strenuously for a stronger CSCE role and a rapid expansion of its duties and resources.[14] His position received vocal support from Czechoslovakia, Poland, and Hungary. The Czechoslovaks offered, as early as April 1990, a rather detailed plan for a new pan-European security institution, within which there would be a 'permanent Commission on Security'.[15] Polish Foreign Minister Krzysztof Skubiszewski, speaking to the North Atlantic Assembly on 29 November 1990, argued for a parallel development of *both* an enlarged NATO and an all-European security system.[16] Meanwhile, prominent US newspapers editorialized about the need to think anew about the potential for collective security in the form of a European Security Council.[17]

Unfortunately, as walls fell, playwrights became presidents, and tyrants were overthrown, American policymakers congratulated themselves for their triumph over communism and concentrated on protecting old US preroga- tives as NATO's dominant alliance partner. Because of that myopia, US leaders lost a chance to prepare for the onslaught of unattended problems from the eastern half of Europe. President George Bush, speaking at the Helsinki CSCE summit in 1992, admitted as much when he said that, even in 1990, 'we did not appreciate what awaited us.'[18]

When the second CSCE summit was held in Paris during late November 1990, signing the CFE treaty, blessing German unification, and broadly denoting the end of the Cold War with the 'Charter of Paris' were the principal agenda items. And, although the United States consented to the establishment of minimal institutions for CSCE – a tiny secretariat in Prague, a Conflict Prevention Center in Vienna, and an Office of Free Elections in Warsaw – the American position on collective security remained far more doubtful than that of most of Washington's European allies.

As noted above, the new noncommunist governments in East-Central and Southeastern Europe joined with Genscher in 1989–90 to call for pan- European collective security. Varying proposals came from Skubiszewski and former Czechoslovak foreign minister Jiri Dienstbier. In contrast to these larger and progressive visions, the 'NATO-first' American position severely limited CSCE's structure, staff (until late 1992, only 17 diplomats and support personnel), and budget (totaling a few million dollars per year).

Bush administration foreign policy tethered CSCE, precluding until late 1990 any metamorphosis into a post-Cold War mechanism for collective security. Although Bush spoke often of 'prudence,' his policy exhibited a reticence towards CSCE born of the fear that an invigorated CSCE would supplant the North Atlantic Alliance. These fears were expressed behind a facade of rationality – that CSCE's consensual process would make it incapable of action, that its size alone meant cumbersome and irresolute response to crises, and that states would not submit themselves to CSCE authority.[19]

By 1991 the East Europeans began to back away from pan-European solu- tions, recognizing that the only position compatible with US views was a NATO-centered policy. Given their dependence on US and other NATO members' financial largesse, East European leaders began pilgrimages to Brussels, and 'Atlantic Clubs' or similar groups sprouted from Sofia to

Warsaw, all in close collusion with American embassies. Visionary statesmen in the fledgling democracies of post-communist Europe had not abandoned their convictions about the importance of collective security; rather they knew that the alternative was not feasible without Washington's support.[20]

Without particular enthusiasm from the United States, a high-level consultative network was agreed upon in a supplemental document of the November 1990 Paris CSCE summit.[21] Foreign ministers form the core of this network, meeting as a 'Council' at least once a year. A 'Committee of Senior Officials' serves as CSCE's coordinating body, convening an average of once a month in 1991 and less frequently thereafter (as CSCE processes became accepted practice). Other intersessional meetings (e.g., symposia or seminars), and noninstitutional 'mechanisms' by which member states convene to respond to specific problem areas (e.g., 'unusual military activities'), formed the bulk of CSCE's presence prior to 1992. Thereafter, the range of other endeavors has continued to expand – seminars on the 'human dimension' and forums on economic issues have been long-winded and minimally productive. More tangibly, the High Commissioner on National Minorities (former Dutch foreign minister Max van der Stoel) has been highly effective on a meager budget as an early warning and mediating office in the Hague.[22] Likewise, the Forum on Security Cooperation – meant to 'harmonize' various arms control agreements in the aftermath of German unification, the Warsaw Pact's demise, and the dissolution of multinational states – has made limited but useful progress. Major review conferences regarding the 'human dimension' also continue, most recently in Budapest from 10 October to 2 December 1994.

Activity within and around CSCE was frequent, visible, and time-consuming. Beset by a lack of political will among its largest and most powerful members, however, CSCE's institutions have not been invested with the resources or capacity to do much more than talk, observe, and report. Opportunities lost in 1989–92 continue to be lost after the Helsinki II summit. Notwithstanding a few bright spots, such as the High Commissioner on National Minorities, the CSCE has none of the imprimatur of Washington and other Western capitals. As a consequence, although CSCE does much more in the mid-1990s than it has ever done, it has relatively little to show for all of its motion.

Policy Failure: The Obsession with NATO

Glaring by its absence is any American willingness to think beyond NATO-provided Euro-Atlantic security. Instead, US policymakers have sought to deflect attempts to develop a robust, well-endowed companion to NATO – a true Euro-Atlantic security organization that might emerge from the nucleus of CSCE. Instead, the United States continues to regard CSCE as a tertiary player in a post-Cold War Europe.

Since 1989 providing life-support for NATO – revised roles, new structures, altered vocabulary – has remained far more important to the US State Department and Pentagon than thinking about what might be in America's best interests as we fast approach the twenty-first century. American officials at NATO and the US State Department have busily undertaken the recoding of the venerable Atlantic alliance during the first half of the 1990s. A new appendage created in late 1991, the North Atlantic Cooperation Council (NACC), included all NATO and former Warsaw Pact members, and was meant, somehow, to address the hemorrhaging security in the Continent's eastern half.

But few people in Eastern Europe, Russia, or other post-Soviet states were impressed with NACC. Although the East Europeans were able to see the security umbrella, NACC did not open it. This second-class association with NATO for former WTO members was a pallid and risky substitute for robust collective security that acts to prevent conflict and ameliorate threats. People in the eastern half of Europe understood that reality so clearly that they sought new bilateral and regional alliances and associational ties with every existing 'Western' institution, while simultaneously turning up the heat for NATO membership. The Poles and Hungarians were the most vocal in lobbying for NATO membership during 1992 and 1993, but other states (e.g., Bulgaria) were not far behind.[23]

At the March 1992 opening of the Helsinki follow-up meeting, even as ominous signs mounted that fighting in Bosnia, Moldova, and the Caucasus would intensify, US Deputy Secretary of State Lawrence J. Eagleburger spoke only of incremental changes in CSCE. He encouraged an expansion of CSCE's activities in democratic institution-building, adding to its longstanding work in human rights and arms control.[24] But he offered no suggestions for additional CSCE authority concerning the increasingly crucial security issues.

At NATO's Oslo meeting in April 1992, another step was taken toward ensuring that NATO alone would decide if military forces would be deployed within Europe as peacekeepers and/or peace-enforcers. NATO leaders announced that the Alliance would be willing to consider a CSCE request for NATO military assets to serve in a peacekeeping role.[25] Although much of the press coverage of that pronouncement conveyed the sense that NATO's public relations apparatus wanted – i.e., that this was a step forward, for the first time enabling CSCE to call upon NATO – the Oslo agreement was not particularly supportive of CSCE. Given that CSCE's decision-making process remained 'consensus minus one,' NATO will only rarely receive such requests and, even then, can act only when all of NATO's 16 members agree. And, of course, the agreement can also be seen as NATO's marker that deploying military force is its business, and that any future development of collective security will be limited to roles other than those already staked out by the North Atlantic alliance.

NATO's hesitant, minimal steps in Bosnia are a product of such muted enthusiasm for becoming an agent of a collective security organization. A chain of command in which NATO implements decisions made by U.N. commanders is met with no enthusiasm in Brussels, and the 'finger-pointing' among NATO members and between NATO and the United Nations has been debilitating and has undermined the effectiveness of the peacekeeping operation.[26]

But the United States has remained tied irrevocably to NATO, which is deemed by national officials to be the *sine qua non* of American presence in Europe and the best means of ensuring Washington's interests. NATO is so deeply enshrined in these perceptions of its security and national interests that its metamorphosis has been the *leitmotif* of US-West European relations during both the Bush and Clinton administrations, within which all other issues (responses to Balkan crises, German reunification, force reductions, etc.) are framed. At NATO's Rome summit in November 1991, after a prolonged intra-alliance 'strategic review', there was clear evidence that the United States had dug in its heels; NATO was to remain the single pillar of Euro-Atlantic security, with everything else in distinctly supporting roles. US President George Bush declared at the Rome summit that 'the NATO alliance was the guarantor of security and stability in Europe and could not be replaced, even in the long term.' More than a year earlier, Secretary of State James Baker stated the same position clearly and unequivocally – that 'only NATO can continue to guarantee European security and stability.'[27]

When NATO leaders met again in Brussels in January 1994, the survival of the Alliance was still at stake, but with added urgency. As noted above, East Europeans – particularly the Poles and Hungarians – had made NATO membership an acute issue during 1993, relentlessly arguing that their ability to remain stable, democratic and outside a renewed Russian orbit depended on entry into the North Atlantic alliance.[28]

By the fall of 1993 the United States had developed a vague response to the NATO enlargement issue in the concept of Partnership for Peace (PFP). The meaning and significance of PFP was not entirely clear when first announced publicly at a NATO defense ministers' meeting in October 1993. It vaguely connoted more than the talking-shop of the NACC, but far less than NATO membership, with which would come guarantees of Article 5 of the Washington Treaty (an attack on one is an attack on all).

By the time of the NATO summit in January 1994 the closing communiqué could include several articles on PFP, each stressing the real, active, concrete nature of Partnerships, e.g., by 'creating an ability to operate with NATO forces in fields such as peacekeeping.'[29]

Threading the needle between Eastern Europe's plaintive cries for more security and Moscow's objection to enlarging NATO required a skillful rendering of words and deeds. Commitments without the mutual guarantees, a path toward NATO membership without signposts, military cooperation without a political alliance – these and many other juxtaposed phrases imply an attempt by the United States and its principal allies to offer something to Europe's eastern half without providing either anything very costly or anything very substantial.[30]

The wars in the former Yugoslavia have spotlighted a grand failure of Western, and specifically American, post-Cold War policy. The Charter of Paris of November 1990 commits all states of the Euro-Atlantic region to 'build, consolidate, and strengthen democracy . . . to safeguard . . . freedom of expression, tolerance of all groups . . . and equality of opportunity . . .'[31] The Charter's linkage of regional peace and security to the domestic environments of all states for the first time implies a collective responsibility to ensure democracy, the rule of law and human rights so that all may live peacefully. Specifically, the Charter asserts the right of collective engagement in internal affairs of states:

> We emphasize that the commitments undertaken in the field of the human dimension of the CSCE are matters of direct and legitimate concern to all participating States and do not belong exclusively to the internal affairs of the State concerned. The protection and promotion of human rights and fundamental freedoms and the strengthening of democratic institutions continue to be a vital basis for our comprehensive security.[32]

But these implied responsibilities ring hollow when there is no willingness to enforce commitments. As aggression, genocide ('ethnic cleansing'), and other atrocities went unanswered in Bosnia, Western and US priorities became clear. Such a willingness will not come from Washington as long as national interests define security and national power augmented by alliances are thought to be the premier means of ensuring it.

Only a clouded vision, or none at all, would see security to be well served by the hand-holding function of NACC, the competitive lapdog behavior encouraged by PFP as former Warsaw Pact members try desperately to be first to sign up or first to hold maneuvers with NATO forces, or by post-hoc battlefield policing by UN blue helmets. Soothing talk in Brussels or carnage cleanup in Bosnia are inhumane substitutes for the ultimate security of conflict prevention.

Roots of Blindness

How can such a misguided policy be explained? Individual self-interest may provide some of the answer, as careers are endangered by the slippage of NATO's preeminence. There was also some talk in Washington among policymakers, members of Congress, and think-tank experts of letting the Europeans – particularly the French – demonstrate in the Yugoslav catastrophe their incapacity to resolve crises without NATO, and especially without US leadership.[33] This desire to demonstrate NATO's indispensability led some observers to suspect that US policy regarding CSCE was a calculated effort to ensure its failure in the growing conflicts of Europe's eastern half. In conversations with many of the key policymakers in the United States and Europe, I have found little corroboration for such a conspiracy thesis. Nevertheless, the thought that Europe's indecisiveness and disunity would become apparent, absent American 'resolve,' was a hope that many in Washington have been unable to conceal.

The most often cited rationale for minimalizing CSCE was the danger of linking 'national security' to a large, amorphous forum when American national interests were not threatened by turmoil in the Balkans or Caucasus. To 'take a pass' on Yugoslavia, as one senior Bush adviser told me in the spring of 1992, was a direct consequence of judging that US national interests were unaffected by ethno-nationalist warfare, and that involvement in multilateral efforts would needlessly intermingle American concerns with those of other states.

Hence, US officials made no effort to heighten CSCE's profile, and let the European Community and, ultimately, the United Nations try to deal with the political and security dimensions of the growing Yugoslav crisis. Not until 1994, when the 'failure' of multilateral institutions had been amply demonstrated, did the great powers act in concert as a 'contact group' in an effort to bring an end to the vicious Bosnian conflict.

Thus stated, the US position regarding the broad issue of collective security, and its specific applicability in Yugoslavia, has the ring of rationality. But underlying that mindset is the deeply troubling ideology of political realism. Political realism, or *realpolitik,* is an appealing concept for those who seek assurances amidst what some writers have called the 'new world disorder'. As uncertainties and dangers of the post-Cold War environment become evident, interest in older, comfortable paradigms such as *realpolitik* has grown.

Realists argue that, after the demise of a bipolar concentration of power, nation states will return to a general struggle for power, defined primarily in military terms, as they pursue national interests. National interests require that states seek 'military capabilities sufficient to deter attack by potential enemies', and that peace and stability 'result through the operation of a balance of power propelled by self interest'.[34] Realist tenets emphasize power as the fundamental commodity of international relations, national interests as the guiding principles of policymakers, and balances of power as the means by which to pursue such interests without war.

That reasoning is at the core of both America's aloofness toward collective security and of the US decision to 'take a pass' on Yugoslavia. Not until the body count and graphic horrors of ethnic cleansing made it impossible to turn away did American policy move perceptibly. America's power and interests are thought to be embedded in a tried and trusted NATO, while any proportional diminution of the US role (e.g., in a larger body without a preponderant American military weight) would throw national interests into the cauldron of collective decision-making, which the United States does not control.

Both Washington's passivity toward the Yugoslav tragedy and the aversion to CSCE are direct consequences of the belief that America's status as the world's last superpower renewed an old standard for foreign policy commitments – 'clear national interests'. According to realist reasoning, unless such unequivocal interests are at stake, commitments of American political, economic or military resources should not be undertaken. By this logic, based on the two crucibles of political realism (power and interests), one uses power only when interests are threatened; to do so when clear national interests are not threatened would damage security.

But this policy assumes that, as the century draws to a close, unambiguous national interests exist, that such interests can be defended by national power alone, and the exercise of power in the name of national interests will produce security. Even after one of the most exhaustive and exhausting reviews of US defense strategy and force structure ever conducted, the Clinton administration's own 'Bottom Up Review' came up with a vision of American power projection that is unguided by any clear national security strategy and is increasingly unaffordable.[35] Defining national interests and matching power to those interests have become an extremely murky enterprise.

The Clinton administration has adopted Bush administration policies and the same disjointed realist logic. Against Saddam Hussein, the United States led and dominated the 'coalition' forces. The adversary was malevolent, and the war's result was sold to the American public as an unqualified victory. Power used to protect interests (oil, allies such as Saudi Arabia, etc.) seemed to beget security. But as that victory proved to be far less glorious, and the policies that led to the original crisis were traced to the White House, the linkage between power, national interests, and a twenty-first century understanding of security grew tenuous.

The Bush administration's spurious syllogism has gone unchallenged by Bill Clinton. Clinton, too, has signed on to the old adage that national interests must guide security policy, and that power must be the principal instrument of such policy. By accepting these norms, neither Bush nor Clinton has been able to provide a strategy for post-communist Europe. Threats in the region, from turmoil and collapse in nascent democracies to economic dislocation, migration and the spread of warfare, are *transnational* and *systemic,* affecting not the lives of Americans today, but the potential for Americans to live in peace and prosperity in the future. Husbanding military resources by avoiding peacemaking commitments, for example, does less to conserve power than to erode the bases for strength.

Mistaking woodenheadedness for realism, George Bush's foreign policy stayed the course and headed for rocky shoals. Bill Clinton has failed to take any corrective action. By eschewing collective security, we have become increasingly less relevant to Europe's future, more isolated with our missiles and our marines, and unable to offer meaningful alternatives to recurrent strife throughout the Continent's eastern half.[36] And, by denying to ourselves any tool for trying to ameliorate threats, we are left with an unpalatable choice – launching a costly great power intervention after the killing has begun or taking a seat from which to watch the slaughter.

CSCE could have been far more, and could have been a path to avoid Yugoslav-style wars. The US adherence to a misplaced political realism, evident in both the Bush and Clinton presidencies, has led both to CSCE's stunted development in the post-Cold War era, and to unmitigated tragedy in southeastern Europe. Were we to realign US post-Cold War strategy dramatically, backing unequivocally a fully institutionalized Euro-Atlantic collective security system, we might yet avoid worst-case scenarios in Moldova, Kosovo, and Macedonia, as well as in the Caucasus, Crimea, and other potential hot spots. The time for accomplishing that task, however, has become exceedingly short.

Scenarios for Collective Security

The genesis of regional collective security can only follow one of two routes. Either an existing institution must metamorphose, becoming a organization to dampen threats effectively, or a new companion entity must be inaugurated.

NATO's functional and territorial expansion – thereby adding to an alliance for common defense both the geography and responsibilities of a more all-inclusive regional collective security organization – has been advocated strongly by American analysts.[37] Indeed, that route has become the default option for US and Western policy. No one has had the political will to create a Euro-Atlantic collective security system, so the metamorphosis of

NATO, the European Union, the Western European Union, and the Council of Europe – an amalgam of allegedly interlocking institutions – has become the pragmatic alternative. As all struggle to broaden and/or deepen, they may yield some of the results sought through a more idealistic collective security organization.

At the moment, however, NATO remains the only credible security architecture. No matter how real the Soviet and Warsaw Pact threat was for several decades, NATO unquestionably succeeded in keeping the United States engaged in Europe, while contributing to West European integration by minimizing fears of a resurgent Germany.

For NATO, however, winning in the short term has meant losing in the long term. Gone is an unambiguous adversary that gave NATO a clear *raison d'être*, and an unarguable threat with which to forge unity and diminish domestic opposition to military spending. Since 1989 NATO has struggled to come to grips with the end of at least one phase of its career; the purpose for which it 'lived' is no more.

After Europe's tectonic political shifts in the late 1980s and early 1990s, NATO has sought to repackage and reinvent itself. After strategic reviews. defense planning papers, conferences, North Atlantic Council sessions and Alliance summits, NATO has been trimmed, broadened, and stretched. Military forces available to Supreme Allied Commander Europe have decreased significantly, while restructuring has meant an abandonment of forward deployment.

Beyond those specifically military changes, NATO has had to confront the immense political challenge of how to behave toward erstwhile Warsaw Pact adversaries. NATO's response to that challenge has been to drift toward expansion, with no one at the helm. Not wanting NATO's preeminence in the security domain to be subordinated to any other organization, the United States and Western Europe have offered first the NACC and then, in January 1994, Partnership For Peace (PFP).

The drift toward danger is evident in several respects. Military cooperation under the auspices of PFP implies an obligation to improve the capability and compatibility of East European forces. But such 'NATO-ization' is expensive, and no one knows from whom the money is to come.

Second, Partnerships will not create partners, at least not within Europe's eastern half. PFP fosters an unseemly contest among these states for Western attention and resources, and competition rather than collaboration. If one state were to gain rapid advancement into NATO circles, its neighbors would not be sanguine, suspecting that NATO's guarantees could become a shield for pressures and intimidations.

Also damaging is the continued absence in PFP of clear markers on the path toward NATO membership. President Clinton reassured Poles while at

Warsaw in early July 1994 that they will be at the head of the line.[38] But will NATO's security guarantees be provided first to those who behave best or to those who need it the most? Specific criteria and the relative weight of each factor for entering NATO are unstated.

Finally, none of the former Warsaw Pact countries have been offered any security guarantees with PFP, but all must fulfill new responsibilities. For NATO and for the proto-democracies in Eastern and post-Soviet Europe, the gap between expectations and responsibilities is unhealthy. For regional security, that gap constitutes a real and present danger.

All of this means that PFP has fostered a security race, the losers of which will exhibit a security envy pushing them toward other patrons – Russia, Germany or possibly other states such as France, Italy, and Turkey that have served such a role in the past century for one or more states in Eastern and Southeastern Europe. NATO leaders have said repeatedly that NATO is open to more members – not if, but when. The pertinent questions, however, are who and why, not if or when.

The terrible mistake is being made of again drawing lines in Europe, despite rhetoric to the contrary. Rather than seeing security as indivisible and collective, it appears that the Western powers will offer guarantees to those they like best, not to those whose peace and prosperity are most endangered. Furthermore, the Western governments continue to imply that the route to the secure environs of NATO lead through PFP's scheme for *military* co-operation.

Yet that is only one component of security. NATO's role in the twenty-first century should not mix and confuse the roles of an alliance for common defense and an organization for collective security. NATO should be NATO. Rather than attempting to transform into a larger, indistinct organization that mixes roles, ends and means, NATO should retain its West European and North American focus – where membership and capacity to fulfill responsibilities are coextensive, and where interstate conflicts are no longer plausible.

A credible military defense for North Atlantic democracies is a substantively different enterprise than is threat abatement for the Vancouver to Vladivostok hemisphere. Proliferation, mass migration, terrorism, and other transnational threats are palpable but unaffected by most unilateral or multilateral military contingencies. Air, naval, or ground forces can do little to mitigate these perils and offer only a blunt and rarely successful response to such new threats.

For threat abatement, NATO must have the help of a strong companion organization in which membership is universal. Such an organization would extend confidence building, early warning, and other conflict resolution mechanisms, as well as undertaking observer and peacekeeping missions. Those are the roles of a fully-institutionalized regional collective security organization, not an alliance that exists to plan for power projection and war fighting. The United Nations, overtaxed financially and slow to act, cannot fulfill such regional missions – and need not in Europe, where ample regional resources exist.

NATO's future role ought to be to ensure that threat abatement works – to provide the essential guarantee absent when previous experiments with collective security ended in tragedy. Neither half of the security equation will alone suffice; alliances to enhance military capacities meant to deter or defeat threats and collective security organizations designed to minimize and mitigate threats need each other.

Generating a new Euro-Atlantic collective security organization will thus depend on NATO and its principal members. The metamorphosis of NATO itself is not the answer. The devastation in both the Balkans and Caucasus, and the dangers at other flashpoints such as Moldova and Crimea, as well as the sheer cost of trying to halt ethno-nationalist warfare once it has produced martyrs and monuments to fuel more atrocities, may foster heightened political will in the mid and late 1990s to build other institutions.

And, as the peril of new threats that cannot be mitigated by NATO or its appendages becomes more acute, a forum such as a CSCE summit might provide the starting point for developing a follow-on organization. Prolonged negotiations are inevitable, but the start should be soon.

The precise outline of a Euro-Atlantic collective security organization lies beyond the scope of this analysis. Universal membership would be essential, but the consensual nature of CSCE decisions could not continue. Actions in the realm of security must be taken by a smaller subset of the total membership, and decisions within such a commission ought to be valid if supported by a majority.

Many tasks and responsibilities related to security in Europe need to be vested in a permanent commission on security. That commission should subsume many of the confidence building efforts, arms control and harmonization negotiations, transparencies and observations that reveal neighbors' military plans, and other tasks. Some capacity to deploy peacekeeping forces should also be present – to keep feuding factions apart while adjudication, arbitration, or other conflict-control mechanisms are utilized. Small numbers of such units should be maintained and dispersed in multinational garrisons throughout Central Europe.[39] Contingents from all member states, proportional to their population, could be assigned to the Euro-Atlantic organization, with accompanying financial and material assets.

These desiderata aside, the purpose of supporting collective security is neither to replace the UN's global efforts nor to supplant NATO. NATO has a place, albeit a much smaller place, in Euro-Atlantic security in the post-Cold War era. UN blue helmets must be available to police truces and the aftermath of carnage in many continents. But the larger needs of Euro-Atlantic security are not for defensive alliances or for ceasefire monitoring and disengagement undertaken by the United Nations. Rather, the principal need is one of conflict prevention and the reduction of transnational threats.

For these tasks, no institution exists, and no one is prepared. Small, disjointed NGO efforts, and courageous solo endeavors (e.g., the CSCE High Commission for National Minorities) will not suffice. Nothing that NATO might begin to do, and nowhere to which NATO might expand, will help diminish ethnonationalism, covert proliferation, mass migration, or other threatening phenomena.

The most difficult path is all that remains – a fundamental realignment of priorities in US and West European security policies, away from protecting NATO by adding to it, and toward addressing the kinds and intensity of threats confronting the region. For that goal, there must be strategic vision in Western capitals, of which little has been present thus far.

NOTES

1. This comment by Silajdzic was repeated by Bosnian diplomats to the author in Washington, DC in July 1992, and later by American diplomats involved in the Helsinki summit. Silajdzic is now Prime Minister of Bosnia-Herzegovina.
2. Max Kampelman, 'Foreword,' in *Enforcing Restraint: Collective Intervention in Internal Conflicts*, (ed.) Lori Fisler Damrosh (NY: Council on Foreign Relations Press, 1993), p.vii.
3. Arguably the most prominent of the neorealists, at least insofar as he has articulated a view on post-Cold War security, is John Mearsheimer. His article 'Back to the Future: Instability in Europe After the Cold War,' *International Security* 15/4 (Spring 1990), pp.5–56 is widely cited. Kenneth N. Waltz and other members of an earlier generation of realist theorists have also commented on the post-Cold War epoch, emphasizing the state, its power and interests. See, e.g., Kenneth N. Waltz, 'The Emerging Structure of International Politics', in US Senate, *Relations in a Multipolar World: Hearings before the Senate Foreign Relations Committee*, Part I, 101st Cong., 2d sess, 26, 28, and 30 Nov. 1990.
4. That extreme formulation can be found in Mearsheimer.
5. Those views can be found in Christopher Layne and Benjamin C. Schwarz, 'Should NATO Close Shop?' *Christian Science Monitor*, 10 March 1994, p.19. A more detailed treatment of the subject is contained in Christopher Layne and Benjamin C. Schwarz, 'American Hegemony – Without an Enemy,' *Foreign Policy* 92 (Fall 1993), pp.5–23.
6. A recent example of such criticism is Josef Joffe, 'Collective Security and the Future of Europe: Failed Dreams and Dead Ends,' *Survival* 34/1 (Spring 1992), pp.36–50. A more balanced treatment is Richard K. Betts, 'Systems for Peace or Causes of War? Collective Security, Arms Control and the New Europe', *International Security* 17/1 (Summer 1992), pp.5–43.
7. One intriguing, simulation-based study that gives rise to these conclusions is Thomas R. Cusack and Richard J. Stoll, 'Collective Security and State Survival in the Interstate System,' *International Studies Quarterly* 38 (March 1994), pp.33–59.
8. For a compilation of all agreements approved by CSCE Heads of State and Government during the Helsinki Follow-Up Meeting, see *Final Document From the 1992 Helsinki Follow-Up Meeting* (Washington: Helsinki Commission of the US Congress, 1992).
9. Robert Mauthner, 'Ministers Prepare For European Security Summit,' *Financial Times*, 2 Oct. 1990, p.2.

10. *The Conference on Security and Cooperation in Europe: An Overview of the CSCE Process, Recent Meetings and Institutional Development* (Washington, DC: Commission on Security and Cooperation in Europe, Feb. 1992), p.1.
11. Ibid., p.2.
12. Sen. Dennis DeConcini and Rep. Steny Hoyer, 'Letter of Transmittal,' in *From Vienna to Helsinki: Reports on the Inter-Sessional Meetings of the CSCE Process* (Washington, DC: Com. on SCE, April 1992), p.iii.
13. Ibid., p.4.
14. Hans-Dietrich Genscher offered several explanations of a pan-European security framework. See, for instance, his speech at the Tutzing Protestant Academy on 31 Jan. 1990. Hans-Dietrich Genscher, 'German Unity Within the European Framework,' in *Statements and Speeches* 13/2 (NY: German Infor. Center, 1990). Another example was Genscher's speech at the CSCE Conference, 11 April 1990, in *Statements and Speeches* 13/8.
15. For a report on the Czechoslovak proposal, see Edward Mortimer, 'Prague Suggests New Security Set-Up,' *Financial Times*, 4 April 1990, p.2.
16. Krzysztof Skubiszewski, Minister of Foreign Affairs of the Republic of Poland, 'Poland and European Security,' statement given to the North Atlantic Assembly, London, 29 Nov.1990, (mimeo, distr. by the Foreign Ministry, Republic of Poland).
17. E.g., see 'How to Make Europe Secure,' *New York Times*, 18 June 1990, p.A18.
18. Author's notes.
19. Those arguments were used by Bush administration officials in the National Security Council and in the Dept. of State during the author's conversations with them in 1990 and 1991. While serving as senior foreign policy adviser to House Majority Leader Richard Gephardt, I repeatedly sought explanations for the Bush administration's refusal to offer more than a limited acknowledgement of CSCE's potential role.
20. Author's interview with former Czechoslovak foreign minister Jiri Dientsbier, Prague, Czech Republic, 2 May 1994.
21. That supplementary document provides details about how the Committee of Senior Officials will work as well as organizational matters concerning the Conflict Prevention Center, a secretariat in Prague, and what was then called an Office of Free Elections in Warsaw. The Charter of Paris for a New Europe, with supplemental document, repr. in Stefan Lehne, *The CSCE in the 1990s: Common European House or Potemkin Village?* (Vienna: Austrian Inst. for Int. Affairs, 1991).
22. During the summer of 1993, the author served as a consultant to the CSCE's High Commissioner on National Minorities.
23. The flavor of the Polish pro-NATO campaign can be surmised from press accounts such as Juliusz Urbanowicz, 'Suchocka to NATO: Let Us In!' *Warsaw Voice*, 12 Sept. 1993, p.4.
24. For an analysis of Eagleburger's opening speech at the Helsinki follow-up meeting, see Commission on Security and Cooperation in Europe, *Digest*, March 1992, p.2.
25. For a brief discussion of this peacekeeping potential, see Heinz Gartner, 'The Future of Institutionalization: The CSCE Example', in *Redefining the CSCE: Challenges and Opportunities in the New Europe*, (ed.) Ian M. Cuthbertson (NY: Inst. for East West Studies, 1993), pp.240–41. Interviews at NATO HQ, Brussels, and at the NATO Defense College, Rome, by the author corroborate this view.
26. E.g., see Roger Cohen, 'Finger-Pointing by NATO Allies Delays Help for a Bosnian Town', *New York Times*, 22 Jan. 1994, p.A1. By the spring of 1994 NATO leaders, such as US Ambassador Robert Hunter, were asserting that they already had a sufficient UN mandate and that NATO could initiate attacks, not merely do so at the request of the United Nations. See Gillian Tett, 'NATO Air Strike Ultimatum to Serbs', *Financial Times*, 23–24 April 1994, p.2. Various internal documents underscored NATO's uneasiness about acting as the UN's army. See, e.g., the report of the Defence Planning Committee, Document DPC-D (93)6, 'Peacekeeping: The Implications for Defence Planning', 11 May 1993; and an 11-page working paper from the NATO defence planning staff from the same period (but undated), 'With the UN Whenever Possible, Without When Necessary.'
27. President Bush quoted in *Financial Times*, 5 Nov. 1991, p.3; Baker's comments in R.C. Longworthy, 'Uncertainty NATO's New Foe,' *Chicago Tribune*, 19 June 1990, p.1.

28. The Poles left no stone unturned in trying to find evidence that everyone was ready for NATO membership, including the Army's officers. See, for instance, a report on a survey of Polish officers in 'We and They in NATO,' *Rzeczpospolita*, 7 Sept. 1993, p.1.

29. 'Declaration of the Heads of State and Government Participating in the Meeting of the North Atlantic Council,' *Europe: Documents*, No. 1867 (Atlantic Document no. 83, 12 Jan. 1994), p.2.

30. Author's conversations with delegations from NATO member states and East European observers at the NATO summit, Brussels, Belgium, Jan. 1994.

31. Lehne.

32. Ibid.

33. Author's discussions with members of Congress and senior committee staff, June–Dec.1991.

34. These succinct summaries of realist views in international politics are those of Charles W. Kegley and Eugene R. Wittkopf, *American Foreign Policy: Pattern and Process*, 3rd ed. (NY: St. Martin's Press, 1987), p.76.

35. Those are among the judgments made in Andrew F. Krepinevich, *The Bottom-Up Review: An Assessment* (Washington, DC: Defense Budget Project, Feb. 1994).

36. The French, of course, have long been anxious for a Europe that provided for its own defense and security. It comes as no surprise, therefore, that French leaders have been most vocal in noting the 'obsolescence, or . . . wholly inadequate' nature of current instruments for defense and security, and that the 'split between the United States and Europe . . . is slowly becoming fact' requiring soon a 'Council of Greater Europe' and a 'real European security council.' These comments, by French National Assembly President Philippe Seguin on 25 Jan. 1994, were reported in *Atlantic News*, no. 2591, 26 Jan. 1994.

37. Two excellent examples of creative thought on this issue are Jeffrey Simon, 'Does Eastern Europe Belong in NATO?' *Orbis* 37 (Winter 1993), pp.21–35; and Ronald D. Asmus, Richard L. Kugler and F. Stephen Larrabee, 'Building a New NATO,' *Foreign Affairs* 72 (Sept.–Oct. 1993), pp.28–40. Another recent example, written by two British NATO parliamentarians, suggests explicitly two 'new core functions' for NATO – 'crisis management outside the treaty area' and 'projecting stability to former adversaries'. See Bruce George and John Borawski, 'Sympathy for the Devil: European Security in a Revolutionary Age,' *European Security* 2/4 (Winter 1993), p.482 of pp.475–90.

38. See Ruth Marcus, 'Clinton Assures Poles of NATO Membership, Eventually,' *Washington Post*, 8 July 1994, p.16.

39. A recent Polish idea, clearly meant to bring a permanent NATO presence onto Polish soil, was Grzegorz Kostrzewa-Zorbas, 'NATO Regional Peacekeeping Center in Central and Eastern Europe: A Proposal,' *European Security* 2/4 (Winter 1993), pp.585–602.

Ending Europe's Security Dependence

DAVID GARNHAM

When American troops were first sent to Western Europe during the Korean War, no one foresaw a permanent deployment. General Dwight D. Eisenhower told Senate committees in 1951 that American troops in Europe would provide 'the needed active strength pending the time that the European nations can build up their own defense forces'.[1] Astonishingly, more than four decades later and with the Cold War won, President Clinton still plans to keep 100,000 US troops in Europe. Nonetheless, continued European security dependence on the United States is anachronistic in a world where: there is no Soviet threat, former Warsaw Pact members clamor to join NATO, America's economic and technological preeminence is substantially diminished, and the European Union possesses its own embryonic defense component, the Western European Union (WEU).[2]

Public Goods Justifications

Both public and private goods arguments are frequently employed to justify Western Europe's anomalous dependence. The public goods argument prevailed during the Cold War. It assumed that European security was vital to America's national interest (which the two world wars seemed to demonstrate), and that Europe alone was too weak to deter and defend against the Soviet military threat. Therefore, the United States needed to expend large resources and take large risks to protect NATO-Europe. A generation of American leaders believed that reasoning. It also comforted Europeans: America would not abandon Europe if vital US interests were at stake, and Europe's *amour-propre* was satisfied by the inference that no charity was involved (and therefore no obligation) when Americans habitually spent more per capita to defend Europe than the Europeans themselves spent.

The public goods rationale is no longer credible. During the final Cold War years over one-half of American defense spending was earmarked for European contingencies.[3] If not fully convincing, it was at least plausible then to argue that Western Europe alone could not deter the Soviet threat. Now, there is no superpower menace to the security of Western Europe.

Recent defense pronouncements and policies by the principal NATO countries (US, UK, France, and Germany) reveal how profoundly the threat has withered during the last decade. Even General Colin L. Powell, the former chairman of the US Joint Chiefs of Staff, candidly admitted just after the 1991 Gulf War, 'I'm running out of demons. I'm running out of villains'.[4]

Most of the major West European governments apparently have a similar view of the threat environment, and they are making decisions about military force structures and defense spending levels accordingly. Before unification, the combined armies of the two Germanys totaled 667,000 active duty personnel. The German *White Book* released in March 1994 lists the Bundeswehr's size as 357,000. Although the force will be maintained at that level for the next two years, further reductions are planned for later in the decade – cuts that could possibly take personnel levels as low as 300,000.[5] German defense spending declined 11 per cent, from DM 54.5 billion to DM 48.5 billion ($30 billion), between 1990 and 1994. This means that Germans, who are approximately as rich per capita as Americans, now spend only about one-third as much per capita for defense.

The 1994 French defense review echoed Germany's low threat assessment. According to Defense Minister François Léotard, 'France has not known for many decades such an absence of a major, direct, aggressive, military threat on its borders.'[6] The French *Livre Blanc* of February 1994 envisages six scenarios for using French forces. Several are quite minor, and the most demanding, 'Resurgence of a major threat against Western Europe,' is described as 'very improbable during the next 20 years. . . .'[7] Like other countries, France responded to the Cold War's end by reducing the size of its military forces. However, spending (currently 3.4 per cent of GDP) remained more stable than in other principal NATO military powers. The military budget is scheduled to remain constant during the next several years – which may prove difficult as the government also plans to reduce the budget deficit from FF301 billion ($56 billion) in 1994 to FF275 billion ($51 billion) in 1995.

British military personnel declined 17 per cent between 1990 and 1994 to 254,000 and will continue to shrink to 242,000.[8] As a percentage of GDP, military spending declined from more than 5 per cent in the early 1980s to 3.8 per cent in 1992–93, and is projected to fall to 2.9 per cent in 1996–97[9]. These cuts are driven by budgetary considerations rather than an explicit reappraisal of the strategic environment, but the benign international environment apparently allows such reductions. In March 1993 British Defence Secretary Malcolm Rifkind conceded that 'it is undeniable that the direct threat posed to the United Kingdom and her allies is lower than it has been for many years.'[10]

Turning to Washington, the principal putative achievement of Les Aspin's brief tenure as Secretary of Defense was the so-called 'Bottom-Up Review' (BUR) of 1993.[11] Most analysts agree the review was more top-down than bottom-up. One interpretation sees the Clinton administration's prior decision to reduce defense budget authority below the level contemplated by the Bush administration as the driving force for the BUR.[12] A second interpretation sees the BUR as a 'highly politicized document designed to exaggerate the threat environment and preserve as much as possible of the Pentagon's budget and force structure.'[13] Whatever the actual motive, there is an obvious imbalance between the goals articulated by the review and the funds available to attain them.[14] That shortfall arises because the BUR recommends excessive and unaffordable objectives, especially 'forces sufficient to fight and win two nearly simultaneous [1991 Gulf War size] regional conflicts',[15] with sufficient numbers 'to act unilaterally, should we choose to do so'.[16]

The Pentagon likes these goals, for they justify most existing military forces and missions, but they exceed what the United States needs and can afford. A capacity for unilateral action is essential, but the ability to fight simultaneously *two* conflicts comparable to 'Desert Storm' is over-insurance. Two such large threats would probably not arise simultaneously, and if they did, it is likely that one engagement could be postponed or handled by allies.

Eighteen months before the BUR, when Aspin still chaired the House Armed Services Committee, he authored a somewhat bolder analysis.[17] Then, Aspin's preferred alternative (Option C) called for fewer army, naval, and especially air forces than the BUR. Nevertheless, former Pentagon officials Dov Zakheim and Jeffrey Ranney estimated it would require 4.5 per cent of GDP to support the force structure contemplated.[18] If their estimate is accurate, the BUR might require 5 per cent of GDP. Given current domestic political realities, few serious analysts believe that 5 per cent of GDP will be available for military spending.

The BUR was an obvious exercise in justifying Pentagon business as usual. As the Defense Budget Project commented, 'the Pentagon bureaucracy has proceeded as most bureaucracies do when left on their own in a very different operating environment: they attempt to 'fit' the new situation to existing planning and resource allocation processes.'[19] Even so, the BUR identifies no menace that approaches the magnitude of that once posed by the former Soviet Union.[20] Even the failure of Russian political reforms could not recreate an equivalent danger. If an ultranationalist leader such as Vladimir Zhirinovsky replaced reformers, years of rebuilding would still be needed before the Russian threat began to approximate that of the former Soviet Union. As General James Clapper, Director of the Defense Intelligence Agency, told Congress in January 1992, Russia 'will have no capacity to directly threaten the United States and NATO with large-scale military operations'.[21] Although it may be convenient to cooperate with European allies to address common dangers, Europe faces no threat that the WEU member states cannot manage with their own military resources.

To some, tragic events in the former Yugoslavia – especially the protracted Bosnian war, which has cost more than 200,000 lives – seem to prove Europe's inability to manage its security. It is more likely, however, that Europe declined to become deeply involved in the war because essential interests were not jeopardized. It is true, as George Kennan has written, that the Bosnian war 'is primarily a problem for the Europeans. It is their continent, not ours, that is affected.'[22] But even for Western Europe Bosnia was chiefly a 'humanitarian' problem. Watching televised images from the war was agonizing, and the perceived impotence of the European Union and the WEU was embarrassing, but the strategic stakes were modest. Although some commentators lamented 'the erroneous assumption that in the violent disintegration of Yugoslavia there were no vital Western interests at stake',[23] the actions of European leaders showed their complacency.

West European officials were too discreet to declare explicitly that Europe's vital interests were not threatened in the former Yugoslavia, but they issued few bold calls for action. British foreign secretary Douglas Hurd described his country's interests in the Bosnian civil war as: 'to stop the war from spreading', 'to keep people alive, to relieve cold and hunger', and 'to help efforts for a negotiated peace'.[24] Hurd had earlier told the Royal Institute of International Affairs (on 27 January 1993) that 'to impose and guarantee order in the former Yugoslavia would take huge forces and huge risks over an indefinite period – which no democracy could justify to its people. British troops there have a humanitarian not an enforcing role. . . .'[25]

WEU and European Union documents reflect a similar assessment that vital interests were not imperiled. For example, in early 1994, Jean Marie Caro, a former president of the Assembly of the WEU, expressed dismay that the situation in the former Yugoslavia had 'deteriorated'. But rather than emphasizing threats to vital interests, he deplored the fact that 'events in Bosnia-Herzegovina have put Europe entirely to shame and betrayed a powerlessness to intervene on the part of Europe's security organisations as a whole.'[26]

Private Goods Arguments

There are several private goods arguments that have been advanced for preserving Europe's security dependence. Some analysts assert that security dependence is linked to other goals, especially international trade. Princeton University political scientist Joanne Gowa argues that trade generates security externalities. Trading with an adversary has a negative impact on security, she contends, but inter-allied trade produces a positive security externality. Gowa found that between 1905 and 1985 trade was more common within than between alliances.[27]

Security and trade were clearly linked during the Cold War.[28] It is not obvious, however, that this effect persists as alliances dissolve (the Warsaw Pact) or decay (NATO). In the absence of salient security threats to NATO-Europe, the Alliance has already faded as an incentive for Europe's deference to the United States in other issue areas. For example, it took seven years to negotiate GATT's Uruguay Round agreement, three years longer than the 'final' date set for an agreement, and in the end the increasingly important film and television sector was excluded because Europe (at French insistence) rejected Washington's demand for liberalization.[29]

American military spending nearly equals the global defense spending of all other nation-states; it is more than double the combined spending of the other four permanent members of the UN Security Council.[30] The American defense budget is five to ten times larger than those of Japan, Germany, France, or the United Kingdom. Given that enormous disparity, Europeans are perhaps as likely to perceive a threat to their interests from the United States as to make concessions to Washington because of the close security connection. Prominent French political figures, including Jacques Delors and Roland Dumas, have already explicitly proposed that Europe balance against the United States.[31]

A second private goods argument, embraced by some American analysts, sees security dependence as usefully containing future European influence and discouraging great power ambitions by the principal West European states. A hoary Cold War era jest (attributed to NATO's first Secretary-General, Lord Ismay) described NATO's role as keeping 'the Americans in, the Russians out, and the Germans down'. With the Cold War won, the United States might use NATO to keep the European Union 'down.' Consider the language contained in the preliminary draft of the Bush administration's Defense Planning Guidance document.[32] It specified that, 'a dominant consideration underlying the new regional defense strategy. . .[is] to prevent any hostile power from dominating a region whose resources would, under consolidated control, be sufficient to generate global power. These regions include Western Europe, East Asia. . . .' The United States was to maintain dominant military power capable of 'deterring potential competitors from even aspiring to a larger regional or global role'.[33]

After unleashing a firestorm of criticism from allied governments, those offending statements were expunged from the final version, but the underlying logic remained. Moreover, prominent members of the American foreign policy community unabashedly advocate continued US hegemony. Columnist Charles Krauthammer wrote that the alternative to American dominance is:

> Japanese carriers patrolling the Strait of Malacca and a nuclear Germany dominating Europe. We have had 40 years of competition

with one heavily armed nuclear superpower. Do we really want to devote the next 40 years to competition with two, three, any such countries – countries such as Germany and Japan that have historically displayed far less prudence in their drive for hegemony than even Stalin's Russia?[34]

Henry Kissinger expresses sentiments similar to those of the draft defense guidance document in his latest book. He argues that the United States has two options in the post-Cold War era: either to remain aloof from international affairs, but poised to intervene when the balance of power needs correction, or to remain engaged in an ongoing effort to preserve the balance. Kissinger believes the first approach, which Britain followed under Palmerston and Disraeli during the second half of the nineteenth century, is poorly suited to the American temperament, which he contends lacks the required capacity to act for *raisons d'état*. The second approach, which characterized Bismarck's Germany, is more suitable in Kissinger's view.[35] He further argues that:

> The domination by a single power of either of Eurasia's two principal spheres – Europe or Asia – remains a good definition of strategic danger for America, Cold War or no Cold War. For such a grouping would have the capacity to outstrip America economically and, in the end, militarily. That danger would have to be resisted even were the dominant power apparently benevolent, for if the intentions ever changed, America would find itself with a grossly diminished capacity for effective resistance and a growing inability to shape events.[36]

This thesis, of course, raises interesting questions for Europe. As *The Economist* asks, 'What policy is Mr. Kissinger suggesting towards development of an enlarged European Union capable of acting as a single unit?'[37] Kissinger implies that this possibility threatens American interests, and that the United States should preclude that danger by active engagement in European affairs.

Even if one accepts the legitimacy of Kissinger's concerns, it is not clear that continued European dependence is the best way to contain Europe's power. Economic capabilities are the essential building blocks of political and military power, so diverting scarce resources to military spending undermines national power and economic competitiveness. As a percentage of GDP, the United States spends twice as much as Germany and four times more than Japan. That disparity seriously handicaps American competitiveness. America's relatively high defense burden saps funds needed for investment, and protracted underinvestment erodes the economic foundation of political and military power. If the other Organization of Economic

Cooperation and Development (OECD) countries are now America's principal competitors, US interests are better served when these competitors bear the full cost of their defense. As foreign policy analyst Christopher Layne argues, 'if the emerging great powers are compelled to internalize their security costs, they no longer will be free to concentrate primarily on trading-state strategies that give them an advantage in their economic competition with the United States.'[38]

The third private goods argument is that security dependence increases Europe's willingness to support interventions favored by Washington. Examples include US access to British airbases to bomb Libyan targets in 1986, participation by British and French troops in the Gulf War of 1991, and the deployment since 1992 of European peacekeepers in Bosnia-Herzegovina. This argument is reinforced by Samuel Huntington's thesis that the emerging axis of international conflict is cultural, between separate 'civilizations.' If, as Huntington expects, future conflicts will often pit 'the West' versus 'the Rest,' the United States may need its European allies as much as it did during the Cold War.[39]

The 1991 Gulf War demonstrated that a determined American administration can sometimes twist allied arms to share the cost of military interventions. However, the lack of combat participation by Germany and Japan, like France's rejection of flights over French territory to bomb Libya in 1986, shows the limits of that leverage. Even Japan's ($13 billion) and Germany's ($11.5 billion) substantial financial contributions to the Gulf War effort were modest compared to America's massive spending to defend those countries over several decades.[40] Defending allies to win their support during crises may not be a cost-effective strategy.

Even when the European allies do choose to support American policies, they are better equipped to lend significant aid if they are not receiving a free ride from the United States. Dependence on the United States undermines their incentive to build military assets that contribute to cooperative missions.

The Real Reasons for Continuing Dependence

The publicly stated justifications are not the principal reasons why European dependence continues, however. The decisive factors are inertia and domestic politics.

The status quo is fiercely defended, even within the Clinton administration, which is less Eurocentric than its predecessor. Prominent bureaucrats, congressional leaders, and administration appointees sometimes fail to distinguish NATO's value as an instrument of American policy from the fallacious view that it is an end in itself. That tendency is illustrated by Clinton's insistence that an important US interest in Bosnia is 'showing that NATO, the world's greatest military alliance, remains a credible force for peace in the post-Cold War era'.[41] Ronald Steel properly points out that 'the purpose of NATO is to protect its members from wars, not to get them into one. Interventionists should argue the merits of their cause, not maintain that they need to find a job for NATO after the cold war.'[42]

As the apparent costs of Europe's dependency decline, policy inertia is reinforced. During the Cold War, the major potential cost was existential: America's nuclear guarantee and NATO's policy of nuclear first-use risked America's very survival. Now, the nuclear threat is largely hypothetical, and NATO treats nuclear arms as 'weapons of last resort'. Without conspicuous threats, conventional military risks are also reduced, and the financial burden dwindles as American troop deployments in Europe shrink from 311,000 in 1990 at the end of the Cold War, toward 100,000. At some lower level of deployment – perhaps 50,000 – a residual force stationed in Europe might even benefit the United States by being near to potential trouble spots in the Middle East and elsewhere.

European attitudes, especially in Britain, also reinforce the policy inertia regarding NATO and Europe's security dependence on the United States. William Wallace of the Royal Institute of International Affairs wrote a decade ago that, 'For most of the past two decades British governments have remained firmly oriented at the highest level of political relations to the bilateral relationship with the United States, as the first priority of British foreign policy . . . .'[43] It may be an exaggeration to assert, as a German analyst recently did, that 'The "Three Circles Concept" developed by Winston Churchill in 1945 . . . has still not been replaced by a new list of foreign policy maxims.'[44] But London certainly considers the 'special' Anglo-American relationship much more important than Washington does.

Indeed, when American officials talk of a 'special' European relationship they are now as likely to mean Germany as Britain. In contemplating a hypothetical Labour government in Britain, President Bush remarked dismissively, 'If we do have a special relationship, it will continue I'm sure.'[45] President Clinton clearly considers Germany more 'special' than Britain. Although no Clinton administration official has said so explicitly, there are increasing indications of Germany's rise and Britain's fall in America's esteem. *The Economist* editorialized that 'Bill Clinton is at best indifferent to Britain, at worst openly hostile. . . . America is sensibly looking to Germany and France as key European interlocutors.'[46]

That trend actually predates the Clinton administration. John Dickie describes how Germany replaced Britain as the most important European power in the estimation of the Bush administration, noting that as early as May 1989, Bush depicted Germany and the United States as 'partners in leadership'. Dickie then describes the continued deterioration of US–UK relations during the Clinton administration – including the US proposal in 1993 to make Germany and Japan permanent members of the UN Security Council, despite London's obvious lack of enthusiasm.[47]

An even clearer indication that the United States was according a higher priority to relations with Bonn came in July 1994. During an interview by ZDF German television on 1 July Clinton was asked pointedly, 'Is Germany still the most important ally of the United States?' He responded:

> Germany is a critically important ally; always has been, certainly since the end of the Second World War. And I think if you look to the future, the kinds of things we have to work together on, the way our interests tend to converge, and the way we see the world, the relationship I have enjoyed with Chancellor Kohl, all the things we work together on – Russian aid, international peacekeeping, a whole range of issues, trying to find a solution in Bosnia – the German people and the American people and their governments need to work very, very closely together, not only for the well-being of Europe, but indeed, for the entire world.[48]

When pressed during a joint press conference with Chancellor Kohl whether the US relationship with Germany was becoming more important than Washington's special relationship with Britain, Clinton attempted to finesse the question. Nevertheless, his answer was revealing. In describing the relationship with Britain, he stressed historical factors and the ties of common culture. The focus with regard to Germany, however, was more forward looking. The result was likely to be:

> [A] common partnership that is unique now because so many of our challenges are just to Germany's east. What we are going to do in Central and Eastern Europe. What will be our new relationship with Russia; will it continue as strongly as it now seems to be doing. So there's a way in which the United States and Germany have a more immediate and tangible concern with these issues, even than our other friends in Europe.[49]

Although the policy inertia that is so pronounced in Britain is somewhat weaker in Germany – and even more so in France – it is still substantial. If Washington avoids becoming too threatening or overbearing, European governments will probably remain comfortable with long-established diplomatic relationships, the possibility to consume more security than they buy, and the potential use of America to prevent domination by Germany (or another European power).

The fitful growth of European security structures does indicate some ambition for greater European autonomy. The Maastricht Treaty created the European Union and sketched out in Article J.4 a 'common foreign and security policy . . . including the eventual framing of a common defence policy'. It also proclaimed the WEU to be 'an integral part of the development of the union' which will 'elaborate and implement decisions and action of the union which have defence implications'.[50]

The persistent tension between France's vision of WEU as the European Union's security dimension and Britain's image of WEU as the 'European Pillar of the Atlantic Alliance', was blurred by defining WEU's 'role as the defense component of the European Union and as the means to strengthen the European pillar of the Atlantic Alliance'.[51] According to the declaration on Western European Union appended to the Maastricht treaty, 'WEU member states agree on the need to develop a genuine European security and defence identity and a greater European responsibility on defence matters.'[52]

Support for European security institutions is encouraged by changes in the international system, especially in American behavior. Europe remains very important to Washington, but its relative priority declined when the Clinton administration elevated Asia's importance. Secretary of State Warren Christopher has criticized the 'Eurocentrism' of past US foreign policy and argued that 'Western Europe is no longer the dominant area of the world.'[53] Washington's recalibration of its attention to Asia and Europe is related to the administration's emphasis on economic issues. When the Asia-Pacific Economic Cooperation Conference (APEC) was held in Seattle in November 1993, an unidentified 'senior administration official' commented that APEC represented 'a distinctive imprint of the Clinton presidency to put international economics on the front burner of foreign policy for the first time.' This was appropriate, the official contended, for 'East Asia . . . represent[s] a larger economy than either North America or Western Europe.' The White House noted that 'for 50 years of the Cold War, we were focused on the East–West relationship and also on the West-West relationship. And security defined those relationships. In a sense, we now are shifting from an East–West focus, perhaps, to a West-East focus.'[54]

The Bosnian war was also significant; it revealed that Washington would not always manage Europe's conflicts. European perceptions were also affected by dwindling American troop strength in Europe and the Clinton administration's praise for European security initiatives. The latter position was openly in contrast to the qualms, if not outright hostility, expressed by the Reagan and Bush administrations. At NATO's January 1994 summit the United States supported the Alliance's explicit recognition of WEU's contribution to Atlantic security. The meeting's final declaration declared:

> We give our full support to the development of a European Security and Defence Identity which, as called for in the Maastricht Treaty, in the longer term perspective of a common defence policy within the

European Union, might in time lead to a common defence compatible with that of the Atlantic Alliance. The emergence of a European Security and Defence Identity will strengthen the European pillar of the Alliance while reinforcing the transatlantic link and will enable European Allies to take greater responsibility for their common security and defence. The Alliance and the European Union share common strategic interests.

We support strengthening the European pillar of the Alliance through the Western European Union, which is being developed as the defence component of the European Union. The Alliance's organization and resources will be adjusted so as to facilitate this. We welcome the close and growing cooperation between NATO and the WEU that has been achieved on the basis of agreed principles of complementarity and transparency. In future contingencies, NATO and the WEU will consult, including as necessary through joint Council meetings, on how to address such contingencies.

We therefore stand ready to make collective assets of the Alliance available, on the basis of consultations in the North Atlantic Council, for WEU operations undertaken by the European Allies in pursuit of their Common Foreign and Security Policy. We support the development of separable but not separate capabilities which could respond to European requirements and contribute to Alliance security.[55]

Especially for London, Washington's endorsement of European security initiatives increased incentives for European collaboration while reducing concern that closer intra-European security relations threatened Anglo-American relations.[56]

France is now more sympathetic toward NATO than at any time since withdrawing from the integrated military structure in 1966. That reaction is probably related to Washington's partial disengagement from Europe, which reduced French fears of American domination and, perhaps, even raised fears of abandonment. The French *Livre Blanc* pledged to participate in the 'genuine renovation' that is needed if the Atlantic Alliance is to 'better take into consideration the European identity, reinforce the coordination of its political and military structures, remain the essential link for consultation between Europeans and North Americans, and finally open itself to other European countries to organize a dialogue and cooperation with them'.[57]

The sluggish pace of European security cooperation is often criticized, but there are several signs of progress. For example, multinational military exercises are proliferating. These include the French-sponsored Farfadet exercise in June 1992, Italy's 'Ardente '94' exercise – with participation by France, Spain, Greece, the Netherlands, Turkey and the United Kingdom – and other

1994 exercises sponsored by Spain (Transmontana) and Britain (Purple Nova).

In addition, beginning in July 1992 – and since 1993 under the codename 'Sharp Guard' – cooperative WEU and NATO Adriatic Sea naval operations have prevented shipping from entering the territorial waters of the Federal Republic of Yugoslavia (Serbia and Montenegro) in violation of UN Security Council resolutions. 'Sharp Guard' also prevents arms from entering the former Yugoslavia. Between November 1992 and July 1994 nearly 37,000 ships were challenged, and more than 3,400 were inspected or diverted. Naval forces were contributed by Belgium, Denmark, France, Germany, Greece, Italy, The Netherlands, Norway, Portugal, Spain, Turkey, and the United Kingdom (as well as Canada and the United States).

WEU's Council of Ministers decided in 1991 to locate a center for satellite data interpretation and training at Torrejon, Spain. The center is eventually intended to give Europe space-based means of observation to verify arms control agreements and monitor security crises and environmental threats. The WEU Assembly has examined the issue of defending Europe against missile threats, and in May 1995 the WEU Council of Ministers will decide whether to create a European earth observation satellite system, as recommended by the Assembly.

WEU absorbed the former Independent European Programme Group (IEPG) as the Western European Armaments Group (WEAG).[58] The Maastricht Treaty specifically mentions creating a European armaments agency, and at their semiannual Franco-German summit in May 1994 Chancellor Kohl and President Mitterrand agreed to establish an armaments agency to coordinate weapons development programs and rationalize the French and German research programs. The agency, scheduled to commence operations in the summer of 1995, will be linked to the WEU and open to other European countries. In June 1994 defense manufacturing firms from Belgium, Denmark, France, Germany, Great Britain, Italy, Norway, Portugal, Spain, Sweden, and Turkey, agreed to work to create a pan-European defense industrial base.[60]

Building on the experience of the Franco-German Brigade created in 1986, the Eurocorps is evolving. Although France sees Eurocorps as 'the core of the future European army',[61] its ultimate role is still not entirely clear. When operations begin in October 1995 its tasks will include the defense of the WEU and NATO allies, participation in UN peacemaking or peacekeeping operations, and humanitarian missions. Eurocorps' members now include France, Germany, Spain, Belgium, and Luxembourg. In peacetime these troops remain under national command (or NATO command in the case of Germany).

Although such initiatives strengthen Europe's real world capacity for self-defense, that is not their principal purpose. They are endorsed, or resisted, by European leaders principally as symbols of European unification. For example, German sensitivities were bruised by exclusion from the 50th anniversary commemoration of the D-Day landings. So despite some vociferous objections in France, President Mitterrand invited Eurocorps troops, including 200 German soldiers, to parade down the Champs Elysées on Bastille Day 1994. Of course, many Europeans oppose all initiatives that appear to 'deepen' the European Union. When British Prime Minister John Major vetoed the candidate at the Corfu summit (June 1994) favored by France and Germany to succeed Jacques Delors as European Commission president, Franz-Olivier Giesbert wrote in *Le Figaro*, 'The British refuse that Europe be more than a free trade zone. They dream only of enlarging it still more to dilute it and drown it in contradictions.'[62]

The symbolic character of European security structures limits their ability to replace NATO in its key role in European security. As long as the West Europeans continue to see common foreign and security policies primarily as means to measure progress toward European unity, rather than as tangible instruments for defending Europe, neither the WEU nor the larger European Union will qualify to replace the Atlantic Alliance. Europe is unlikely to cross that threshold until the American security blanket is further withdrawn – or if America's military hegemony causes Europeans to see the United States as more threatening than reassuring.

US Domestic Politics

Domestic American politics is a second unspoken obstacle to reducing US defense commitments to Europe still further. It is regrettably true, as Randall Forsberg has written, that 'the US defense budget has become a gigantic federal public works program. . . . The real obstacle to deep and rapid cuts in military spending is not foreign threats but domestic unemployment. . . .'[63] Clinton's successful 1992 presidential campaign stressed economic themes. The economy is likely to again be the prime issue when Clinton runs for reelection in 1996, and defense spending has a large impact. To be reelected, Clinton must win California, but California's fragile economy has been battered by both base closings and reduced military procurement. In recent years, southern California alone has lost 300,000 defense jobs. To placate their constituents, most politicians are prepared to fund redundant military bases or wasteful military procurement. A notable case was the Bush administration's proposal to rebuild Homestead Air Force Base in Florida after it was devastated by Hurricane Andrew in August 1992, even though the base had been slated for closure before the storm.

During the last decades of the Cold War, 'burden sharing' was a major issue of intra-Alliance politics. Many Americans, including members of Congress, believed that increased defense spending by the NATO-European countries (which was typically less than half the US level as a percentage of GDP) would allow reduced American spending. Now, the incentive to reduce defense spending to pare the deficit or to fund other programs is offset by domestic political pressure to slow the decline of Pentagon spending. In this context, NATO is a politically useful justification for current military budgets, and there is little domestic political pressure to goad the Europeans to spend more.

This situation is unlikely to change before 1997. If America's economic recovery continues and President Clinton is reelected, however, lower unemployment rates and a president relieved of reelection concerns might seriously challenge entrenched proponents of the status quo.

Conclusion

For nearly 50 years the United States outspent the Europeans on defense and Washington largely controlled the responses to European security threats. Although many Americans and Europeans are comfortable with this status quo, its alleged benefits are illusory. It is especially unwise for America to subsidize the security costs of major economic competitors. One astute French analyst pointed out that the most novel danger identified by the BUR is the 'potential failure to build a strong and growing US economy'. This concern echoes President Clinton's stated belief that if the United States fails to reestablish its economic power, 'we will no longer be a superpower', and Les Aspin's declaration that, 'The most important thing that the United States can do for its security is to reinforce its economy.'[64] America's financial resources are now so pinched that implementing the laboriously won General Agreement on Tariffs and Trade agreement was threatened by the temporary need to replace $10 billion in lost tariff revenue. Deeper cuts in defense spending would facilitate deficit reduction, reduce a major obstacle to economic growth, and level competition between Europe and the United States. It would also create incentives for Europeans to maintain military assets that could make meaningful contributions to future multinational operations.

The policy of active engagement to preserve the balance of power, as Henry Kissinger advocates, presumes that the United States knows against whom to balance. But what is the threat? Is it Russia risen from the ashes? Or the European Union? Or united Germany? Or Japan? Or China? Or some threat as yet unidentified? Kissinger himself has described how difficult making that decision can be. He describes how during the interwar years Britain based its policy:

on the mistaken belief that France was already too powerful and that the last thing it needed was a British alliance. Great Britain's leaders considered demoralized France to be the potentially dominant power and in need of being balanced, while revisionist Germany was perceived as the aggrieved party in need of conciliation. . . . There was no hope whatsoever of maintaining a balance of power in Europe so long as Great Britain considered the primary threat to be a country [France] whose nearly panicky foreign policy was geared to fending off another German assault.[65]

The United States has often backed ostensibly friendly regimes that later threatened American interests. President Saddam Hussein of Iraq is the principal recent example, but others include Panama's General Manuel Noriega and the Afghan 'freedom fighters'. These cases suggest that the United States is ill-equipped to implement successfully the Bismarckian policy that Kissinger recommends.

With much smaller threats, and somewhat stronger European security structures, NATO-Europe is competent to defend itself. The United States can reduce military spending to three per cent of GDP and prune force levels below the BUR's recommendation. European deployments are an obvious place to cut (to a residual level of 50,000) and such a step is politically feasible, for German chambers of commerce are poorly equipped to lobby American politicians. The combined effect of policy inertia and domestic politics makes that goal difficult to achieve, but even at three per cent of GDP, most NATO-European governments (and Japan) would still spend significantly less for defense than the United States.

NOTES

* I appreciate comments by Joseph Lepgold on an earlier version of this article.

1. Quoted in Phil Williams, *The Senate and US Troops in Europe* (London: Macmillan, 1985), p.71.
2. In May 1994 the WEU established a counterpart to NATO's Partnership for Peace by admitting nine central and East European countries – Bulgaria, Czech Republic, Estonia, Hungary, Latvia, Lithuania, Poland, Romania and Slovakia – as 'associate partners.'
3. See Richard Halloran, 'Two Studies Say Defense of Western Europe Is Biggest US Military Cost', *New York Times*, 20 July 1984, p.A2.
4. Quoted in Jim Wolffe, 'Powell Sees Opportunity for US to Reduce Military Strength', *Defense News*, 8 April 1991.
5. *The Week in Germany*, 18 March 1994, p.2.
6. François Léotard, 'Défense: un consensus actif,' *Le Figaro*, 4 March 1994.
7. *Synthèse du Livre Blanc* (Washington, DC: French Embassy, 1994). The second largest contingency is a regional conflict that threatens vital national interests, e.g., a state possessing nuclear weapons.
8. See *Survey of Current Affairs*, June 1994, pp.157–8.

9. 'Postponing Pain', *Economist*, 30 April 1994, p.64.
10. Malcolm Rifkind, 'Defence in the 90's', Speech in London, 30 March 1993 (NY: British Inf. Services), p.3.
11. When Aspin was appointed chairman of the Foreign Intelligence Advisory Board, the White House described the Bottom-Up Review as 'the most thorough, comprehensive guide to defense requirements available.' 'President Announces Appointment of Les Aspin as Member and Chair of the President's Foreign Intelligence Advisory Board', White House, Office of the Press Secretary, 26 May 1994.
12. See Kim R. Holmes and Baker Spring, 'Aspin's Defense Review: Top-Down, NOT Bottom-Up', *Armed Forces Journal International* 131/1 (Aug. 1993), pp.39–40.
13. David Isenberg, 'The Pentagon's Fraudulent Bottom-Up Review,' Cato Inst. Policy Analysis no. 206, 21 April 1994, p.1.
14. See, e.g., Dov S. Zakheim and Jeffrey M. Ranney, 'Matching Defense Strategies to Resources: Challenges for the Clinton Administration', *International Security* 18/1 (Summer 1993), pp.51–78. For the period 1995–99, the Senate Armed Services Committee estimates a $60 billion funding gap; the General Accounting Office foresees a shortfall of $150 billion. See Eric Schmitt, 'Pentagon's Budget May Not Cover Its Strategy, Planners Say,' *New York Times*, 1 Aug. 1994, p.A8.
15. Les Aspin, *The Bottom-Up Review: Forces for a New Era* (Washington, DC: Dept. of Defense, 1 Sept. 1993), p.10.
16. Ibid., p.6.
17. See Les Aspin, *An Approach to Sizing American Conventional Forces for the Post-Soviet Era: Four Illustrative Options* (Washington, DC: House Armed Services Committee, 25 Feb. 1992).
18. Zakheim and Ranney (note 14), p.72.
19. Andrew F. Krepinevich, *The Bottom-Up Review: An Assessment* (Washington, DC: Defense Budget Project, Feb. 1994), p.61.
20. The principal threats identified by the BUR are:(a) Spread of nuclear, biological, and chemical weapons, (b) Aggression by major regional powers or ethnic-religious conflict, (c) Potential failure of democratic reform in the former Soviet Union and elsewhere, (d) Potential failure to build a strong and growing US economy. 'Defense Strategy for the New Era', *Defense*, no. 6 (1993), p.3.
21. Quoted in Aspin (note 17).
22. George F. Kennan, 'The Balkan Crisis: 1913 and 1993,' *New York Review of Books*, 15 July 1993, p.6.
23. Henk Vos and James Bilbay (co-rapporteurs), 'NATO, Peacekeeping and the Former Yugoslavia', Draft Interim Report, Sub-Committee on Defence and Security Co-Operation Between Europe and North America (Brussels: NATO, May 1994). Electronic version; no pagination.
24. Douglas Hurd, 'Why We Will Not Be Dragged Into the Quagmire', (NY: British Inf. Services, 3 March 1994), pp.1–2. Repr. from the *Evening Standard* (London). Former Prime Minister Margaret Thatcher presented the minority argument that the West did have 'real and important strategic interests in Bosnia' including international credibility, deterring Serbia and other potential aggressors, and possible 'floods of refugees'. Margaret Thatcher, 'Stop the Serbs. Now. For Good', *New York Times*, 4 May 1994, p.A15.
25. Also see 'Britain's Peacekeeping Role in Former Yugoslavia: Questions and Answers,' (NY: British Inf. Services, Jan. 1994), especially p.2. According to Defence Secretary Malcolm Rifkind, 'Bosnia is a snapshot of the kind of highly complex, politically fraught, multinational operation which will increasingly face us in the future. The dividing line between pure defence and humanitarian aims will become increasingly blurred, with important implications for public pressure on us to get involved.' Rifkind, p.9.
26. Jean-Marie Caro, 'Towards Association of the Countries of Central Europe with WEU', Seminar on WEU's Point of View on Developments in Central and Eastern Europe, Warsaw, 11–12 Feb. 1994. Electronic version; no pagination.
27. See Joanne S. Gowa, *Allies, Adversaries, and International trade in strategic goods. Trade* (Princeton, NJ: Princeton UP, 1994), pp.3–10. Also see Robert J. Art, 'A Defensible

Defense: America's Grand Strategy After the Cold War,' *International Security* 15/4 (Spring 1991), pp.39–42.

28. In the West, the explicit function of COCOM (Coordinating Committee for Multilateral Export Controls) was to prevent interbloc trade in strategic goods.

29. In April 1994 the European Commission issued a discussion paper on audio-visual policy which calls for tightening a current (since 1991) regulation that requires television broadcasts be at least 50 per cent of European origin. See 'Battling for the Box,' *Economist*, 9 April 1994, p.52; and 'Television of Babel,' *Economist*, 5 Feb. 1994, p.52.

30. Calculated from data in IISS, *The Military Balance, 1993–1994* (London: Brassey's, 1993).

31. See David S. Yost, 'France and the Gulf War of 1990–91: Political-Military Lessons Learned', *Journal of Strategic Studies* 16/3 (Sept. 1993). p.354.

32. The heavily amended version was signed by Defense Secretary Dick Cheney in May 1992.

33. Quoted in Barton Gellman, 'Pentagon Plan Aims to Preclude Emergence of a Rival Superpower', *Washington Post*, 11 March 1992, p.A4.

34. Charles Krauthammer, 'What's Wrong With the 'Pentagon Paper'?' *Washington Post*, 13 March 1992, p.A25.

35. Henry Kissinger, *Diplomacy* (NY: Simon & Schuster, 1994), pp.166–7.

36. Ibid, p.813.

37. 'Henry Kissinger Weighs In', *Economist*, 14 May 1994, p.94.

38. Christopher Layne, 'The Unipolar Illusion: Why New Great Powers Will Rise', *International Security* 17/4 (Spring 1993), p.49.

39. See Samuel P. Huntington, 'The Clash of Civilizations?' *Foreign Affairs* 72/3 (Summer 1993), p.41. One empirical analysis of ongoing ethnopolitical conflicts during 1993–94, however, found no evidence that inter-civilizational cleavages were becoming more prominent. See Ted Robert Gurr, 'Peoples Against States: Ethnopolitical Conflicts and the Changing World System', Presidential address, Annual Meeting of the Int. Studies Assoc., Washington, DC, 1994.

40. Of the German total, 60 per cent went to the US. See Gunther Hellmann, 'Germany and Alliance Burden-Sharing in the Gulf War', paper presented at the conference 'Friends in Need: Alliance Burden-Sharing in the 1991 Gulf War', Georgetown Univ., Washington, DC, 2–3 April 1994, p.2. Also see Danny Unger, 'Japan and the Gulf War: Making the World Safe for Japan-US Relations,' paper presented at the conference 'Friends in Need', p.9.

41. President Clinton, radio address to the nation, 19 Feb. 1994. Electronic version.

42. Ronald Steel, 'Beware of the Superpower Syndrome,' *New York Times*, 25 April 1994, p.A11.

43. William Wallace, *Britain's Bilateral Links Within Western Europe*, Chatham House Papers 23 (London: Routledge & Kegan Paul, 1984), p.10.

44. Reinhard Meier-Waiser, 'Britain in Search of a Place "at the Heart of Europe"', *Aussenpolitik* 45/1 (1994): 16. The Three Circles Concept ranks Britain's foreign policy priorities as the United States, the Commonwealth, and Europe.

45. Quoted in Peter Stothard, 'Bush to End US Coolness to Kinnock', *The Times*, 17 April 1990, p.1.

46. 'Mr Major Goes to Washington,' *Economist*, 26 Feb. 1994, pp.17–18. 'Bagehot' observed that in Feb. 1994 'Anglo-American feelings reached their sourest for four decades.' 'A Battered Rolls-Royce', *Economist*, 12 March 1994, p.68. The *New York Times* also noted the growing ties between Washington and Bonn. See 'The German Special Relationship', editorial, *New York Times*, 18 July 1994, p.A10.

47. See John Dickie, *'Special' No More: Anglo-American Relations: Rhetoric and Reality* (London: Weidenfeld, 1994), esp.pp.207–55.

48. White House, Office of the Press Secretary, 1 July 1994. Electronic version, no pagination.

49. White House, Office of the Press Secretary, Press Conference by President Clinton and Chancellor Kohl, The Chancellery, Bonn, Germany, 11 July 1994.

50. Quoted in Committee for Parliamentary and Public Relations, Western European Union: Information Report, Part 2 (Brussels: WEU, Feb. 1993). Electronic version; no pagination.

51. WEU Council of Ministers, Communiqué, Luxembourg, 9 May 1994. Electronic version; no pagination.

52. Quoted in Committee for Parliamentary and Public Relations.
53. Quoted in Stanley Sloan, 'Transatlantic Relations in the Wake of the Brussels Summit', *NATO Review*, April 1994. Electronic version; no pagination.
54. White House, Office of the Press Secretary, 'Background Briefing by Senior Administration Officials', Washington, Nov. 16, 1993. Electronic version; no pagination.
55. Declaration of the Heads of State and Government Participating in the Meeting of the North Atlantic Council Held at NATO HQ, Brussels, 10–11 Jan. 1994, NATO Press Communiqué M-1(94)3, 11 Jan. 1994. Electronic version; no pagination.
56. For a German perspective on British perceptions, see Meier-Waiser (note 44), p.17.
57. However, this is within the context of continued French commitment 'to the principles that have constantly guided our attitude for 30 years' including nonparticipation in the integrated military organization. *Synthèse du Livre Blanc*, sect. 3, 'Le cadre international.'
58. Three former IEPG members continue to participate in WEAG, although their WEU status is either as observer (Denmark) or associate countries (Norway and Turkey).
59. Quoted in Agence France-Presse, AFP-Matin-Actualité, 1 June 1994, distr. by the French Embassy, Washington, DC Electronic version; no pagination.
60. See *News from France*, 1 July 1994, p.5.
61. Ibid., 17 Dec. 1993, p.5.
62. Quoted in Agence-France Presse, AFP-Matin-Actualité, 27 June 1994, distr. by the French Embassy, Washington, DC. Electronic version; no pagination.
63. Randall Forsberg, 'Defense Cuts and Cooperative Security in the Post-Cold War World,' *Boston Review* 17 (May–July 1992), p.5.
64. Quoted in Gen. Bernard de Bressy, 'Une révision de fond en comble des forces armées américaines', *Défense nationale* 50 (Feb. 1994), p.103.
65. Kissinger (note 35), pp.251–2.

Conflicting Agendas and
the Future of NATO

TED GALEN CARPENTER

Efforts to rejuvenate NATO have acquired new urgency on both sides of the Atlantic in the past two years. The nations of Central and Eastern Europe seek admission to the Alliance at the earliest possible date and warn of dire consequences for the well-being of the entire Continent if NATO fails to address the political and security problems of their region. They view the Partnership for Peace (PFP), proposed by the Clinton administration and endorsed by the existing members of NATO at the Alliance's January 1994 summit meeting, as merely an interim step on the path to full membership. Moscow lobbies for a 'special relationship' with the Alliance and emphasizes that Russia must not be excluded if NATO is enlarged or Europe risks again being divided into antagonistic military blocs. The West European nations want to preserve the Alliance and the transatlantic security link that it symbolizes, but they remain divided and ambivalent about shielding and stabilizing Eastern Europe. American political leaders and foreign policy experts engage in concerted efforts to find a credible new mission for NATO in the post-Cold War era, lest the Alliance succumb to irrelevance.

All of the diverse factions embrace the premise that NATO serves an important purpose in post-Cold War Europe and must be preserved. Yet their motives and objectives vary widely. Although they speak of the same organization, they have markedly different images of the Alliance and the purposes it should serve.

To the East Europeans, NATO represents a desperately needed security shield to protect them from Russian domination – and possibly future German domination as well. Conversely, Russian leaders view the Alliance as a potential threat to Moscow's longstanding political, religious, economic, and security interests in Eastern Europe. From their perspective, the most feasible way to neutralize that threat is to be included in NATO's policy organs and work to guarantee that the Alliance is transformed into a nebulous pan-European security forum instead of becoming a mechanism for creating a new *cordon sanitaire* on Russia's western border. German officials want NATO to move the frontiers of Western Europe's security zone to the east, thus providing badly needed strategic depth in the event that Russia again becomes an expansionist power. Bonn also sees the Alliance as a multilateral arrangement to protect growing German political and economic interests in

Eastern Europe without risking the inevitable accusations of imperialism that would arise if Germany sought to play a more active military role unilaterally.

When the other West European nations think of NATO's future role, they contemplate a continuation of the Alliance's traditional function: employing US strength as insurance against Russian expansionism or intimidation and to constrain Germany's power. America's enthusiasm for a post-Cold War NATO arises from the desire to preserve the only institution that guarantees continuing US influence in Europe's affairs and the fear that, without Washington's oversight role, Europe might succumb to the same destructive national rivalries that led to the two world wars.

Whatever the merits of the various motives and objectives, their great diversity raises serious doubts about NATO's viability. Indeed, many of the agendas seem fundamentally incompatible. The problem of conflicting agendas is likely to become most acute if expanding the Alliance's security jurisdiction (and ultimately, perhaps, its membership) becomes the focus of NATO's new mission. But even if the Alliance confines itself to its traditional role and geographic coverage, the problem may grow worse as the spirit of transatlantic solidarity wanes without a credible common security threat. In marked contrast to its relatively well-defined role during the Cold War, NATO in the post-Cold War era faces the daunting task of trying to be all things to all people.

The East European Agenda: Obtain Security Guarantees

The goals of the East Europeans are unambiguous; they want membership in NATO as soon as possible and the full protection of the Alliance's security guarantees. Czech President Vaclav Havel expressed the view of many of his colleagues when he urged the Alliance to consider his country, Poland, Hungary, and Slovakia (the four Visegrad powers) as 'prime candidates for early membership,' with the other 'post-Communist countries' brought in at a later date.[1] Although the East European states continue to hope for an affiliation more substantial than the Partnership for Peace, they embrace even such limited measures. The Visegrad powers, the Baltic republics, and other East European states have signed the documents required to join the PFP and have agreed to participate in joint military exercises.

In most of their public statements, East European leaders avoid identifying specific potential enemies, preferring instead to cite general security concerns. Laslo Kovacs, chairman of the Hungarian parliament's Foreign Affairs Committee, typified this oblique approach when he stated, 'The security risk we now face stems from the instability of the region rather than a traditional military threat.'[2]

Despite such diplomatic rhetoric, East European officials have rather definite security threats in mind. Privately, some leaders still express fear of Germany's long-term ambitions, although even the most paranoid types concede that the notion of a Fourth Reich is rather far-fetched at the moment. A much more pressing concern is Russia. Havel offers a revealing hint of the principal source of his worry when he discusses how the West should react to the emergence of a new hardline government in Moscow. If that event occurred, the West would 'make the most fatal possible mistake' by adopting a policy of appeasement, Havel warns. The East Europeans' fear of a new wave of Russian expansionism was evident even before the surprisingly strong showing of Vladimir Zhirinovsky's ultranationalist Liberal Democratic party in Russia's December 1993 parliamentary elections. Since then, their desire for NATO protection from a neo-imperial Russia has intensified.

Poland's President Lech Walesa has been the most outspoken in warning of Russian revanchism and in seeking the shelter of NATO's security umbrella. During President Clinton's visit to Warsaw in July 1994, Walesa stated that he was 60 per cent apprehensive about peace with Russia and only 40 per cent optimistic that Moscow would not order troops into Poland at some point. An American military, as well as an economic, presence was necessary, he contended, to change that pessimistic assessment.[3]

The East European nations believe that membership in NATO would give them the security guarantee contained in Article 5 of the North Atlantic Treaty. Article 5 declares that an attack on one member shall be considered an attack on all, and it obligates every signatory to render assistance to the treaty partner under assault. But even many Western proponents of NATO's expansion are uneasy about obliging the existing members to defend the nations of Central and Eastern Europe, given the potential for conflict in that region.

Some advocates of enlargement have tried to get round the problem by suggesting an expansion that would – at least initially – be devoid of Article 5 obligations. National Defense University senior fellow Jeffrey Simon, for example, promotes the concept of 'associate membership' as a way station for new NATO members. The Central and East European countries would then have the right to consultations under Article 4 but would not be entitled to Article 5 guarantees.[4] RAND Corporation scholars Ronald Asmus, Richard Kugler, and F. Stephen Larrabee adopt a similar approach to avoid the thorny issue of Article 5 commitments.[5] The PFP also incorporates that distinction by giving participants a right to consultations without binding promises of assistance.

Such schemes may deserve high marks for creativity, but they are not likely to impress the East Europeans. Politically, it is difficult to imagine how an alliance could long endure with two classes of members: a first class entitled to military assistance from its allies under Article 5 and a second class that would receive only the thin gruel of Article 4 consultations in the event of trouble. There is a glaring conflict between the agendas of Western proponents of expansion and the governments of Central and Eastern Europe that seek to join NATO. The former seem to regard enlargement primarily as a political exercise to enhance European 'stability'. The latter, however, regard NATO as a lifeline to guard their independence from powerful adversaries – especially a revanchist Russia. To those governments and populations, NATO's great appeal is precisely the obligations of mutual assistance set out in Article 5. Apprehensive Central and East European nations want reliable protection, not merely consultations.

The cool initial reception that some East European officials gave the PFP confirms that goal. Hungarian Defense Minister Lajos Fur's reaction to the PFP was quite candid. 'Hopefully it's a step toward NATO integration, which is our aim. But unfortunately it does not give us what we need – a guarantee of security.'[6] During Clinton's visit to Prague in January 1994, Havel also made that point, stating that while the Visegrad powers welcomed the PFP as 'a good point of departure', those countries 'do not regard the Partnership for Peace as a substitute for [full NATO] membership, but rather as a first step toward membership.'[7] Slovakia's government adopted a similar position in its memorandum formally accepting the PFP.

> The Slovak Republic fully comprehends the gradual process of creating security mechanisms which ensure stability throughout the European continent, that has found its expression in proposals and programmes raised by the NATO summit. At the same time, the Slovak Republic deems it necessary to stress that it will proceed in its initiatives aimed to achieve full membership in NATO and the security guarantees which are a prerequisite for the successful accomplishment of its economic transformation and strengthening of its democracy.[8]

Such desires on the part of Russia's former Warsaw Pact allies create difficult enough problems for NATO, including the potential to embroil the Alliance in nasty confrontations with Moscow. Similar goals on the part of several former Soviet republics are even more troublesome, since NATO's acquiescence would require an Alliance presence in Russia's 'near abroad' – a step that Russian leaders have made clear would be highly provocative. It is not merely a hypothetical problem; the three Baltic states express the same eagerness as Poland, Hungary, the Czech Republic, and other Russian neighbors for NATO membership and Article 5 security guarantees.[9]

The East European nations may not be satisfied with the paper guarantee of protection that comes with NATO membership, even if it includes Article 5 security commitments. Sooner or later – and probably sooner – they will want NATO, including US, tripwire forces in their countries to make the treaty provisions credible. A subtle but revealing hint of that intent came from Hungary's ambassador to the United States during an interview with Free Congress Foundation President Paul Weyrich on National Empowerment Television. When asked whether his country would want Western troops as well as Alliance membership as a tangible expression of NATO's security commitment, the ambassador replied merely that it was 'too early' to consider that issue.[10] He could just as easily have stated that such a step would not be necessary, or that Hungary had no desire for any foreign troops on its soil, but instead he chose a response that had very different implications. Walesa has also spoken of the need for a US military as well as economic presence in Poland.

It would hardly be surprising if the East Europeans wanted NATO tripwire forces. American proponents of expansion who argue otherwise ignore the history of the Alliance during the Cold War. One of the earliest and most consistent aspirations of the West Europeans was to get and keep a US troop presence on the Continent.[11] Without that presence, European leaders stated privately (and sometimes publicly), they could never be certain that the United States would honor its pledge to defend them if war actually broke out. Not only did the allied governments want US forces stationed in Europe, they wanted them (along with nuclear weapons) deployed in forward positions so that they would be certain to be caught up in the initial stages of a Soviet offensive. A persistent theme of the transatlantic relationship throughout the Cold War was the West European effort to deny US policymakers the luxury of choice.[12] If the West Europeans were unwilling to trust the US treaty commitment to aid them, despite the importance to America's own security of keeping Western Europe out of Moscow's orbit, the East Europeans, who recognize that their region has never been as important to the United States, would have an even greater reason to want the tangible reassurance provided by a NATO tripwire force that included US military personnel.

Russia's Agenda: Obstruct or Neutralize NATO

Boris Yeltsin caused a brief stir in international circles in September 1993 when he seemed to indicate that Russia would not object if Poland and other Central European states sought to join NATO. That position had little support among Russia's political and military elite, however, and in a 30 September letter to Western leaders, Yeltsin retracted his earlier statement. Subsequent comments by Russian policymakers indicate a marked lack of enthusiasm for proposals to expand NATO.

At the same time, they realize that given its current weakened state, Russia may not be able to block enlargement. The Yeltsin government has therefore adopted a 'damage limitation' strategy – insisting that if expansion takes place, it must include Russia. Russian policymakers apparently assume that if Russia is inside the NATO tent, Moscow can prevent the Alliance from being an anti-Russian association. If their strategy proved successful, NATO would be transformed from a US-dominated military alliance into an innocuous pan-European collective security organization. As an interim measure, Russian leaders are seeking a higher status for Russia within the PFP. That special arrangement would recognize that Russia is a great power with nuclear weapons and that its views must be given more weight than those of the smaller East European states. If NATO conferred such a special status on Moscow, the Alliance would also implicitly be acknowledging Russia's extensive interests in Eastern Europe. Indeed, Moscow's ultimate goal may be to make the region a joint NATO-Russian protectorate. The United States and its European allies have deflected Moscow's bid for an enhanced position in the PFP, offering only the vague assurance that the Alliance's relationship with Russia will be 'broader' than the relationship with the other members of the Partnership.[13] Although Russia agreed to join the PFP in June 1994, it has since reconsidered and continues to press for a more influential status.[14]

The pervasiveness of Russian opposition to an expanded NATO that excludes Russia can be gauged by the comments of Foreign Minister Andrei Kozyrev, easily the most pro-Western member of Yeltsin's foreign policy team. On the eve of the January 1994 NATO summit, Kozyrev presented his government's case in the pages of *Frankfurter Rundschau*. Russia 'has no right to stipulate who may and who may not join NATO', he conceded, but it does have the right to insist on the principle, 'enshrined in NATO's articles, that states that NATO remains open to any democratic European or Atlantic state wanting to become a member.'[15]

Kozyrev contended that there was no shortage of simple, superficially appealing solutions to Europe's security problems. '[T]hey essentially consist of the extension of Western institutions, whose existence was justified in the Cold War era, to the countries of Eastern Europe. . . . Here the main attention goes to the quickest possible integration of the Central European countries into Western military-political structures.'[16]

Such an approach, he stated, was based on two myths: that there was a security vacuum in Central Europe, which would inevitably become the site for either Russian domination or a destructive Russian-German rivalry, and that Russia was moving to adopt a nationalist-imperialist policy.

> The solution is produced by taking these two statements together: NATO should protect the countries of Central Europe against the inevitable thrust from the east. The 'guardhouse on the Rhine' should

thus be shifted to the banks of the Bug. This request is substantiated by references to the West's 'moral obligation' toward the democracies in the region and by reflections about the 'natural geopolitical interests' of the Western nations themselves.[17]

Kozyrev cautioned that if NATO's leaders acted upon such assumptions, they would strengthen extremists in Russia who argue for a revival of the Russian empire to resist an attack from the West. A Western strategy based on a worst-case scenario, therefore, was particularly dangerous because it could become a self-fulfilling prophecy. Such concerns expressed by a moderate like Kozyrev must be taken seriously. If even the most pro-Western elements of Russia's political establishment conclude that they cannot abide an expansion of NATO that excludes their country, it is certain that the hostility is far more intense among stridently nationalist elements. Former vice-president Alexander Rutskoi, for example, even denounced Russia's stated intention to join the PFP. 'It is a humiliating agreement,' he fumed. 'The "Partnership for Peace" program is nothing but a means of making Russia submit to America's will.' He added that Russia's role had become that of a 'bootlicker'.[18]

Responding to the Asmus, Kugler and Larrabee article, Alexei Pushkov, Deputy Editor of *Moscow News*, excoriated their reasoning. 'Expanding NATO membership to include East European countries while leaving Russia aside,' he warned, 'would be playing with fire.' Pushkov ridiculed the notion that enlargement proposals were motivated merely by a desire to assist fragile democracies and market economies in the region and to promote general stability. 'Military-political alliances do not exist for the sake of abstraction or charitable purposes. They are always directed against someone or something.' In this case, the inescapable conclusion 'is that NATO expansion to Eastern Europe can be directed only against one country: Russia.' He summarily dismissed assurances to the contrary. 'The security and economic "confidence-building" measures that the RAND analysts offer up to allay Russian concerns are designed to justify the ugly-looking idea of a new *cordon sanitaire* between the West and Russia.'[19]

Andranik Migranyan, a member of Yeltsin's presidential council, expresses similar suspicions about Washington's motives for wanting to extend NATO eastward.

Clearly Russia has reasons to oppose NATO's expansion to its borders. The US, through the alliance, intends to preserve its military and political leadership in Europe. The expansion of NATO – initially through the Partnership for Peace – is a real step on the way to fillirtg the power vacuum [in Eastern Europe], with the ultimate goal of restraining and disciplining Russia itself.[20]

Moscow would, in fact, have valid reasons to worry about NATO's enlargement. Great powers have usually been more concerned about competitors' capabilities than about their intentions – because intentions can change quickly. And for all the talk of NATO's being largely a political organization in the post-Cold War era, it remains a military alliance with impressive capabilities. Even Russians who are not closet aggressors might be uneasy about having such a powerful military association perched on Russia's borders.

Yeltsin and his foreign policy team seem uncomfortable with the emphasis on NATO as the principal institution for dealing with Europe's post-Cold War security problems.[21] Writing in the pages of the US journal *Foreign Affairs*, Kozyrev gives the Partnership for Peace at best a backhanded endorsement, saying that it answers the need of defining Russia's relationship with the Alliance 'for now'. His coolness toward the Alliance is evident when he cautions that the PFP must not 'stimulate NATO-centrism among the alliance's policymakers or NATO-mania among impatient candidates for membership'.[22]

Kozyrev and other Russian officials have repeatedly advocated strengthening the Conference on Security and Cooperation in Europe (CSCE) as an alternative to an expanded NATO. According to Kozyrev:

> The creation of a unified, non-bloc Europe can best be pursued by upgrading the Conference on Security and Cooperation in Europe into a broader and more universal organization. After all, it was the democratic principles of the 56-member CSCE that won the Cold War – not the NATO military machine. The CSCE should have the central role in transforming the post-confrontational system of Euro-Atlantic cooperation into a truly stable, democratic regime.[23]

Russia's reasons for preferring the CSCE to NATO are not hard to fathom. NATO is an organization dominated by the Western powers, especially the United States, and it has a pronounced military emphasis. Conversely, the CSCE has virtually no military component beyond a vague commitment to the concept of peacekeeping. Its principal focus is on political dialogue and conflict resolution by peaceful means. It is highly improbable that such an organization could pose a military threat to Russian interests. Furthermore, because all decisions in the CSCE, even on minor matters, must be made by consensus, Moscow would exercise a legal veto over policies it disliked. Finally, given its growing network of clients among the other former Soviet republics, Russia could expect to exert more influence in CSCE councils than it could hope to do in NATO. Only if NATO were transformed into a virtual organizational twin of the CSCE would it become acceptable to Russian leaders as the leading security institution in Europe.[24]

The Divided and Ambivalent West Europeans

The West European allies are badly split on the issue of NATO expansion. Bonn has been the most inclined to support membership for the Visegrad countries and perhaps some of the East European countries as well. At the same time, members of the German foreign policy community are nearly unanimous in opposing membership for Russia. Defense Minister Volker Rühe has stated bluntly, 'If Russia were to become a member of NATO, it would blow NATO apart. NATO would become like the United Nations of Europe. This isn't going to work, and why should we lie about it or be ambiguous about it.' Rühe added that unlike Russia, the Central European nations deserve to join NATO because 'they belong to the European system and they were artificially separated from it.'[25]

As *Washington Post* columnist Jim Hoagland observes, the reasons for Bonn's desire to expand NATO into Central and Eastern Europe are understandable. 'With the outcome of the Russian revolution still uncertain, Germany would prefer to push NATO's frontier to the east so that any fighting would be done on Polish soil, rather than on German territory. Getting Poland into NATO means Germany would cease being NATO's eastern frontier guard and would move to the center of Europe, psychologically and geographically.'[26] An expanded Alliance would also provide a security shield for growing German political and economic influence in Eastern Europe without arousing the intense opposition that could be anticipated if Bonn attempted to play the role of regional military stabilizer unilaterally.

Nevertheless, there appears to be some dissension even within Germany's foreign policy bureaucracy. Rühe has pushed the expansionist agenda – continuing the policy preferences of his predecessor, Manfred Wörner. Other policymakers, especially those in the Foreign Ministry, express greater hesitation. They fear that enlarging NATO would be provocative to Moscow – especially if that step were taken while Russia was still grappling with its internal political and economic woes and coming to terms with the implications of the loss of its East European empire.[27]

Britain, France, and several other European members of NATO are noticeably reluctant to involve the Alliance in the volatile security affairs of Eastern Europe. British Field Marshal Sir Richard Vincent, the Chairman of NATO's Military Committee, cited a variety of potential perils, most notably those arising from the fragile nature of many of the democratic regimes in the region and the plethora of ethnic and territorial disputes.[28] Boris Biancheri, Italy's ambassador to the United States, mentioned similar concerns and indicated that his government believed that the Alliance should be extremely wary of admitting the East European states as members.[29] In an usually candid moment, Rühe conceded that his country and the United States were the only NATO members that were 'enthusiastic' about expanding the Alliance and that some signatories were distinctly cool toward the idea.[30]

For many of the West Europeans, NATO expansion may simply be the unavoidable price of preserving the transatlantic security tie and keeping the United States engaged in Europe's security affairs. They understand that enlarging the Alliance entails certain risks, but they also recognize that unless NATO finds a more credible mission than guarding the Fulda Gap against an invasion by a nonexistent Warsaw Pact led by a defunct Soviet Union, an eventual US military withdrawal from Europe becomes increasingly probable.

Despite occasional displays of annoyance at the United States for its domination of NATO – and Washington's sometimes high-handed disregard of European interests and policy preferences – the West European powers would like to forestall US disengagement for several reasons. At the most basic level, Washington's security commitment to NATO provides a significant financial subsidy to Western Europe's defense – approximately $90 billion a year. The departure of American forces from the Continent – much less a US withdrawal from the North Atlantic Treaty – would confront West European governments with an unpalatable choice: either increase their military spending to compensate for the loss of Washington's military support or continue to underfund their military establishments, despite the volatile political and security environment in Russia and Eastern Europe, and thereby accept a higher level of risk.

The nations of Western Europe would also prefer to maintain the security tie to the United States as a long-range insurance policy against both a revanchist Russia and a dominant Germany. Although the former danger seems remote at the moment, the West Europeans cannot assume that Russia will always remain weak, cooperative, and democratic. The desire of the other West European states to use America's power and influence as a counterweight to Germany's growing strength is perhaps a more immediate concern, even though it is a motive that is less frequently discussed in public. The comment attributed to NATO's first secretary-general, Lord Ismay, that the Alliance existed to 'keep the Russians out, the Americans in, and the Germans down,' still resonates with many of Germany's neighbors.[31] Indicative of lingering suspicion was the apprehensive reaction of Britain and other West European states to German reunification.[32]

The West European nations still have not resolved their ambivalent attitudes about several important issues. Those issues include the degree to which they are willing to accept Washington's dominance of NATO; the political, economic, and military role of Germany; the nature of Western Europe's relationship with Central and Eastern Europe; and Russia's place in the post-Cold War European order. Given the scope of such unresolved matters, it is hardly surprising that of all the factions with an interest in NATO's future, the West European states (excepting Germany) have the least well-defined policy positions.

Washington's Agenda: Preserving US Leadership

US supporters of NATO are concerned about the implications of instability in Eastern Europe and would like to pacify the region as well as keep it out of Moscow's orbit. Nevertheless, their principal objective, like that of the West Europeans, is to preserve NATO as an institution. They view expansion as a necessary means to that end, recognizing that NATO needs a credible new mission or the Alliance may not be politically sustainable in the long term. Although the US and West European goals are compatible on that score, there are other important differences that are likely to produce more than a small measure of friction.

Whereas the West Europeans want to preserve NATO to retain the America's financial subsidy of their defense and the assurance of US protection if another major expansionist threat emerges, the priority goal of American Atlanticists is to preserve Washington's waning influence in Europe. What NATO partisans in the United States fear is not that the Europeans will be unable to manage their own affairs, but that they will be too successful and therefore have no further need for the United States. Senator Richard Lugar (Republican-Indiana) is quite candid on that point, warning that if NATO fails to provide a credible solution to the problems faced by the European powers, 'they will ultimately seek to deal with these problems either in new alliances or on their own.'[33]

American objections to that scenario are usually couched in terms of warnings about the danger of 'renationalized' foreign and military policies throughout Western Europe. According to the renationalization thesis, without America's stabilizing presence and leadership role, the deadly cycle of nationalistic rivalries will resume, with alarming implications for European – and global – stability.[34] Such concerns, while not entirely without foundation, are overblown.[35]

Moreover, the specter of renationalization is frequently used to conceal more mundane worries. American Atlanticists fear that greater independence by the West Europeans will mean a loss of status for the United States and – perhaps more substantively – a loss of economic influence. Both concerns were evident in former UN ambassador Jeane Kirkpatrick's lament about efforts to promote political and economic unity among the West Europeans: 'The most important conversations about the future organization of the Western world are taking place without any US participation.'[36]

It is not coincidental that Kirkpatrick and others who express apprehension about America's possible exclusion from Europe's affairs are also among the loudest proponents of new missions for NATO. Maintaining NATO is crucial, they argue, because it is the only significant European institution in which the United States has a seat at the table. (Indeed, Washington occupies the seat at the head of the table.) In contrast, the United States has no way of participating in decisions reached by the European Union. NATO leadership is the principal 'leverage' – perhaps the only remaining meaningful leverage – Washington has to guarantee that its political and economic interests on the Continent will be respected by the major West European powers.

But Washington's ability to translate its dominance in the transatlantic security relationship into comparable influence on such nonmilitary matters as trade, monetary policy, and out-of-area diplomatic initiatives was overrated even during the Cold War.[37] The allies typically made just enough (frequently grudging) concessions on those issues to prevent an open breach in the Alliance.

If the United States found it difficult to exercise effective leverage when the importance of its military protection to the West Europeans was quite substantial, it is likely to encounter even greater problems in the post-Cold War era. The value of the US security guarantee has depreciated with the demise of the Soviet threat. Although the West European nations wish to retain defense ties with the United States as a long-term insurance policy and a valuable financial subsidy, US protection is no longer irreplaceable.

Secretary of Defense William Perry tacitly conceded the modest extent of US leverage when he pleaded with Congress to refrain from making demands for greater burden sharing. (The House of Representatives had passed an amendment to the Defense Authorization Bill for fiscal year 1995 threatening to reduce the number of US troops stationed on the Continent if the European members of NATO did not pay a greater portion of the expenses associated with the deployment of those forces.) 'It is unrealistic to expect that our allies can be convinced to increase host nation support and other contributions', Perry stated.[38]

Representative Barney Frank (Democrat-Massachusetts), the principal sponsor of the amendment, dismissed Perry's objections as 'nonsensical'. Frank contended that 'if it [the troop presence] is really important, the Europeans should be willing to pay.'[39] But that is precisely the point; the presence of US forces, while desirable from the perspective of the West Europeans, is not so crucial that they are willing to make significant financial sacrifices. If US officials fear that the allies are unwilling to placate the United States on this narrow burden-sharing issue – which involves only a few billion dollars a year – expectations that those countries will capitulate on trade and monetary matters involving far greater stakes are more unwarranted.

Washington's desire to preserve NATO – especially if preservation requires undertaking new missions in Central and Eastern Europe as desired by Germany and its eastern neighbors – is a case of investing new capital in a declining asset. US leaders need to ask whether NATO, however important it may have been during the Cold War, still serves America's best interests.

Assessing America's Real European Interests

Reconciling the many competing objectives for and demands on NATO in the post-Cold War period is problematic, at best. It is difficult to see, for example, how any version of the Alliance can satisfy both the East Europeans' desire for NATO protection from Russia and the Kremlin's insistence that NATO not only include Russia but also recognize a special Russian sphere of influence in the region – especially in the near abroad.[40] Implementing the goal of the West European nations to preserve NATO without involving the Alliance in the risky mission of preventing instability in Eastern Europe would be equally daunting. That 'status quo' approach is not only unacceptable to the East European states, it runs counter to the policy preferences of NATO's largest and most influential European member, Germany. A more subtle but nevertheless troublesome problem exists in trying to reconcile the West European view of the transatlantic security relationship primarily as hedge against Russian or German expansionism and the American view of NATO as a vehicle for continuing the dominant US role in Europe.

Thus far, the reaction among policy experts to such dilemmas has largely been evasion, delay, and obfuscation. Western (especially American) proponents of new missions for NATO are disturbingly vague about the timing and scope of expansion, whether Article 5 commitments should be given to new members, and whether the Alliance should merely seek to keep Eastern Europe out of Russia's orbit or attempt to dampen all conflicts in the region, whatever their source.[41] The Partnership for Peace is the perfect vehicle for and symbol of such conceptual confusion. As British journalist Edward Mortimer observes, the PFP is 'transparently a device for gaining time, for postponing invidious choices'.[42] But such choices cannot be postponed indefinitely.

Given the likelihood that NATO cannot satisfy the many diverse objectives, the United States would be well advised to seek an alternative strategy for protecting its European interests. The essential prerequisite for such a policy change is to define those interests in a more rigorous manner than is usual in most discussions of NATO and America's post-Cold War role.

The United States does have legitimate interests in Europe, but they are relatively narrow and specific. Not every unpleasant development that occurs somewhere in Europe ought to be a matter of grave concern to American policymakers. Yet whenever critics of an excessively interventionist policy attempt to distinguish between vital and peripheral matters, NATO proponents reflexively respond with cries of 'isolationism'.[43]

But it is hardly isolationism to suggest that many, or even most, disturbances in Europe will not affect America's security. The pertinent issues are how to define America's European interests – separating relevant from irrelevant matters – in a way that makes sense in the post-Cold War setting and how to defend and promote those interests in the most low-risk, cost-effective manner.

The lack of appropriate discrimination is evident in the comments of National Security Adviser Anthony Lake. 'If there is one thing this century teaches us', he insists, 'it is that America cannot ignore conflicts in Europe.'[44] Lake misses the crucial point that both of the conflicts in which the United States ultimately intervened were wars involving all of Europe's great powers. Such serious disruptions of the international system had significant potential to place American security interests at risk. (Although in the case of World War I, the United States confused a shift in the European balance of power – one that Washington could have tolerated, albeit with some discomfort – with a complete breakdown that would have posed a dire threat to America's security.)

Not every conflict in Europe necessarily has wider strategic implications. That is particularly true if the dispute does not involve rival alliances of European great powers. There is no validity to the assumption that more limited struggles, especially those involving small powers in Eastern Europe, are destined to escalate to continent-wide conflagrations that will automatically drag in the United States.[45]

Several variables determine whether a conflict is merely of regional importance or whether it has wider implications that might impinge on US interests. Those variables include the location and scope of the armed struggle; the number of nations involved; and especially the size, influence, and power of the key belligerent states. Some conflicts might warrant a US response, but others would not. The argument that the United States must be concerned about all European conflicts is not justified historically or logically.

The basic American interest in Europe is to prevent any power or combination of hostile powers from achieving a hegemonic position and thereby controlling the major industrial states of Western Europe. Such a massive disruption of the European balance of power could pose a serious threat to America's security. A major motive for the US entry into both world wars as well as Washington's willingness to become a member of NATO was to prevent Western Europe from being at the disposal of a large, aggressively expansionist state.

No comparable hegemonic threat exists today, nor is there a credible one on the horizon. Russia has monumental economic and political woes that will likely keep it occupied for years. Its military spending has plunged to little more than $20 billion a year, and the readiness of Russia's armed forces continues to decline as well.[46]

That is not to say that Russia will never seek to reemerge as one of the world's great powers. It is, in fact, already making limited efforts to do so, primarily by attempting to contain (and perhaps manipulate) conflicts in its near abroad. President Yeltsin and other Russian officials have openly claimed that Russia has a legitimate sphere of influence in that region. Given the historical record, it is also probable that Moscow will eventually seek to defend and promote some interests elsewhere in Eastern Europe. But there is no evidence that Moscow will be able to pursue more extensive ambitions in the foreseeable future, even if it were inclined to do so. Certainly, Russia does not pose a serious conventional military threat to Western Europe. It is important for US policymakers to distinguish between the hegemonic ambitions of a totalitarian Soviet Union during the Cold War and the normal behavior of a great power that seeks to carve out a modest sphere of influence in regions along its perimeter.[47] The former posed a serious threat to America's security; the latter does not.

There is even less to fear from the only other credible candidate for a European hegemonic power – Germany. It is probable that Germany will gradually play a more assertive role in world affairs. Bonn's growing use of economic leverage in the European Union, as well as in Eastern Europe, and its declared desire for a permanent seat on the UN Security Council are indications of that trend. Nevertheless, Germany is far from becoming a military powerhouse. Indeed, German military spending and force levels are declining, not rising – a curious strategy for any nation with expansionist ambitions.

Whatever the accuracy of the judgments made by US policymakers of the two world wars and the Cold War, there is at least a legitimate American security rationale for preventing a hegemonic challenger from gaining a valuable geopolitical objective. A smothering strategy – using NATO to pacify every portion of the Continent, however remote and obscure, and resolve every ethnic feud or territorial dispute that might lead to armed conflict – is quite another matter.

It is necessary to distinguish between the relevance of Western Europe and Eastern Europe from the standpoint of America's interests. Vice-President Al Gore expresses the new conventional wisdom when he contends; 'The security of the states that lie between Western Europe and Russia affects the security of America.'[48] Such a statement is without historical foundation. Eastern Europe has never figured prominently in this country's strategic calculations. Keeping Western Europe out of hostile hands is an important (although not, as Atlanticists typically argue, a vital) American security interest.[49] The political status of Eastern Europe simply does not have the same relevance.

The ability of the United States to tolerate Soviet domination of the region throughout the Cold War confirms that point. Occasional suggestions for a military 'rollback' strategy were dismissed by liberal and conservative administrations alike. That refusal to incur the costs and risks of securing a friendly Eastern Europe contrasted sharply with the willingness to assume significant burdens and dangers decade after decade to keep Western Europe out of Moscow's orbit. The burden of proof is rightfully on those who contend that the independence and stability of Eastern Europe have now become so important that the United States must risk being entangled in the conflicts of that region through an expanded NATO.

Yet that is the import of the comments of Secretary of State Warren Christopher. Meeting with the foreign ministers of nine Central and East European countries in July 1994, Christopher assured them that the security of their region was a vital interest of the United States. 'Peace and stability in Europe require that the nations of Central and Eastern Europe be strong, independent, democratic and secure', he stated in opening comments to the group. 'The United States has a vital interest in ensuring that goal is achieved.' Placing additional emphasis on that theme – and implicitly rejecting the legitimacy of even a limited Russian sphere of influence – Christopher stated, 'For the United States there must not and cannot be a so-called gray zone of instability in Central and Eastern Europe.'[50]

Christopher's comments illustrate the tendency of US foreign policy officials to use the concept of 'vital interests' in a careless fashion. Declaring something to be a vital interest implies a willingness on the part of the United States to risk a major war to defend it. Otherwise, the term is simply an empty rhetorical flourish. If Christopher is to be taken at his word, Washington must be willing to incur the risk of war not only to keep Eastern Europe out of Moscow's sphere of influence but to oust indigenous undemocratic regimes and suppress internecine struggles as well as conflicts between states, however small, throughout the region. That would constitute an unprecedented expansion of US responsibilities in Europe for which there is little evidence of domestic support and no compelling justification.

Leading the Alliance on a mission to establish and maintain political stability throughout Central and Eastern Europe would constitute an attempt to micromanage the Continent's security affairs. In the absence of a great-power challenger, which could dominate the Continent and thereby increase its threat potential to the United States, America can afford to view lesser regional and internal conflicts with considerable detachment. The struggles currently taking place in Eastern Europe may be important to the parties directly involved, and perhaps to their immediate neighbors, but virtually none of them has the potential to disrupt even the European, much less the global, balance of power. Those disorders do not reach (in most cases they do not even approach) the threshold at which US military involvement might be warranted.

Beyond NATO: Encouraging 'Europeans-Only' Successors

Instead of offering the NATO allies new assurances of America's enduring commitment to every aspect of the Continent's security, Washington should stoke the embers of European realism. That effort would begin by stressing that there are rigorous limits to the risks that America is willing to take and the costs it is willing to bear. A new US approach would also acknowledge that while European and American security interests may overlap, they are by no means identical. The policy implication of such candor is that the West Europeans would be wise to create robust security organizations of their own.

Beyond the expansion issue, which has dominated the debate about the future of NATO, lies a far more important question that needs to be addressed. The underlying premise for the Alliance was a fundamental compatibility of interests between the United States and its European allies. Although that argument seemed convincing during the Cold War, when the Western democracies faced a powerful common adversary, the validity of assumptions about transatlantic solidarity is far more questionable in the post-Cold War era. There is growing evidence that the economic, political, and even security interests of the United States and the major powers of Western Europe are diverging in ways both obvious and subtle.

Indeed, the very notion of a transatlantic security community in the post-Cold War era is dubious. Owen Harries, editor of the *National Interest*, even questions whether 'the West' exists as a meaningful concept any longer.

> [P]roposals for what amount to a new NATO are based on a most questionable premise: that 'the West' continues to exist as a political and military entity. Over the last half century or so, most of us have come to think of 'the West' as a given, a natural presence and one that is here to stay. It is a way of thinking that is not only wrong in itself, but is virtually certain to lead to mistaken policies. The political 'West' is not a natural construct but a highly artificial one. It took the presence of a life-threatening, overtly hostile 'East' to bring it into existence and

to maintain its unity. It is extremely doubtful whether it can now survive the disappearance of that enemy.[51]

Harries points out that despite the many common roots of their civilizations, there was little concept of political unity between the United States and Europe before World War II. Indeed, each side tended to view the other with either suspicion or contempt. Despite the rhetoric of solidarity, the actions of the United States and the major powers of Western Europe since the end of the Cold War have again suggested more disharmony and rivalry than unity.

> [A]s soon as the Soviet Union disintegrated, what we immediately started to hear propounded on both sides of the Atlantic – and what we were still hearing from President Clinton during the July [1993] Tokyo summit – was a tripartite or tripolar version of the world, with Europe and the United States again constituting not one but two separate sides of the triangle, and with Japan/Asia as the Third. Far from stressing the continuing existence of 'the West', once free of a Soviet threat many Europeans immediately began anticipating, often with ill-concealed glee, a post-Maastricht United Europe that would supplant the United States as the dominant economic – and ultimately political – force in the world.[52]

Developments in several policy areas have generally confirmed Harries's analysis. Certainly the bitter confrontations between the United States and various West European countries during the Uruguay Round of the General Agreement on Tariffs and Trade (GATT) were hardly symptomatic of Western solidarity. Equally caustic exchanges on economic and fiscal policy – including intense US efforts to pressure the German government to lower its interest rates – likewise indicated friction rather than harmony. And there have been nasty scraps over such security issues as the formation of the Franco-German Eurocorps and the strengthening of the Western European Union.[53]

The pertinent question for American policymakers is whether it makes sense from the standpoint of national interests to preserve a transatlantic alliance that was designed for a vastly different era to deal with a mutual threat that no longer exists. That point is important, not only because America's continued leadership of NATO involves significant financial costs, but because the new missions being contemplated for the Alliance would entail grave risks.

American leaders should not only resist suggestions to enlarge NATO's security jurisdiction, they should seriously consider a policy that moves precisely in the opposite direction – toward giving the Alliance a well-earned retirement. As part of that reassessment, Washington must recognize that the concept of an Atlantic Community, however valid it may have had during the Cold War, no longer has the same relevance. Rather than strive to preserve an outdated transatlantic alliance, Washington would be better advised to encourage the European states to form new security structures or to strengthen such existing bodies as the Western European Union and the Eurocorps as replacements for NATO.

Such 'Europeans-only' organizations would bring to an end Western Europe's military reliance on the United States. Although that would probably mean a further dilution of American influence in European affairs, the benefits would appear to outweigh the drawbacks. Devolution of security responsibilities would resolve the problem of the West Europeans' 'free riding' on the US security guarantee – an annoying phenomenon that has cost American taxpayers hundreds of billions of dollars during the history of the Alliance and sparked numerous, acrimonious burden-sharing disputes. Phasing out NATO would also end Western Europe's unhealthy dependent mentality on security issues, which has rendered the European powers so tentative and ineffectual in dealing with the region's disputes in the post-Cold War period. The major European powers would have to take responsibility for security problems instead of always looking to the United States as a *deus ex machina* to provide solutions. Finally, Europeans-only organizations would be more appropriate for dealing with the purely local or regional conflicts and quarrels of post-Cold War Europe.

Adopting a policy based on a limited, 'arms-length' US security relationship with Western Europe is not without tradeoffs and risks. Nevertheless, that course is more realistic than attempting to perpetuate an alliance that must search for new missions to justify its existence and must satisfy an assortment of conflicting, if not mutually exclusive, expectations. The 3rd Marquis of Salisbury, the late nineteenth-century British statesman who was three times prime minister, once observed that the most common error in politics is clinging to the carcasses of dead policies. Efforts to preserve NATO – an alliance designed to prevent the domination of Europe by a powerful, totalitarian Soviet Union during the Cold War – confirm Salisbury's observation.

NOTES

1. Vaclav Havel, 'New Democracies for Old Europe', *New York Times*, 17 Oct. 1993, p.E17.
2. Quoted in Celia Woodard, 'Hungary Winces as West Defers Its NATO Membership', *Christian Science Monitor*, 28 Oct. 1993, p.3. See also Pavel Bratinka, 'The Challenge of Liberation: The View from the Czech Republic', Svetoslav Bombik, 'Returning to Civilization: The View from Slovakia', Jerzy Marek Nowakowski, 'In Search of a Strategic Home: The View from Poland', and Tamas Waschler, 'Where There's a Will . . .: The View from Hungary', in *NATO: The Case for Enlargement* (London: Inst. for European Defence

and Strategic Studies, 1993), pp.13–35.

3. Paul Bedard, 'Walesa to Clinton: Russians Coming', *Washington Times*, 7 July 1994, p.A11.

4. Jeffrey Simon, 'Does Eastern Europe Belong in NATO?' *Orbis* 37/1 (Winter 1993), p.33. Former ambassador Edward L. Rowny makes a similar proposal, outlining an interim membership 'that grants all rights except those under Article V'. Edward L. Rowny, 'NATO and the Difference', *Washington Times*, 15 March 1994.

5. Ronald D. Asmus, Richard L. Kugler, and F. Stephen Larrabee, 'Building a new NATO', *Foreign Affairs* 72/4 (Sept.–Oct. 1993), pp.35–6.

6. Quoted in David Ottaway and Peter Maass, 'Hungary, NATO Grope Toward New Relationship', *Washington Post*, 17 Nov. 1993, p.A.32.

7. Quoted in Ann Devroy and Daniel Williams, 'Clinton Boosts A-Arms Pact in Ukraine', *Washington Post*, 13 Jan. 1994, p.A1.

8. Press Release, Memorandum of the Government of the Slovak Republic on joining Partnership for Peace, Bratislava, 1 Feb. 1994, p.1.

9. Comments by officials in Latvia and Estonia are quite candid about the desire for NATO membership to protect their countries' independence from a neo-imperial Russia. See 'Minister on "Partnership for Peace" Expectations', 4 Feb. 1994; 'Foreign Affairs Minister on Plan', 7 Feb. 1994, *Foreign Broadcast Information Service Daily Report, Central Eurasia*, 7 Feb. 1994, pp.70, 72; and Lennart Meri, 'Estonia, NATO and Peacekeeping', *NATO Review* 42/2 (April 1994), pp.6–8.

10. Interview on National Empowerment Television, 20 Jan. 1994.

11. For discussions of this point, see Lawrence S. Kaplan, *NATO and the United States: The Enduring Alliance* (Boston, MA: Twayne, 1988), passim; Christopher Layne, 'Atlanticism Without NATO', *Foreign Policy* 67 (Summer 1987), pp.22–45; Ted Galen Carpenter, 'United States NATO Policy at the Crossroads: The Great Debate of 1950–1951', *International History Review* 8 (Aug. 1986), pp.389–415; and idem, 'Competing Agendas: America, Europe, and a Troubled NATO Partnership', *NATO at 40: Confronting a Changing World*, (ed.) Ted Galen Carpenter (Lexington, MA: Lexington Books, 1990), pp.29–42.

12. Christopher Layne, 'Continental Divide: Time to Disengage in Europe', *National Interest*, No.13 (Fall 1988), pp.13–27, and Layne, 'Atlanticism Without NATO' (note 11).

13. Craig R. Whitney, 'NATO Bends to Russia to Allow It a Broader Partnership', *New York Times*, 19 May 1994.

14. Steven Greenhouse, 'Russia and NATO Agree to Closer Military Links', *New York Times*, 23 June 1994, p.A3.

15. Andrei Kozyrev, 'Partnership for United, Peaceful, and Democratic Europe', *Frankfurter Rundschau*, 8 Jan. 1994, translated text in *Foreign Broadcast Information Service Daily Report: Central Eurasia*, 10 Jan. 1994, p.7.

16. Ibid., p.5.

17. Ibid.

18. Interview in *L'Espresso* (Rome), repr. in *Foreign Broadcast Information Service Daily Report: Central Eurasia*, 15 June 1994, p.7.

19. Alexei Pushkov, 'Building a New NATO at Russia's Expense', letter to the editor, *Foreign Affairs* 73/1 (Jan.–Feb. 1994), pp.173–4.

20. Andranik Migranyan, 'Unequal Partnership', *New York Times*, 23 June 1994, p.A23.

21. For an overview of the attitudes of Russian officials, see Gerhard Wettig, 'Moscow's Perception of NATO's Role', *Aussenpolitik* II (1994), pp.123–33.

22. Andrei Kozyrev, 'The Lagging Partnership', *Foreign Affairs* 73/3 (May–June 1994), p.65.

23. Ibid.

24. At a CSCE meeting in Sept. 1994, Russia even proposed creating a new 5-nation committee within the CSCE that would be able to exercise a veto over NATO military actions. Reuter, 'Russia Pushing CSCE Veto', repr. in American Forces Information Service, *Current News*, 15 Sept. 1994, p.2.

25. Quoted in 'NATO Membership for Russia Doubted', *New York Times*, 10 Sept. 1994, p.A3. Also see the similar reasoning of Christoph Bertram, the respected diplomatic correspondent for *Die Zeit*. Christoph Bertram, 'The New West, the New East', *Washington Post*, 10 July

1994, p.C7.
26. Jim Hoagland, 'When Russia and Germany Talk . . .' *Washington Post*, 17 May 1994, p.A17. For a rare critical view by a German scholar of the wisdom of extending the Alliance eastward, see Holger H. Mey, 'New Members – New Mission: The *Real* Issues Behind the New NATO Debate', *Comparative Strategy* 13 (1994), pp.223–9.
27. Christopher Bobinksi, Bernard Gray, and Bruce Clark, 'NATO Begins First Exercises in Poland', *Financial Times*, 13 Sept. 1994, p.2.
28. David White, 'Military Chief Fears for NATO Expansion', *Financial Times*, 3 Dec. 1993, p.A11.
29. Andrew Borowiec, 'Italian Envoy Urges NATO Not to Look East', *Washington Times*, 3 Dec. 1993, p.3.
30. Bruce Clark, 'Ruehe Raises Polish Hopes Over NATO', *Financial Times*, 19 July 1994, p.2.
31. Quoted in Gregory F. Treverton, *America, Germany, and the Future of Europe* (Princeton, NJ: Princton UP, 1992), p.153. For a discussion of NATO's 'double containment mission' throughout the Cold War, see Wolfram F. Hanreider, *Germany, America, Europe: Forty Years of German Foreign Policy* (New Haven, CT: Yale UP, 1989), pp.6–11, 142–3, 157.
32. For examples of that reaction, see Ted Galen Carpenter, *A Search for Enemies: America's Alliances after the Cold War* (Washington, DC: Cato Inst., 1992), pp.36–7. The intensely hostile response of Britain and several other West European states to Bonn's suggestion for a 'inner core' (led by Germany) within the European Union is a more recent manifestation of suspicions about German intentions. James Blitz, Michael Lindemann, and David Buchan, 'Major Hits Out Against "Two-Tier" Europe Move', *Financial Times*, 8 Sept. 1994, p.1.
33. Richard Lugar, 'NATO: Out of Area or Out of Business: A Call for US Leadership to Revive and Redefine the Alliance', remarks to the Open Forum of the US State Dept., 2 Aug. 1993, p.7.
34. Articulate expressions of the renationalization thesis can be found in John J. Mearsheimer, 'Back to the Future: Instability in Europe after the Cold War', *International Security* 15/1 (Summer 1990), pp.5–56; Charles L. Glaser, 'Why NATO is Still Best: Future Security Arrangements for Europe', *International Security* 18/1 (Summer 1993), pp.18, 21–3; and Simon (note 4), pp.23–4.
35. Ted Galen Carpenter, *Beyond NATO: Staying Out of Europe's Wars* (Washington, DC: Cato Inst., 1994), pp.139–40.
36. Jeane Kirkpatrick, 'An Active Europe, a Passive United States', *Washington Post*, 25 Nov. 1991, p.A21.
37. For discussions, see David P. Calleo, Beyond *American Hegemony: The Future of the Atlantic Alliance* (NY: Basic Books, 1987), passim; and Alan Tonelson, 'The Economics of NATO', in *NATO at 40* (note 11), pp.93–107.
38. Quoted in Philip Finnegan, 'Perry Raps Budget Focus', *Defense News*, 25–31 July 1994, p.1.
39. Quoted in ibid.
40. E.g., see the statement of Russian Defense Minister General Pavel S. Grachev that all portions of the former Soviet Union rightfully constitute a Russian sphere of influence. Stephen Kinzer, 'With Eye on Russia, Lithuania Courts NATO', *New York Times*, 25 Sept. 1994, p.A10. President Boris Yeltsin expressed essentially the same view in his 26 Sept. 1994 speech to the United Nations. John M. Goshko, 'Yeltsin Claims Russian Sphere of Influence', *Washington Post*, 27 Sept. 1994, p.A10. Important discussions of Russia's policies in the near abroad include Maxim Shashenkov, 'Russian Peacekeeping in the "Near Abroad",' *Survival* 36/3 (Autumn 1994), pp.46–69; John W.R. Lepingwell, 'The Russian Military and Security Policy in the "Near Abroad",' ibid.: pp.70–92; Karen Dawisha and Bruce Parrott, *Russia and the New States of Eurasia: The Politics of Upheaval* (NY: CUP, 1994); and Victor Kremenyuk, *Conflicts in and around Russia: Nation-Building in Difficult Times* (Westport, CT: Greenwood, 1994).
41. For a more detailed discussion of the gossamer quality of the various proposals for NATO's new missions, see Carpenter, *Beyond NATO* (note 35), pp.13–18.
42. Edward Mortimer, 'The Better Part of Valour', *Financial Times*, 2 Feb. 1994, p.10.
43. Even a sophisticated scholar such as Univ. of Chicago Professor Charles L. Glaser resorts to

that distorted and simplistic analysis. See, e.g., his criticisms of the writings of Christopher Layne, Earl C. Ravenal, and the late Eric Nordlinger. Glaser (note 34), pp.8–9.

44. Anthony Lake, 'Bosnia: America's Interests and America's Role', Remarks at Johns Hopkins Univ., Baltimore, MD, 7 April 1994, p.1.

45. Several serious conflicts in the late nineteenth and early twentieth centuries – most notably the Austrian-Prussian Seven Weeks War (1866), the Franco-Prussian War (1870–1), and the Balkan Wars of 1912 and 1913 – did not become Continental wars.

46. Therese Raphael, 'Yeltsin's Military Might', Wall Street Journal, 23 Sept. 1993, p.A16. See also, Ann Ignatius, 'Russian Now Fields a Potemkin Military', Wall Street Journal, 2 July 1993, p.A4; and 'Russian Mothballing 3 Carriers', Washington Post, 15 Feb. 1994, p.A4.

47. For a discussion of that crucial distinction, see Stephen Sestanovich, 'Giving Russia Its Due', National Interest, No.36 (Summer 1994), pp.3–13.

48. Vice-President Gore, 'Forging a Partnership for Peace and Prosperity', Address before a conference sponsored by the Inst. of World Affairs, Univ. of Wisconsin, Milwaukee, WI, 6 Jan. 1994, US Dept. of State Dispatch, 10 Jan. 1994, p.15.

49. For a discussion of the distinction between vital and conditional (important but nevertheless secondary) security interests, see Carpenter, A Search for Enemies (note 32), pp.170–9.

50. Quoted in Susanne Hoell, 'Eastern Europe's Security Called Vital US Interest', Washington Times, 8 July 1994, p.A16.

51. Owen Harries, 'The Collapse of "The West",' Foreign Affairs 72/4 (Sept.–Oct. 1993), pp.41–2.

52. Ibid., p.48.

53. See Jonathan G. Clarke, 'The Eurocorps: A Fresh Start in Europe', Cato Inst. Foreign Policy Briefing No.21, 28 Dec. 1992; and idem, 'Replacing NATO', Foreign Policy 93 (Winter 1993–94), pp.22–40.

Notes on Contributors

Coral Bell is a Visiting Fellow at the Strategic and Defense Studies Centre of the Australian National University, Canberra. She was formerly Professor of International Relations at the University of Sussex. Her primary field of research is the relationship between strategic and diplomatic decision-making, particularly for the central balance powers. Bell is currently working on a book entitled *The Defences of Peace*.

Jonathan G. Clarke, a syndicated columnist for the *Los Angeles Times* and an adjunct scholar at the Cato Institute, is a former career diplomat in the British Diplomatic Service. His articles have appeared in publications that include *Atlantic Monthly*, *Foreign Policy*, *National Interest*, and the *Washington Post*, and he is a frequent guest on BBC and Canadian Broadcasting Corporation radio programs. His forthcoming book, *After the Crusade: American Foreign Policy for the Post Superpower Age* will be published by Madison Books in June 1995.

Hugh De Santis is Professor of International Security Affairs at the US National War College in Washington, DC. Previously, he was a senior staff member of the RAND Corporation and senior associate at the Carnegie Endowment for International Peace, where he directed the European Security Project. A former career officer in the Department of State, he also served on the Policy Planning Staff of Secretary of State George Shultz in 1983–84. De Santis is the author of *The Diplomacy of Silence*, for which he was awarded the Stuart Bernath Prize, and has also written numerous articles on foreign affairs and appeared on many radio and television talk shows.

David Garnham is Professor of Political Science at the University of Wisconsin at Milwaukee. His research focuses on international conflict and defense policy. He is the author of *The Politics of European Defense Cooperation: Germany, France, Britain, and America* (1988) and has also written articles, book chapters, and conference papers on Western European security issues and US-Western European relations. His current research compares the policy cultures of the G-7 countries and draws implications for American leadership.

Joseph Lepgold teaches in the School of Foreign Service and Department of

Government at Georgetown University in Washington, DC. His areas of interest include the evolving post-Cold War security system and domestic-international linkages in world politics. He is the author of *The Declining Hegemon: The United States and European Defense, 1960–1990*. Lepgold is currently working on two edited volumes, on burden sharing in the 1991 Gulf War and on the future of collective security, as well as a book-length manuscript on domestic-international linkages in US foreign policy.

Daniel N. Nelson is Director of Graduate Programs in International Studies at Old Dominion University in Norfolk, Virginia. He previously served as a foreign policy consultant in Senator Tom Harkin's presidential campaign and as House Majority Leader Richard Gephardt's senior foreign policy adviser. Nelson's articles have been published in journals that include *Foreign Policy*, *Survival*, and *European Security*, and he has appeared on such programs as 'The MacNeil-Lehrer Newshour' and National Public Radio's 'Morning Edition.' Nelson is the author of several books, most recently, *Security After Hegemony* in 1993. He is also a founder editorial board member of *European Security*.

Benjamin C. Schwarz is an analyst at the RAND Corporation in Santa Monica, California. His articles on foreign and defense policy have appeared in *Foreign Policy* and other policy journals, as well as in such publications as the *New York Times* and the *Los Angeles Times*.

Notes on the Editor

Ted Galen Carpenter is Director of Foreign Policy Studies at the Cato Institute which was founded in San Francisco in 1977 and moved to Washington, DC in 1981. He is the author of *A Search for Enemies: America's Alliances after the Cold War* and *Beyond NATO: Staying Out of Europe's Wars*. Carpenter is also the editor of four books on defense and foreign policy issues, including *NATO at 40: Confronting a Changing World*. He has contributed chapters to 14 books on international relations, and his articles have appeared in numerous policy journals including *Foreign Affairs*, *Foreign Policy*, *World Policy Journal*, *International History Review*, and *National Interest*. He is a frequent guest on television and radio news and public affairs programs in the United States, Canada, and Europe. Carpenter received his BA and MA in US history from the University of Wisconsin at Milwaukee and his PhD in US diplomatic history from the University of Texas.

9 780714 641713